Manufacturing Freedom

Manufacturing Freedom

*Sex Work, Anti-Trafficking Rehab, and the
Racial Wages of Rescue*

Elena Shih

UNIVERSITY OF CALIFORNIA PRESS

University of California Press
Oakland, California

© 2023 by Elena Shih

Library of Congress Cataloging-in-Publication Data

Names: Shih, Elena, author.
Title: Manufacturing freedom : sex work, anti-trafficking
   rehab, and the racial wages of rescue / Elena Shih.
Description: Oakland, California : University of
   California Press, [2023] | Includes bibliographical
   references and index.
Identifiers: LCCN 2022040591 (print) | LCCN 2022040592
   (ebook) | ISBN 9780520379695 (cloth) | ISBN
   9780520379701 (paperback) | ISBN 9780520976870
   (ebook)
Subjects: LCSH: Human trafficking victims—Services
   for—United States. | Rehabilitation centers—China. |
   Rehabilitation centers—Thailand. | Pay equity. |
   Human trafficking victims—Abuse of. | Women
   migrant labor—Abuse of. | Economics—Moral and
   ethical aspects.
Classification: LCC HQ314 .S45 2023 (print) | LCC
   HQ314 (ebook) | DDC 362.88/510973—dc23/
   eng/20220919
LC record available at https://lccn.loc.gov/2022040591
LC ebook record available at https://lccn.loc
   .gov/2022040592

Manufactured in the United States of America

32 31 30 29 28 27 26 25 24 23
10 9 8 7 6 5 4 3 2 1

For my parents, Ruby and Davi

Contents

Preface   *ix*

Introduction: The Slave-Free Good   *1*
1. The Business of Rehab: Ethical Consumption, Social
   Enterprise, and the Myth of Vocational Training   *26*
2. Manufacturing Freedom: Racialized Redemptive Labor
   and Sex Work   *53*
3. Bad Rehab: House Moms, Shelters, and Maternalist
   Rehabilitation   *84*
4. Trafficking Benevolent Authoritarianism in China   *111*
5. Vigilante Humanitarianism in Thailand   *135*
6. Quitting Rehab: The Promises and Betrayals of Freedom   *161*
   Conclusion: Redistribution and Possibilities for
   Global Justice   *181*

Acknowledgments   *201*
Methodological Appendix: The Embodied Currencies and
   Debts of Global Feminist Fieldwork   *207*
Notes   *217*
References   *237*
Index   *267*

Preface

I first heard the phrase *human trafficking* on two separate occasions in the fall of 2002. The first was when cast mates in my college production of *The Vagina Monologues* voted to donate the proceeds of our ticket sales to the Coalition to Abolish Slavery and Trafficking (CAST), one of the United States' oldest anti-trafficking organizations, founded in 1998. This was significant because in previous years the student production had donated the show's proceeds to domestic violence or reproductive rights organizations, in line with the play's commitment to raise funds in support of efforts to combat violence against women. At the time, interest in human trafficking was just beginning to arrive on college campuses, whereas now, two decades later, it has a sizable and well-established home among student activists and in academic centers.

The other episode occurred while I was interning as a Mandarin legal intake counselor at the Asian Pacific American Legal Center (APALC) in Los Angeles. When I started my internship, I was trained to help attorneys provide legal assistance through the Violence Against Women Act (VAWA) to new immigrants whose experiences with domestic violence may have prevented their access to US citizenship. In 2003, APALC took on a few T-visa (trafficking visa) cases. This was a new category of visa that had been introduced in 2000 through the federal Trafficking Victims Protection Act (TVPA). As I found myself caught between translating the complicated migration histories of immigrant women and helping attorneys comb through and fill out abundant legal paperwork, one jarring disconnect was clear: the onerous US legal standards for proving trafficking victimhood failed to match the ways that migrant women chose to tell their own stories.

In the two decades that I have studied and been a part of the anti-trafficking movement, I have heard the statement "I first heard of / learned about human trafficking when . . ." countless times, phrased almost as testimony, for activists to situate the newness of the problem within their particular expertise and intervention. It has become a vital part of the testimonial tradition in what Carol Vance calls the "melo-drama" of the anti-trafficking movement. By contrast, I have also worked alongside activists in the United States and across the global South who refuse to call themselves anti-trafficking activists. They refuse to apply for funding that is allocated for the cause of combating trafficking because they feel it has overshadowed and co-opted the work of long-standing migrant, labor, and sex work organizing. Yet, each year, a seemingly growing chorus of voices extols the urgency of raising awareness about human trafficking. In 2010, the priority to increase human trafficking awareness encouraged President Barack Obama to declare January 11 "National Human Trafficking Awareness Day" in the United States; and in 2016, the United Nations declared July 30 "World Day Against Trafficking in Persons."

By the time of this writing, global efforts to combat trafficking have reached a fever pitch, uniting actors as diverse as Hollywood celebrities, NFL quarterbacks, faith-based communities, and students on college campuses. As an eager young college graduate, I was not immune from the allure of the growing global fight to combat human trafficking. I first moved to China in 2004 to research human trafficking at the Bei-jing University Center for Women's Law Studies and Legal Aid, as a Fulbright Fellow. Founded after the 1995 Beijing World Conference on Women, this was the first women's legal aid organization in China. When I arrived at the center, a group of generous legal aid practitioners trained me to be a legal intake counselor and to understand how they mobilized gender rights within the Chinese authoritarian state. Our cases fell into two categories: domestic violence and migrant worker wage theft. In 2005, Legal Aid won the first public-interest litigation case on sexual harassment in the workplace, a victory it regarded as the most tremendous achievement of the year. No one in our office—clients, lawyers, or policy makers—spent their time talking about human traf-ficking, though they did entertain my stated research interests and pro-vided me access to the limited number of government documents being produced on the topic. Among this preeminent group of women's legal aid workers, "human trafficking" was understood by its literal Chinese translation, "kidnapped and sold," and simply did not resonate with any of the cases we encountered through our hotline. In 2010, the center briefly changed its name to the Zhongze Women's Legal Counseling and Service Center, following a crackdown by the government that forced the organization to register under a different name; and, in 2016, the center was formally shut down. In this environment of increased political hostility to civil society organizations—in particular those that work with migrants, workers, and women—it has been surprising to see that the Chinese government has nominally placed human trafficking on its agenda. This book situates the Chinese government's surprising acquiescence to global anti-trafficking policy within the broader restrictions over migrant worker rights and labor organizing.

As a strategy for popularizing anti-trafficking efforts around the globe, many have now rebranded human trafficking as "modern-day slavery." Lyndsey Beutin has shown how this strategy has been tremendously successful in the United States by harnessing American guilt concerning the transatlantic slave trade and chattel slavery and providing a facile contemporary counterpart in which people can become "modern-day abolitionists."[1] The ploy is also extremely dangerous because, as this book shows, the anti-trafficking movement has focused on racialized assumptions about sex trafficking stemming from a global moral panic against sex work.

While critical of the rebranding of human trafficking as modern-day slavery, I have certainly benefited immensely from the institutional support of my research interests through fellowships pursued at academic institutions such as Brown University's Center for the Study of Slavery and Justice and Yale University's Gilder Lehrman Center for the Study of Slavery, Resistance, and Abolition. As an Asian American woman scholar embedded within these elite and well-resourced institutions, I write from a perch that casts as many shadows as I strive to illuminate.

This book is mainly about these long shadows that the anti-trafficking movement casts. In focusing on these shadows, it does not suggest that extreme forms of labor exploitation, debt bondage, and forced labor do not exist. Rather, it argues that we miss a lot when we are driven by global North morality, expertise, and funding, without the input of members of the global South—those very victims that the movement hopes to assist. Like many scholars, lawyers, and activists whom I admire and who have shaped my thinking about this topic, I believe that we sit on a precipice where we risk *too much* awareness concerning human trafficking. The cause has grown so grand that it is now used to police as much as to protect.

By now, most Americans have heard the terms *human trafficking* or *modern-day slavery*. Within the past decade many young Thai and Chinese people I have met have also become familiar with them. The terms' spread has been so robust that in 2015, the late sex worker Carol Leigh warned of an "anti-trafficking industrial complex," whereby boundless benefits are circulated and accrued by those who are working to stop trafficking, though the net positive impact on trafficked people may still be debated.[2] This book recounts the impact on a small but representative group of subjects targeted by the anti-trafficking movement.

Given the intense global interest and urgency focused on trafficking, I have been met with everything from disappointment to outright disdain when I explain that this book does not explore the mechanisms that drive human trafficking, but rather the movement that has arisen to combat it. I now realize that such an explanation creates a false dichotomy. At its core, it presumes that human trafficking—and its variant allegations about freedom, dignity, and modern-day slavery—is an analytic that has been accepted globally. It has not. I push back against the argument that studies of trafficking are somehow distinct from studies of anti-trafficking by suggesting that the anti-trafficking movement is now a power-laden institution that is vital to understanding the shifting fates of working people in the global South.

While conducting research for this book, and even before I knew I would be writing a book, my ethnographic research was characterized by an embodied negotiation of generosity, reciprocity, and debt—at its core probably what the Chinese language simply calls *guanxi,* or the nebulous web of relationship cultivation that underwrites all social exchange. I often traded my personal skills, language ability, and labor to gain research access to anti-trafficking organizations. I also accumulated a serious obligation to share the accounts of the numerous low-wage women workers who generously confided their experiences with me. These ethnographic possibilities and responsibilities have been facilitated by my mobility, class standing, educational status, and institutional affiliations. The fluidity of my access to the wide-ranging people, perspectives, sites, and stories across this movement constantly reminds me of my responsibility to expose structural power and inequality where it might not be obvious—or comfortable to confront.

This is particularly important because such power privileges certain voices and prevents others from being heard. I have attempted to do justice to these accounts throughout these pages. However, this book undoubtedly has its own blind spots, specifically as it still anchors itself within human-trafficking terminology and has benefited from its funding. I hope that as you read it, you see those blind spots as worthy of future consideration, discussion, and redress.

Introduction

The Slave-Free Good

At the annual End Trafficking Now conference in Orange County, California, dozens of young women eagerly flock toward an eight-foot pillar emitting neon-blue light, punctuated by bold black text designating the entrance to a "Freedom Store." The large, tented outdoor venue houses more than a dozen vendors, and a group of friends traces the periphery of tables selling products from around the world, with compelling slogans inviting consumers to "Purchase with Purpose," before being drawn to a booth selling jewelry. The table for the Cowboy Rescue project in Thailand—where I worked as a jewelry maker and volunteer as part of my ethnographic fieldwork between 2008 and 2010—displays a wide assortment of jewelry: rings, bracelets, chokers, and earrings made of silver, gold, colorful gems, and pearls.[1] Two silver necklaces are neatly overlaid on each other like perfect Venn diagrams. They are identical except that each bears a different slogan engraved on its dangling silver-plated dog tag pendant:

"Not For Sale"

"Not Buying"

One customer picks up the "Not Buying" dog tag and inspects it closely. Sensing her curiosity, a salesperson approaches her with rehearsed enthusiasm: "This is our his-and-her series," she says. "You wear the one that says, 'Not For Sale,' and you ask your husband or boyfriend to wear

FIGURE 1. At the End Trafficking Now conference, a large neon pillar marks the entrance to the Freedom Store and urges attendees to "buy cool stuff." Photo by author.

the one that says, 'Not Buying.' Worn together, they are part of our global commitment to end human trafficking." The impassioned vendor continues: "All of our jewelry is handmade by survivors of sex trafficking in Thailand. We run a rescue program in the red-light districts that trains victims of trafficking to become jewelry makers. These jobs allow them to live dignified lives, free from sexual slavery."

A few months earlier, I was hanging out with one of Cowboy Rescue's employees after work. It happened to be my friend Ploy's forty-third birthday, and she wanted two things as part of the celebration: a game of pool and a glass of expensive red wine. As someone who formerly worked in the sex industry, Ploy wielded intimate knowledge of local hot-spots—the best place for noodles, to hem clothes, or to buy secondhand electronics, and certainly the pool hall with the best red wine. Ploy hesitated, however, because the pool hall she wanted to take me to was nestled amid go-go bars in Soi Cowboy, where she was a sex worker for over ten years. Soi Cowboy—the namesake of the Cowboy Rescue project—is one of Bangkok's largest red-light districts, named after an American airman who opened one of the first bars in the area after being stationed in Southeast Asia during the Vietnam War in the early 1970s.

Walking through the crowded street on this hot August evening in 2010, our eyes darted back and forth cautiously before we reached our destination. Once inside, we chose a table in the farthest corner of the bar to avoid being seen by American outreach workers from Cowboy Rescue, who regularly visited the bars in the early evenings to recruit new jewelry makers from among the different workers there. We were nervous because the outreach workers posed a threat to Ploy's job security and safety: being seen inside a bar on Soi Cowboy would constitute a violation of Ploy's employment contract. In the name of freeing them from so-called sexual slavery, Cowboy Rescue contractually forbids its jewelry makers from patronizing the red-light districts where they formerly worked. Once settled in our seats, Ploy—visibly annoyed and understandably a bit on edge—shook her head and pointed to her right shoulder where the Thai word for freedom was stitched neatly just below the organization's logo on the breast of her uniform. "I must wear this uniform to work every day," she said sharply, "but my boss doesn't let me choose where to celebrate my own birthday . . . Do you think this is freedom?"

Manufacturing Freedom takes up Ploy's poignant question in order to expose how the compelling claims of American anti-trafficking organizations often clash with and betray the lives of migrant women workers in the global South. This book takes readers across the global commodity chain of "slave-free goods," an emergent niche market created by the global anti-trafficking movement in the early 2000s. Following this commodity chain not only leads us to, from, and in between the physical sites of production and consumption of jewelry, but also connects the global imperatives and moral sentiments of the anti-trafficking movement with the political and economic circumstances facing migrant women workers in China and Thailand.[2] Ethnographically, I trace jewelry from sites of ethical consumption in the United States back to their very sources of virtuous production in China and Thailand. Understanding the varying roles and perspectives of consumers, activists, and producers exposes the asymmetric power and visibility each differentially wields.

By framing vocational training as victim rehabilitation, anti-trafficking organizations have introduced a widely palatable way to export low-wage women's work throughout the globe. In working alongside and speaking with women in these programs, however, I found that they often contested the labor processes of reform work. They also objected to the individual moral-reform requirements of such organizations—pervasive, but largely invisible in sites of movement organization and jewelry sales. Within such rescue programs, manual labor is embedded in the tactics of moral reform, collapsing transnational moral panics about sexuality and gender-based rights. Claiming that jewelry represents a proxy commodity for freedom from enslavement as well as a virtuous wage, American rehabilitation programs import a *racialized redemptive labor* in which traditional exchanges of wages for labor are replaced with affective commitments between white First World rescuers and their purported victims in Asia. Calling these arrangements "racialized" emphasizes more than the racial identity of the different actors; it names how the structures that allow for First World saving are produced through the histories of colonial and imperial dispossession and reaffirm a racial order of moral righteousness and division of low-wage labor.

While vocational training programs are presented as a technical solution to the moral and spiritual issue of sex work, this solution blurs the political and economic causes behind what activists monolithically characterize as human trafficking. In practice, vocational training does not offer pathways for long-term social mobility or economic independence but, rather, creates new forms of dependence on American aid and intervention and on the global market economy. Despite claiming to revise these dynamics, the global anti-trafficking movement reproduces low-wage women's work by seeking to replace the sale of sex with the sale of jewelry.

This book grounds and specifies some of the claims of the global anti-trafficking movement within local sex, labor, and migrant-worker struggles in China and Thailand. In doing so, it details how these forms of market governance represent new articulations of American empire. The resounding salience of market-based approaches to managing low-wage women's work is not limited to American nongovernmental organization (NGOs) and social enterprises: it must be understood within the global policy goals and nation-state politics of anti-trafficking efforts in China, Thailand, and the United States. Unique state-society and state-market relationships in China and Thailand ultimately shape in-country understandings of and transnational mobilizations around human trafficking. These differing political economic relations in China and Thailand shed light on how market-based social movement organizations mobilize resources in different political economic environments. The same environment in Thailand that favors foreign economic and political capital—through mass tourism, foreign direct investment, humanitarian aid, and the presence everywhere of international foundations and NGOs—is also hospitable to transnational social movements and the private-sector turn to movement accountability. Dozens of foreign international anti-trafficking NGOs operate in Thailand, with varying degrees of registration, transparency, and collaboration with the Thai government, law enforcement, international organizations, and the private sector.

By contrast, the authoritarian Chinese government's strict control of local and global civil society and the market creates a more challenging environment for transnational social movement responses. Comparing the anti-trafficking movement in these two countries reveals how China and Thailand graft existing carceral structures onto the global framework of human trafficking, shaping transnational norms in the interests of the state and the market. While the state is not the target of social action for these rehabilitation projects that have chosen instead to seek change through the market, differences in state power and interest in China and Thailand shape how workers, activists, and consumers understand the moral economy of low-wage women's work. Further, these important distinctions reveal how global movements are reciprocally shaped by local politics regarding gender, sexuality, migration, and rights. These powerful systems make resisting them, and challenging the conflation of sex trafficking with sex work, more difficult. The humanitarian promises of rescue and rehabilitation—central objectives of the global anti-trafficking movement—obfuscate the moral and criminal policing of low-wage women's work. Branding and profiting from the racialized redemptive labor of sex trafficking victims and sex workers in the global South, such rehabilitation programs expose how anti-trafficking efforts fortify structures of racialized global capitalism.

MARKETING A MOVEMENT

Jewelry and other "slave-free goods" are heavily marketed as opportunities for ethical consumption as one popular solution to human trafficking. This form of consumption is racialized via white American sentimentality for the promises of rehabilitation through labor for Asian sex workers. The promotional video for Freedom Unchained, another America anti-trafficking jewelry project that works in China, opens with an Asian woman walking through a wheat field, her face and figure intentionally blurry and out of focus. A narrator, speaking in English in the first person, begins: "I came from a really poor family in the countryside. I was often beaten as a child and I didn't go to school because girls aren't worth much where I come from. When I was fourteen, I left my village and was sent by my family to the city. I needed to find work to support them as we had no money. My friends told me I could get a job working at a hair salon, but when I arrived, I realized I had been tricked into something I never intended to do."

In marketing transnational justice narratives, American organizations like Freedom Unchained, Cowboy Rescue, and others I discuss in this book have had the greatest voice in shaping the contemporary anti-trafficking movement to date. "Xiao Li," for instance, who is referenced throughout Freedom Unchained's marketing materials, is a pseudonym, and the story that appears on marketing materials is, the organization discloses, an amalgamation of experiences and struggles that migrants from rural areas faced.

However, because the jewelry is made with an international and specifically American clientele in mind, all promotional materials are in English and most sales (for both organizations) are made either online or through trafficking-related fair trade shows in the United States. This means that while jewelry producers fingered through the pamphlets on a daily basis—attaching earrings to promotional cardboard or stuffing jewelry bags with small cards that tell you "about this purchase"—jewelry producers in Beijing and Bangkok did not always know what these promotional materials were saying about them.

One afternoon, while packaging jewelry alongside its makers in Beijing, workers asked me to translate the English content of the promotional materials scattered across the table. In Mandarin, I roughly translated the story about "Xiao Li" that appeared on the card to which all earrings were attached. As I finished translating, a growing discomfort swelled among the group. I noticed several eyes darting back and forth between them, an exchange of glances to check one another's reactions. When I asked what was wrong, Bing, a twenty-something woman worker, said that this narrative "distorted parts of some of their lives." Yao chimed in, "There really isn't anyone named 'Xiao Li.'" Rather, they sought to explain together, the narrative seemed to be a

FIGURE 2. Cowboy Rescue and Freedom Unchained's jewelry bags and "About This Purchase" marketing tags. Photo by author.

composite of different kinds of challenges each of them faced growing up in rural farming communities. Despite the depersonalization in this narrative, the name, age, and photographs with blocked-out eyes that adorn all promotional materials offer the consumer a voyeuristic window into what Freedom Unchained claims are symptoms of "human trafficking."

Xiao Li's story—and other stories like hers—stands in for countless victims of trafficking around the world, though their stories are flattened to create the most palatable, marketable versions of struggle. This archetypal tale depicts a woman or child born into poverty and who, faced with limited labor migration opportunities and with family pressures that subordinate girl children, is duped or forced into sex work. The resounding tenor of this message is one of monolithic sexual victimization, which is conveniently and singularly remedied by the intervention of American rescue projects that provide economic alternatives through job training.

During my research, I met and made jewelry with the worker whose life, activists claimed, was the primary template for this story. A fiery and provocative personality, "Xiao Li" had a life history of work, migration, survival, and rehabilitation that was complicated and far too dynamic to be captured in a pithy sales pitch. These distortions and omissions are significant and troubling. Absent at the Freedom Store, for instance, are stories depicting struggle alongside resilience, or ambivalent attitudes toward sex work, stories and attitudes that complicate the notions of "freedom" and "dignity" that many organizations claim their rehabilitation programs deliver. Consumers learn little about the varied constraints and opportunities that low-wage women workers confront as they choose between sex and other, nonsexual types of labor. We don't hear about workers who "fail" out of rehabilitation programs, or what happens to them once they are no longer considered "victims of human trafficking" deserving rescue. Most significantly, we don't hear that most of the women "rescued" by the socially entrepreneurial organizations featured at End Trafficking Now events often do not consider themselves "victims of trafficking" and choose instead to identify as migrant workers, grandmothers, sisters, mothers, girlfriends, wives, and daughters. This fundamental disconnection between employees and employers over what exactly constitutes human trafficking reflects the larger ideological schisms within the global movement to combat human trafficking. It is these disconnects that this book is devoted to unearthing.

TRAFFICKING FREEDOM, TRAFFICKING EMPIRE

Popular American slogans that demand an end to "modern-day slavery" embody the seemingly straightforward and unified objective to combat human trafficking; however, multiple sources of conflict define the movement's significant ruptures. Many organizations have focused exclusively on sex trafficking, framing all commercial sex work as inherently exploitative, while others frame human trafficking more broadly and acknowledge sex work as one of many legitimate forms of women's work and intimate labor, including domestic work, manufacturing, and service professions.[3] Focusing on the exceptional kinds of labor exploitation or sexual violence under the trafficking label has limited the degree to which we understand alternative working arrangements *before* and *after* trafficking that undergird the economic decision-making processes all workers undertake.

As sociologist Elizabeth Bernstein has shown, US efforts to combat trafficking align the unique moral and political goals of evangelical Christians, radical feminists, Democrats, and Republicans, pointing to the ubiquitous "strange bedfellow" coalitions that have come to characterize anti-trafficking efforts. This broad-based interest reflects an underlying desire to reframe a long-standing moral objection to sex work and prostitution within the newer lens of human trafficking.[4] Abolitionist organizations tend to focus exclusively on sex trafficking; these groups find the sale of sex to be distinct from other kinds of work, arguing that it is fundamentally exploitive.[5] The moral panic around sex work has framed sex trafficking as a more urgent concern than nonsexual-labor trafficking in domestic, agricultural, and garment and other manufacturing work, to name a few. The fixation on women's bodies and sex work frames the discourse in ways that have real policy consequences: although ongoing research finds that cases of nonsexual-labor trafficking far exceed those of sex trafficking, most US anti-trafficking interventions have magnetically been drawn to *sex* trafficking.[6] Legal scholars have also argued that humanitarian provisions such as T-visas, which grant citizenship or residency rights to those whom courts ascertain to be victims of human trafficking, have consequences for other migrant groups—most notably irregular and undocumented migrants.[7] Humanitarian policies that anoint a select few human trafficking victims as deserving of state assistance block pathways to migration and citizenship for those in nonvictim categories—typically men and those subjected to forms of labor exploitation portrayed in opposition to sexual labor.[8] This definitional ambiguity surrounding human trafficking is highlighted by distinctions between human smuggling and human trafficking, and between forms of sexual commerce and of labor trafficking, and further complicated by numerous methodological challenges to studying human trafficking.[9]

The widespread appeal of anti-trafficking has created a "rescue industry" whereby the profitability of the anti-trafficking movement generates nefarious circuits of social control veiled as benevolence.[10] Anthropologist Nicola Mai has labeled new strains of global North activism as "sexual humanitarianism," in which social welfare protections for sexual minorities contain the veiled and dubious motives of disciplining sex workers, nonheterosexual/nonbinary individuals, and others at the margins of society.[11] And legal scholar Janie Chuang has warned that the widely expanding public definitions of exploitation, broadened to facilitate human trafficking's increased popularity—what Chuang calls an "exploitation creep"—are gravely detrimental to specific legal categories that are vital to victim protection around the globe.[12]

This book traces these contentious debates starting in the year 2000, following passage of the United Nations Palermo Protocol and the related United States Trafficking Victims Protection Act (TVPA), land-mark legislation that brought human trafficking onto the mainstream global policy agenda. While a discussion of human trafficking circulated among feminists and activists working at international conferences as early as the 1980s—often under the rubric of "violence against women"—the anti-trafficking agenda did not enter the North American mainstream until the United States took political interest and began funding anti-trafficking work in 2000. The UN Palermo Protocol and US TVPA have been used collaboratively for over a decade to govern the transnational social movement to combat human trafficking, spe-cifically by asking countries to ratify the Palermo Protocol and adopt national anti-trafficking laws.

The introduction of the US State Department's Trafficking in Persons (TIP) report in 2000 would serve as the first global ranking mechanism to assess individual countries' progress in conducting anti-trafficking work. This report ranks each nation according to a four-tier system based on its compliance with US "minimum standards" as defined in the US TVPA.[13] Ranking among the lowest in Tier 3 has been punishable by multilateral economic sanctions enforced by the International Monetary Fund (IMF) and World Bank. Janie Chuang cites this, along with other evidence, as an example of the co-constitutive global hegemony that governs this movement, in arguing that the United States has assumed the position of "global sheriff" in the anti-trafficking movement.[14]

The United States as ongoing self-appointed global sheriff of anti-trafficking efforts raises important questions about the varying manifes-tations and impact of American empire in specific sites around the world. New legislative frameworks have been bolstered by specific funding mechanisms, unbridled media frenzy, and unmediated civilian concern that have reshaped the parameters of American activist mobili-zation so that they extend far beyond the legislative arena. The anxieties around human trafficking are difficult to allay, precisely because of a pervasive claim that human trafficking is, as the US Department of Jus-tice and numerous anti-trafficking organizations claim, "hidden in plain sight."[15] Because exploitation and bondage are structural conditions that can invisibilize vulnerable populations, the public has been called upon to increase its vigilance to aid in identification.

As a result, civilians are seeking novel opportunities to participate in the movement, inventing and inviting activist strategies that advocate civilian responsibility and vigilance in identifying trafficking. Such strategies have become institutionalized in dozens of nonprofit organizations that have sprung up in the past two decades. A trenchant ethos of multisectoral collaboration has underscored nonprofit cooperation with law enforcement, exhibiting carceral feminist and carceral protectionist ends.[16] In recent years, paramilitary groups have also emerged. A tactic unifying such paramilitary groups as Operation Underground Railroad and Nvader (both of which I discuss in this book) is the mobilization of American civilian military forces to amplify the policing of trafficking across the global South. To borrow sociologist and Caribbean studies scholar Kamala Kempadoo's coinage, the "war on trafficking" fortifies US empire by mobilizing civilians, nonprofits, law enforcement, and paramilitary organizations to resolve American insecurities around sex, borders, and immigration.[17]

Even anti-trafficking NGO attempts to shine a light on agriculture- or manufacturing-based labor exploitation—as distinct from sex work—focus exclusively on countries in the global South and tend to ignore domestic labor exploitation. Put differently, the binary of Asian "sex slaves" and their white saviors ignores structural racism, xenophobia, and global anti-migrant sentiments. This should be unsettling because, as Lyndsey Beutin powerfully argues, the modern-day slavery narrative has gained prominence precisely because it explicitly conjures the Black suffering of enslavement.[18]

Throughout this book, I refer to human trafficking and forced labor as the law defines them, as opposed to using the more emotionally provocative moniker of "slavery." As the anti-trafficking movement has grown, the modern-day slavery analogy has expanded and threatens to overshadow the unique and distinct history of the enslavement of Africans. Today, nearly any well-meaning citizen with a fleeting interest in trafficking can become a "modern-day abolitionist." This abolitionist nostalgia is detailed throughout this book, in the marketing of William Wilberforce scarves sold by a social enterprise that claims to train victims of sex trafficking in Cambodia to be seamstresses, and in Truckers Against Trafficking, a vigilante organization that confers an annual Harriet Tubman Award to truckers who report to police the sex work they spot on popular US highways. Images also abound of white American former military personnel claiming to build a new underground railroad through the paramilitary organization "Operation Underground Railroad," working in Thailand and several other countries in the global South. These forms of nostalgia are disingenuous in that they capitalize on the guilt and memory of the transatlantic slave trade while concerning themselves only with poverty in the global South. At the same time, they harness a devoted American vigilantism to end trafficking in the service of state and market forces bolstering US empire around the globe.

This book illuminates these forms of American activism and NGO politics as they appear in China and Thailand. In 2008, pursuant to the 2000 UN Palermo Protocol, China and Thailand introduced landmark policies that scripted the international language of human trafficking into their domestic legal frameworks. Migrant-, labor-, and gender-based offenses had previously been captured and categorized under each country's labor, migration, prostitution, and family laws. Both China and Thailand required the formation of new government agencies to manage these anti-trafficking efforts in the early 2000s. While the resonances between China and Thailand are immense, there are still significant differences between authoritarian China and free-market democratic Thailand, raising important questions about the character of global anti-trafficking strategies specific to each political economic context.[19]

Benevolent Authoritarianism in China

The mechanisms that drive human trafficking within and from China are linked to two forms of increased mobility and inequality under global capitalism: widening rural and urban inequality within China, and growing mobility, connectivity, and inequality between China and its Southeast Asian neighbors.[20] China's period of economic reform beginning in 1978 moved the country from a predominantly agricultural economy toward one that encourages domestic manufacturing and opened China's economy to global markets, foreign direct investment, and export opportunities.[21] The effects of economic reform are still evident today: the reliance on migrant labor for industrialization, coupled with widening rural-urban income disparities, has caused one of the largest migration flows in world history.[22] The Chinese women workers who participate in the American anti-trafficking rehabilitation program examined here are part of this migrant workforce to Beijing. As people born with a rural *hukou* (residency permit),[23] they are systematically excluded from accessing resources in urban areas. Rural migrants to Beijing have limited rights to social resources like education and face trenchant structural barriers to finding decent employment opportunities.[24]

China ratified the UN Palermo Protocol in 2010 and signed its first five-year National Plan of Action on Combating Trafficking in Women and Children in 2008, its second National Plan in 2013, and the latest National Plan in 2021. Despite its public acquiescence to international treaties and its being a party to regional cooperative initiatives like the United Nations' Coordinated Mekong Ministerial Initiative against Trafficking (COMMIT) process, China has yet to adopt the international definition of human trafficking, instead acknowledging only the trafficking of women and children for the purpose of forced prostitution, forced marriage, or child kidnapping. The trafficking of men and trafficking for the purposes of nonsexual labor exploitation are notably missing from the Chinese definition.[25]

China's state anti-trafficking response is characterized by strategic partnerships among state entities, global governance organizations, and local and international NGOs, a setup that creates a mechanism for state control over the movement. As part of the rollout of the National Plan of Action, the Chinese government created the Inter-Ministerial Office Against Trafficking (IMOAT), located within the Ministry of Public Security (MPS), which, according to MPS's mandate, focuses primarily on prosecuting and policing trafficking, rather than prevention or victim protection. China's state interest in advancing its economy distances the problem of human trafficking from labor markets, branding it as a criminal issue that can be addressed through various state-led anti-trafficking projects, including improving shelter, raising awareness, and conducting baseline research. In light of China's efforts to appear amenable to partnerships, the global community has enthusiastically engaged the Chinese government's commitment to anti-trafficking efforts on state-mandated terms.

The Chinese government's ratification of the UN protocol and its participation in the transnational anti-trafficking movement according to United Nations norms are unique in that they occur under a regime that has typically resisted global human rights norms. Sex work and the legislative restrictions on sexual commerce in China have been shaped by global and local political economic circumstances.[26] Xin Ren has suggested that the losses women sustained during China's economic reform—including a gendered wage gap, increasing rural and urban inequality, and greater restriction of women's rights across the board—led more to turn to sex work as a means of economic and social mobility. In 1997, the government responded to the increase in sex work with a campaign that explicitly named prostitution and trafficking in women and children as one if the "6 evils of society."[27] Historically, crackdowns on prostitution have been tied to different political moments, including the government's response to a national HIV/AIDS epidemic, its program to clean up the streets before and during the 2008 Olympics, and most recently, its effort to align with global human-trafficking protocols.[28] China's aggressively carceral response to prostitution includes highly contentious mandatory re-education sanctions that many view as legacies of Cultural Revolution–era reeducation-through-labor camps. In 2014 a group of more than one hundred concerned Chinese legal scholars and women's rights activists submitted a letter to the State Council demanding that forced education as punishment for prostitution arrestees be abolished. They noted damning statistics showing that of the 108 detention centers surveyed in the country, 88 percent were used exclusively to detain those arrested for prostitution.[29]

The authoritarianism of the Chinese government is characterized by a state-controlled civil society notoriously intolerant of dissent and popular mobilization.[30] While Chinese authoritarian state repression is well documented, a stream of nuanced research has also sought to understand the more insidious and invisible tactics of state control. Sociologists Ching Kwan Lee and Yonghong Zhang point to trends in rural peasant land expropriation and the government's co-option of grievance petitioning in theorizing that contemporary Chinese state power is maintained through the rote process of "bureaucratic absorption," in which state entities formalize power through putative collaborations with aggrieved populations.[31] Together, these distinct accounts of emergent social protest and state absorption of protests in China provide a rich body of literature concerning "the subjective experiences of subordination" under authoritarianism. Extending this work, my research shows how the Chinese state absorbs and transforms transnational anti-trafficking mobilization rather than repressing it.

Free-Market Democratic Monarchy in Thailand

Since the formal exit of US troops from Southeast Asia in the early 1970s, the commercial sex industry has remained central to the Thai tourist industry's expansion. Scholars of the Thai political economy note that the Thai state explicitly pursues an export-driven economy—planned and funded by IMF and World Bank loans—that privileges not only exports but also tourism and corporate expansion, primarily in Bangkok.[32] Bangkok's rapidly developing economy, alongside Thailand's relative political stability and in contrast to the neighboring countries of Cambodia, Myanmar, and Laos, has also initiated significant flows of undocumented migration from these regions to the nation's capital.[33]

As Thailand's capital and the hub for economic activity, infrastructure, and investment, Bangkok contributes 50 percent of the nation's gross domestic product (GDP), despite being home to less than one-third of the country's population.[34] During the 1970s, as Thailand transitioned from an agricultural to an industrial economy, rural-to-urban labor migration surged. In 1997, following the Asian economic crisis, many migrant workers lost their city employment and moved back to rural areas. However, returning from the urban context, these workers were surprised to discover that the previous decades' shift away from an agrarian economy made agricultural work financially unsustainable. The large rural-urban income disparity continues to the present day, causing a steady stream of migrant workers from all parts of Thailand who seek low-wage employment in Bangkok.[35] Disparities in wealth between rural and urban regions in Thailand have led to successive patterns of internal migration to Bangkok for a range of low-wage service sector opportunities. Alongside other jobs, such as waitressing, domestic work, and retail sales, work in the sex industry is among the prominent forms of employment for female labor migrants within Thailand.[36]

The prevalence of commercial sex tourism—which, many faith-based and abolitionist groups argue, is the primary source of demand for human trafficking[37]—illustrates the relationship between human security and economic development in Thailand. While the sale of sexual services is currently illegal in the country, the Thai government does little to curb the sex tourism industry aside from raids on sexual-entertainment establishments for the purposes of nominally enforcing the law and meeting police quotas. In fact, the government has historically supported sex tourism, owing to the economic profitability of this industry given Thailand's central geographic, military, and economic position in the area.[38] The US military presence during the Vietnam War, including the stationing of American troops in Thailand, and the influx of other foreign troops for "rest and recreation" (R and R) bred one of the earliest infrastructures for tourist exchange and commercial sex tourism in the world.[39]

The prevalence and visibility of the commercial sex industry in Thailand has continually made sex trafficking a priority for American rescue projects.[40] International pressures have forged an aggressive anti-trafficking response that has resulted in a multitiered rescue industry involving the private sector, NGOs, transnational advocacy networks, and new government anti-trafficking entities. The Thai Anti-Trafficking in Persons Act (B.E. 2551; 2008) targets the trafficking of men and women for "exploitation" in a range of "forced labor" situations.[41] Thai anti-trafficking efforts are housed within the Ministry of Human Development and Social Welfare and coordinated among numerous other government entities. The governmental response in Thailand is significantly less centralized than that in China, and law enforcement is coordinated through both the Royal Thai Police and the Thai Department of Special Investigation.

In contrast to China, because Thailand has adopted the UN definition of labor trafficking, the Thai state must balance capital interests in developing export industries and tourism with the transnational concern over labor trafficking. The distinctions between China and Thailand motivate the national comparative research design of this book, which argues that American rehabilitation programs are reciprocally shaped by local and national politics regarding gender, sexuality, migration, and labor rights.

A GLOBAL ETHNOGRAPHY OF A "SLAVE-FREE GOOD"

Two organizations—Freedom Unchained in Beijing and Cowboy Rescue in Bangkok—were ground zero for the ethnography that became this book. Freedom Unchained and Cowboy Rescue were independently founded by American Christian missionaries in 2006. When I began this research in 2008, neither organization was aware of the other's existence, though similarities across organizational practices and motives are abundant. Both organizations conducted biweekly "outreach ministry" to red-light districts in Bangkok and Beijing to identify sex workers—whom the organizations universally labeled victims of human trafficking—who wish to leave the commercial sex industry, and recruit them to be jewelry makers. Workers in both cities were paid wages marginally higher than those of minimum-wage service-sector jobs, and in both cases, workers were compensated not only for the jewelry they produced but also for an hour of Christian worship daily.

The fact that both organizations independently became jewelry-based social enterprises despite previous ignorance of each other's existence is not surprising given the parallel rise of evangelical Christians within the anti-trafficking activist sphere, and given the broader secular turn to market-based forms of humanitarianism and social enterprise.[42] Founders of both organizations were connected to different nondenominational evangelical Christian churches in Los Angeles patronized by congregants who were drawn to the church's explicitly "social justice" mission statements.[43] Both organizations believe that it is the right and responsibility of Christians around the world to step into social justice spaces, because the state alone cannot be trusted or relied on to address injustice.

Likewise, over half of the organizations that sell products through End Trafficking Now's Freedom Store are Christian social enterprises, reflecting the well-documented presence of evangelical Christians within the American anti-trafficking movement.[44] The dominance of evangelical Christianity in the fabric of the contemporary American anti-trafficking movement partially explains the moral backdrop for the overwhelmingly abolitionist, anti-prostitution agenda, rather than an alignment with sex worker rights. These conservative sexual politics have inspired many American anti-trafficking efforts to focus squarely on sex trafficking, as opposed to nonsexual forms of labor exploitation, as outlined in the 2000 UN Palermo Protocol, anti-trafficking's contemporary global governance document. This singular focus also obscures the complex and often contrasting stories workers share about different aspirations and desires.

MORAL MARKETS OF FREEDOM, ABOLITION, AND REHABILITATION

The commodity chain of jewelry made by victims of human trafficking is unique in that it occurs in a market that calls itself a movement. Social enterprise and the ethical consumption of "slave-free goods" are new forms of market governance that reference key features of neoliberal global capitalism in seeking justice outside the state and through the free market. The rise of market-based social movements should not be surprising: in 2010, an *Annual Review of Sociology* article discussed the contentious social potential of markets due to their ties to political stability and their impact on consumer-led commodity chains.[45] Movements that turn to the market often "bypass the state" and have emerged as a venue for many aggrieved populations, ranging from farm workers to environmental justice advocates to the LGBTQ rights movement.[46] Each of these movements turns to the market as a result of decreased state accountability, the emergent dominance of global capital over state power, and the promise of creating alternative political identities through consumption.

The turn to the market, however, raises another set of concerns, as market dynamics have the power to co-opt counterhegemonic interests, as Alexandra Chasin explains with respect to the gay and lesbian rights movement.[47] By branding a rights-based identity movement around gays and lesbians as consumers, the market reinscribed hierarchies based on class and race, catering to the market demands of predominantly white upper-middle-class gay men who have the purchasing power to access the joint satisfaction of consuming goods and services and supporting identity-based ethical branding. Writing over a half-century earlier, Karl Polanyi identified such concerns over the "double movement" when discussing eighteenth-century England's "great transformation" to a market-oriented society.[48] Polanyi's prescient writings have paved the way for economic sociologists to explore the social dimensions of the market, as opposed to employing exclusively rational-actor models.

An astute observer and theoretician of how morality is embedded in markets, Viviana Zelizer sharpens our understanding of transnational social movements with her concept of the "moral market." First elucidated in 1979 to discuss the contexts of life insurance, the "priceless child," and "intimacy," Zelizer's rich theoretical formations offer a toolkit for understanding the social meanings of the "slave-free good."[49] In the near four decades of her writing, the moral market has taken on new forms as neoliberalism has spread around the globe and enthusiasm has increased for social enterprise and corporate social responsibility. When markets and morals collide, their co-constitutive influence on gender and sexuality has proven to be empirical terrain that is ripe for exploration. Among these, Rene Almeling's ethnography of the gendered moral markets of sperm and egg donation, particularly when read alongside Sharmila Rudrappa's study of the global surrogacy market between India and North America, provides insightful analyses into the transnational gendered moral markets in reproduction.[50] Economic sociologist Frederick Wherry's comparative ethnography of ethnic handicrafts, tourism, and fair trade markets in Costa Rica and Thailand further illustrate how moral markets are shaped by different political economic opportunities and constraints.[51] Building on these insights, this book seeks to understand how market-based interventions reinforce forms of power connected not only to gender and sexuality but also to race and nation.

The fair trade food movement, proposed as an alternative development model, has been both heralded and critiqued for being both "in and against the market." Some authors suggest, however, that the movement and the market may be more mutually exclusive. In particular, Daniel

Jaffee's ethnography of the fair trade coffee movement places it on a continuum of "marketness" and embeddedness, suggesting that "fair trade, through its attempt to place a value on the social conditions of production, offers us at least the possibility for re-embedding production into those social and ecological systems."[52] One way the fair trade movement has succeeded in embedding morality in market consumption is through the standardization of fair trade norms and the adoption of the universal fair trade seal of approval. Taking the fair trade movement as a corollary model, this book explores how anti-trafficking social enterprises have embedded in their commodities numerous moral meanings. In lieu of a fair trade seal, we have activist claims marked on price tags and branded in jewelry catalogs, that these goods are produced by victims of "trafficking" on pathways to "freedom," both terms used here to gesture to the numerous ways women workers contest these claims.[53]

Understood through another lens, an established genealogy of critical humanitarianism studies explains why and how social action has been commodified under the conditions of global capitalism. Didier Fassin suggests that a field he calls "humanitarian reason" exists between mutually constituted poles of morality and politics.[54] Nation-states, according to this theory, strategically deploy moral agendas to achieve militaristic, medical, and corporeal hegemonic regimes. Moral agendas inform humanitarian reason through the varying practices and politics of humanitarianism that are firmly entrenched in a "dichotomizing paradigm defined by relationships of difference."[55] Accordingly, empathy and solidarity, two emotional claims of contemporary global humanitarian action, must be understood as deeply embedded in relations of power. This book explores how such relations are intentionally obscured by the putative guise of universal humanitarian benevolence and thus serve as a veil for empire.[56]

The concerned consumers and activists from the global North who design social projects increasingly commodify humanitarianism and social movements.[57] Many global movements have turned to the market to leverage consumer buying power to effect social change, as in the cases of fair-trade coffee, microcredit lending, ethnic handicrafts, and product RED™ goods made and sold to fund HIV/AIDS research—all endeavors that promise to redistribute profits toward alleviating a social problem.[58]

Attuned to sources of power and difference, commentators have focused attention on the race, class, and gender inequalities between humanitarians, rescuers, saviors, and their alleged beneficiaries. Kamala

Kempadoo's writing on the "white wo(man)'s burden," in concert with Teju Cole's "white-savior industrial complex," highlights the interlocking forms of racial, national, and colonial power that underscore contemporary humanitarian acts—and their related sentiments of benevolence and morality—by the global North for the reputed benefit of the global South.[59] Ghanaian British sociologist Samuel Okyere has spent over a decade documenting the intrusion of white and Western anti-trafficking NGOs and activists in Ghana. These interventions claim to address hot-button issues like child labor in Ghanaian mining communities or child fishing on Lake Volta. The harrowing accounts of forced rescue—described by parents as "kidnapping"—recorded by Okyere and his collaborators Nana Agyeman and Emmanuel Saboro detail the abduction of child fishers by American anti-trafficking NGOs. In three accounts of Lake Volta parents whose children were nonconsensually "rescued," villagers expressed shock and horror over "the White Man with the camera" and others who arrived on Lake Volta by speedboat to kidnap their children and place them in forced government detention. The camera is significant in these instances because these images would no doubt serve later as footage for the sensationalist fundraising campaigns that have earned this particular anti-trafficking organization a multimillion-dollar 2021 annual budget. Despite pleas and advocacy, some of these children have not been returned to their families. Even though Okyere coauthored an *Al Jazeera* op-ed with the Ghanaian MP for Afram Plains North Constituency, the honorable Betty N.E. Krosbi Mensah, the American anti-trafficking organization has faced no consequences for its actions. The social capital afforded to white saviors creates what African American studies and communications scholar Lyndsey Beutin identifies as the "white indemnity" that plagues anti-trafficking.[60]

Finally, by centering consumption as a force for action, the organizations discussed in this book center global North feminist consumer identities. Ethel Brooks has developed critiques of simplistic narratives of salvation around the place of child labor in the international garment industry. She notes how consumer boycotts of Bangladeshi garment production, based on alarm about "child labor," represented a kind of consumer protectionism and imperialism, in which US and European groups failed to contextualize child labor in a larger context of global inequality, and often failed to listen to Bangladeshi activists themselves.[61] Further, Maria Mies has argued that the international division of labor, particularly exemplified through global South women producing goods for consumption in the global North, links women together but also disrupts solidarities.[62] Other scholars have also examined the problematic potentials for the corporate co-optation and individualism of consumer politics in the global North, including through racist and colonial depictions of global South women.[63]

The aforementioned theoretical discussions of the market dimensions of social movements, racialized humanitarianism, and the nonprofit industrial complex provide a rich framework in which to discuss global anti-trafficking efforts, which have been characterized as a "rescue industry," the "anti-trafficking industrial complex," and sites of "redemptive capitalism" and "philanthrocapitalism."[64] These market metaphors are particularly apt because human trafficking has often been likened to a market in human beings.[65] Thus, the irony of championing market-based solutions to resolve labor exploitation generated in the first place by global free-market inequality cannot be ignored.[66]

This book exposes how the market-based anti-trafficking movement reinforces American empire and global white supremacy—via humanitarian intervention, ethical consumption, social justice activism, and Western feminism—in China and Thailand. It is equally invested in exploring how market-based governance solutions, once exported to China and Thailand, are then reshaped by local political economies and juridical structures.

THE MANY LIVES OF THE "SLAVE-FREE GOOD"

The book begins by tracing the American architecture of the global anti-trafficking movement and its ties to global labor, sex, and migrant rights. Chapter 1, "The Business of Rehab: Ethical Consumption, Social Enterprise, and the Myth of Vocational Training," opens with an in-home jewelry party in the United States, revealing "slave-free jewelry's" marketability as it is branded and sold. We meet self-described modern-day abolitionists who tout the benefits of social enterprise. The turn toward consumer activism and ethical consumption poses not an alternative to but a vital component of extractive global capitalism and US empire. Integrating scholarship that has critiqued the geopolitical positioning of the United States as "global sheriff" alongside its deeply evangelical ties to Bush-era conservative Christian politics, this chapter demonstrates how and why the American movement has largely prioritized paradigms of "rescue and rehabilitation" over those of "rights." It examines the contemporary anti-trafficking movement in the light of core theories of transnational social movements and markets and looks specifically at the growing regimes of rehabilitation, vocational training, and labor reform as solutions to human trafficking. This chapter concludes that the mission of anti-trafficking rescue reinforces US empire by espousing the corollary goals of salvific evangelism and its ideological refuge in social enterprise.

The furtive duality of the social and entrepreneurial aspects of labor is explored in chapter 2, "Manufacturing Freedom: Racialized Redemptive Labor and Sex Work." Few empirical studies have examined the impact vocational training programs have on their participants.[67] To address this gap, chapter 2 looks at the labor regimes of rehabilitation through vocational training in Beijing and Bangkok, focusing on the lives of women during an eight-hour working day. By transforming sex work into manual labor producing jewelry, anti-trafficking organizations create a transnational moral economy of low-wage women's work. Workers must negotiate the daily exchange between their past as sex workers with the labor-intensive and highly gendered work of making jewelry. These virtuous labor arrangements are heavily regulated by anti-trafficking activists—who also happen to be shop-floor managers and employers. Vocational training—in this case training in the skills of making jewelry—is marketed as a technical solution that unites the global development goals around human trafficking and ethical consumerism, while obscuring the equally present faith-based objectives of missionary work and the abolition of prostitution.

As a key imperative, rehabilitation has come to stand in for both the economic and the moral improvement of "rescued" sex workers. Broadly, chapter 3, "Bad Rehab: House Moms, Shelters, and Maternalist Rehabilitation," examines each organization's efforts to achieve social control once the workday has ended, and also amplifies forms of worker resistance in each country. The chapter is guided by the Asia Pacific Network of Sex Workers' music video parodying Lady Gaga's Grammy Award–winning song "Bad Romance," the lyrics of which express grievances of rescued sex workers living in government and NGO rehabilitation centers in Cambodia. This chapter suggests that rehabilitation becomes "bad" when maternalist invocations of the merits of "rehabilitation" are used to justify social control and to co-opt worker resistance in each place.

The book then shifts to connecting workers' lives in these programs with the larger migrant and sex worker struggles in each country, illustrating that discussions of the global anti-trafficking movement cannot be abstracted from local Chinese and Thai politics around migrant, labor, gender, and sexual rights. I offer a glimpse of how global governance imperatives have emboldened transnational civil society in Thailand, and the Chinese authoritarian state, to seek carceral solutions that turn away from worker rights. Chapters 4 and 5 focus on secular responses to the more generalized problem of labor trafficking, including both sex trafficking and nonsexual labor—in each country.

Chapter 4 travels to China, where transnational anti-trafficking efforts have bolstered state power to the exclusion of labor organizing, thus foreclosing opportunities for labor solidarity. In analyzing the mobilization of transnational human trafficking norms in China, I offer an ethnographic glimpse at the "Migrant Worker Band Project," cofunded by the Chinese government, the United Nations, the International Labor Organization, and several international NGOs. Selecting and training workers to compose and perform songs about human trafficking, this transnational collaboration reveals unresolved contradictions between United Nations definitions and norms regarding labor trafficking on one hand and Chinese legal definitions on the other. The contradiction between the UN and Chinese definitions of human trafficking is amplified under the authoritarian Chinese state, which has largely shaped transnational norms to serve the interests of the nation-state, implementing anti-trafficking initiatives that punish undocumented and irregular migrants, marriage migrants, and sex workers.

While chapter 4 reveals how transnational anti-trafficking efforts and the state work together to exclude labor organizing from the movement, chapter 5, "Vigilante Humanitarianism in Thailand," explores state and NGO collusion in market-based humanitarianism in Thailand, as demonstrated through the lenses of paramilitary anti–sex trafficking interventions undertaken by vigilante forces. It places American anti-trafficking organizations and new humanitarian undertakings, such as "human trafficking reality tourism," in direct conversation with Thai sex worker rights organizations, revealing the tensions between state interests in capital and the transnational human trafficking movement. The combined market forces of sexual commerce, mass tourism, and the anti-trafficking rescue industry have made Thailand a site ripe for market-based interventions against human trafficking.

Alongside a growing global interest in understanding "life after trafficking," chapter 6, "Quitting Rehab: The Promises and Betrayals of Freedom," explores the afterlife of anti-trafficking rescue and rehabilitation. It closely follows four women workers who have left jewelry-making training projects and looks at their life choices and constraints after leaving rehabilitation. Without the "victims of human trafficking" label, these workers no longer benefit from the resources once available to them as docile movement subjects. In most cases, after years of vocational training, workers find that they have no marketable skills in the local economy and are merely reabsorbed into the orbit of global capitalism or state-sponsored heteropatriarchy in the form of precarious low-wage work or marriage.

. . .

In disparate settings ranging from Beijing to Bangkok to Los Angeles, market-based solutions to poverty and inequality have produced facile anti-trafficking interventions that posit freedom against slavery, sex work against manual labor, social movement activists as heroes of sex trafficking victims, ethical consumers as vital supporters of redemptive labor, and the United States against the global South. The alluring techno-politics of vocational training and rehabilitation through labor has created new regimes of racial capitalism feminized on the backs of low-wage workers. Migrant workers—predominantly, though not exclusively, women—are caught in the crossfire of intense geopolitical negotiations for global governance, neoliberal market supremacy, and humanitarian sentimentality. Freedom and rescue are loosely invoked in tandem, by secular and religious organizations alike, to glorify rehabilitation regimes that keep women mired in manual and menial low-wage work. The hallow promises of freedom, rescue, and rehabilitation have the additional consequence of eclipsing local migrant, sex, and labor activism and creating intractable dependencies on American rescue, aid, and intervention.

This book journeys from labor relations on the shop floor to the macroeconomic, political, and legal contexts that shape sexual, migrant, and labor politics in all three countries. Comparing American anti-trafficking rehab projects in China and Thailand offers unique insights into how the transnational anti-trafficking movement is articulated and mobilized under democratic and authoritarian political economic regimes, and into what is left out under the ubiquitous global framing of human trafficking and heroic celebrations of its interventions. In the following chapters, I uncover how transnational social movements in different contexts have refashioned social and political engagement, blurring the lines between the public and private; states, markets, and social movements; secular and religious institutions; and democratic and authoritarian political economic regimes. In sum, the movement has bolstered authoritarian state power in China, global market supremacy in Thailand, and racial vigilantism in the United States—ultimately serving hegemonic interests in state power, global capitalist enterprise, and racial capitalism. I hope that readers draw connections between these findings and other global justice movements, connections illuminating how certain models of transnational justice and Western liberal feminism operate in the service of the state or the market, thus reinstalling the very practices of power they seek to deconstruct.

CHAPTER I

The Business of Rehab

Ethical Consumption, Social Enterprise, and
the Myth of Vocational Training

On a Saturday afternoon in the spring of 2010, I helped facilitate a jewelry party in Culver City, California, a middle-class neighborhood of West Los Angeles. Roughly two dozen women guests had gathered in the home of the party's host, Jane, a long-term volunteer with Cowboy Rescue's operations in Los Angeles. Brought together through their local nondenominational evangelical Christian church, and in anticipation of the night ahead, the women shared their reasons for attending. Several guests stressed the importance of human trafficking as they had learned about it through documentary films like *Born into Brothels* and *Call and Response* or Hollywood features like *Taken*. Others emphasized the growing prominence of human trafficking stories in local and global news media outlets, referencing a particular rash of reporting in the *Los Angeles Times* and *Orange County Register* in previous years. Others shared that they had heard about Cowboy Rescue through church, friends, or annual talks the organization's founder gave to American churches that support their work. Each of these distinct forays into the problem of human trafficking underscored a desire for participants to get more involved in anti-trafficking efforts.

Jane was a long-term Cowboy Rescue volunteer who often offered her home for jewelry parties. Her living room was decorated according to the guidelines of the "Home Jewelry Party Sample Kit," widely available for distribution to potential party hosts through Cowboy Rescue's website. It instructed jewelry party hosts to "set the mood: light some candles, order some Pad Thai, or invite a local Thai masseuse, and say a prayer for trafficked women in your community." As guests snacked on chicken satay skewers, papaya salad, and curry takeout from a local Thai restaurant, Cowboy Rescue's US director of operations, Grace, stood at the front of the living room to describe Cowboy Rescue's work.

Grace read from one of the organization's brochures, which narrated how victims of sex trafficking in Bangkok were rescued and trained to become jewelry makers. She then screened Cowboy Rescue's brief promotional DVD in which several Thai women, their eyes blurred for anonymity, tell their stories of migration and sex work—a fate the NGO has deemed indistinguishable from "modern-day slavery." While hearing about the indignities depicted in the video, participants grew emotional and some wiped tears from their faces. Following the emotional arc of a genre that Carol Vance has labeled "melomentary" to describe anti-trafficking storytelling, the short promotional film concluded on a hopeful note, extolling the promise of rescue and rehabilitation.[1] Vocational training and new jobs as jewelry makers served as the triumphant antithesis of the stories of sexual slavery that began the film.

This narrative and emotional trajectory facilitates a smooth segue into a sales pitch, so natural that it always felt more like the presentation of an opportunity than a fundraising ask. Jewelry that had in the film been described as the object of salvation was neatly positioned around the room, and guests were invited to browse the pieces and learn more about the project. Patrons gently set aside the cocktail-sized paper plates of Thai finger food to admire pearl bracelets that cost from $30 to $50, finger earrings made from semiprecious stones that sell for around $20 a pair, and try on necklaces, the most expensive pieces, which could cost up to $75. Once purchased, each piece of jewelry is inserted into a discrete black velvet bag printed with the NGO's logo and accompanied by a small note that tells recipients "about this purchase." As I helped the host shut down and clean up after the event, we tallied a total of $2,000 earned for the two-hour event—average for a weekend home jewelry party of its kind.

When economist Muhammed Yunus won the Noble Prize in 2006 for the Grameen Bank, his ideas about microcredit lending for impoverished Indian women swept the world as an exemplary development scheme that used the market to ameliorate gender inequality and uneven development. In the past two decades, transnational feminist scholars have illuminated the ways in which microlending weds women to capitalist institutions.[2] Espousing a dangerous claim that women's empowerment must be linked to global capital—and its related metrics of merit and deservingness—such programs create new "entrepreneurial subjectivities" and inextricably tie social mobility to external intervention.[3] Calling attention to a "gendered microfinance chain," sociologist Smitha Radhakrishnan has argued that these characteristically small, high-interest loans allow the state to collaborate with commercial microfinance institutions to carry out predatory and extractive measures on poor women borrowers in India. Equally pernicious, as anthropologist Lamia Karim has found, global lending and development institutions have appropriated cultural tropes of honor and shame in the administration of such programs in Bangladesh.

Like microcredit lending, social enterprise has emerged as one of the primary mechanisms by which social movements turn to the market. This marriage presents an unsettling contradiction when it comes to the movement to combat human trafficking. As Elizabeth Bernstein points out, this contradiction is aptly illustrated through the multinational organization Not For Sale, whose "Freedom Store" sells goods made by trafficked persons across the globe.[4] What is plainly surprising here, as Bernstein notes, is that a movement whose main motto is "Not For Sale" advocates a response rooted in the commodification of victimhood, human suffering, and survival. As evident in the sentiments that circulated through the in-home jewelry party, it is not suffering itself that is being sold but rather the antidote to it.

Activists themselves recognized this contradiction, and many did not consider it troubling. Rather, they saw it as an explicit and critical opportunity. For instance, at the annual Freedom Conference in 2012, an emcee pleaded with audience members to read David Batstone's book *Not For Sale,* which, published in 2003, helped launched the global nonprofit organization of the same name. She waved a copy of the book on stage and praised its wide-spanning content—with chapters dedicated to nearly every continent in the world—laughing as she said, "Please visit our booth, where you'll find this book, despite its title, . . . is actually for sale." Later that night at this very booth, I witnessed a young woman approach the vendor's table, where, in addition to Batstone's book, they also showcased their trademark jewelry branded with the organization's logo. She picked up a leather cuff with a sterling silver plate engraved with the words "Not For Sale." Holding the cuff in her hand, patiently waiting as dozens of people paid for their purchases, she eagerly asked the vendor, "Is this for sale"?

I am a sociologist of markets and movements, and my sociological imagination was tickled by these seemingly ironic moments; however, I understand that they are not fundamentally troubling for most activists seeking an end to human trafficking. A more pressing material criticism that scholars and activists have made is of the gross asymmetry between the profits such events generate and the limited funding that actually reaches victims of trafficking and vulnerable populations. Throughout the course of my research, I witnessed a tremendous amount of money amassed and exchanged at fundraisers, conferences, fairs, seminars, and workshops about human trafficking.

Annual galas like those for the Nomi Network, of "Buy her Bag not her Body" tote bag fame, sell individual tickets to their yearly fundraisers for several hundred dollars each. At Nomi's tenth anniversary gala, individual tickets had jumped to $500 apiece. The nonprofit's newsletter noted that it had "exceeded our fundraising goal of $300,000" during that evening event held at New York's Chelsea Piers Lighthouse.[5] In 2021, Nomi Network reported an annual revenue of just over $3.6 million, supporting its work to provide Cambodian and Indian women impacted by human trafficking with vocational and skills training in sewing as a "pathway to dignified employment."[6] One question continued to emerge throughout my fieldwork as I was caught between the stunning opulence of American fundraisers and the portrayals of victims of trafficking living in abject poverty: How is this profit made invisible as it accompanies endless pleas for more and more fundraising?

In addition to the invisibility of anti-trafficking fundraising as a profitable enterprise, there is another notable obfuscation in American anti-trafficking projects: the religious motives and funding that inspire and undergird such activism. Though often undetectable at large anti-trafficking fairs, on organizational websites, or in mission statements, religious—particularly evangelical Christian—commitments are at the center of the US anti-trafficking policy response.[7] Several high-profile American anti-trafficking organizations, including Operation Underground Railroad (OUR), International Justice Mission (IJM), and Love146, have clear evangelical Christian foundations, both relating to the personal faiths of their founders and evident in their organizational culture. Not one of the organizational mission statements for Cowboy Rescue, Freedom Footprints, IJM, OUR, or Love 146 mentions Christian faith despite the clear faith-based influence on their work.[8] I am less concerned with how these organizations are categorized

FIGURE 3. Nomi Network's signature tote bag, featuring the
"Buy her bag not her body" slogan. The similar Slogan Zip Tote
retails for $30 at Nomi's online store. Photo from https://
nominetwork.org/.

than with how these slippery distinctions allow evangelical priorities to
shape the daily lives of those experiencing anti-trafficking rehabilitation.

This chapter argues that profit and proselytization become invisible
when enshrouded in the sentimentality of entrepreneurship and rehabilitation as pathways to "freedom." Vocational training, in this case in
the skills of making jewelry, is marketed as a technical solution that
brings global development goals to end human trafficking into sharp
focus while obscuring the equally present faith-based objectives of mis-

FIGURE 4. Advertisement for 2019 fundraiser event at Nashville's Franklin Theater to support Operation Underground Railroad. The ad features some of OUR's prominent marketing images. Photo from https://secure.franklintheatre.com/websales/.

sionary work and the abolition of prostitution. Replacing sexual labor with low-wage manual labor, such organizations meld Christian morality and salvific evangelism with secular development goals concerning decent work.[9] Rehabilitation, though couched in a specific American secular tradition of reform, has found a happy marriage with and vital counterpart in faith-based social enterprise.

GLOBAL SOCIAL MOVEMENTS AND RELIGION

Research using global social movement frameworks has found that political power has shifted from the state and dispersed across global governance institutions, trade organizations, NGOs, and the market. Whereas earlier social movements were rooted in specific social identities or particular sites of contention, contemporary social movements seek to address global problems of neoliberal political governance and resource distribution.[10] Environmental justice movements, for instance, address climate change and carbon emissions as globally resonant organizing concerns of the past several decades. Another key example is the global movement for water accessibility, which has assumed a naturally transnational character because rights and access to water tend to traverse the national boundaries across which water flows or is held.[11] The proliferation of the precarious global migrant labor force has also increased the salience of transnational attention to human rights, which also traverse political borders.[12] These issue-based concerns of the day have been characterized by sociologist Peter Evans as "counterhegemonic" in that they are caused by hegemonic systems of global capitalism and neo-liberalism.[13] For that reason, they present key actors with opportunities to engage in moments of counterhegemonic globalization as they utilize the tools and technology of globalization to promote global justice goals.

Faith-based organizations are a critical, though understudied, contingent of contemporary social movement organizations. Christian churches, in particular, have become a cornerstone of state and nonstate partnerships in global urban governance and economic development projects. Religious social movements often suggest that they offer an alternative to state- and government-led interventions. Pointing to evidence of government corruption, inaction, and lack of accountability, evangelical Christians have emerged as important actors in diverse social movement activities, from infrastructural repair post-hurricane and post-tornado in New Orleans and Oklahoma City to curbing gang activity in Guatemala and eradicating the phenomenon of child soldiers in Uganda.[14] Responding to the mass deportation of undocumented immigrants in the United States, churches and synagogues, became some of the few places, other than schools, where it was illegal for US Immigration and Customs Enforcement (ICE) officers to arrest immigrants. These religious institutions have been praised for their ability to act quickly and without state or other bureaucratic oversight.[15]

Historically, missionary work has long been a tool of relational evangelism, justified by the need for economic development and by the promise of salvation in areas of extreme poverty, social crisis, or high medical need in the global South.[16] American-led Christian missionary work in Asia has been critiqued over time for its "civilizing" motives, with moral and spiritual correction serving broader imperialist agendas.[17] Historian Peggy Pascoe's seminal *Relations of Rescue* detailed late-nineteenth-century American Christian missionary efforts to discipline Chinese sex workers in San Francisco's Chinatowns.[18] These historical antecedents reveal how moral reform for Asian sex workers has a long legacy in the form of racist, xenophobic, and gendered projects often filtered through Christian missionary work. A century and a half later, a critical difference is how new forms of racialized moral rehabilitation have sought redemption through, and reaped profit from, sex worker's manual labor.

Most notable about the cases I discuss in this book is not that missionary organizations use the church as a primary source of transnational resource mobilization: after all, as Kathryn Keck and Margret Sikkink note, religious organizations were the earliest examples of transnational advocacy networks.[19] What is novel is the fact that they use the church *and* the market economy to bridge sacred and secular forms of activism. This market-based approach allows Christian anti-trafficking actors to embrace a sense of shared spiritual morality with their consumers, which is then compared to the cultural and spiritual conditions in the Third World communities where they work. Equally, the political situation of the Chinese and Thai states—in particular, allegations of government corruption related to trafficking—often justifies religious responses.

Many Western activists working in China and Thailand pointed to numerous instances when the state did not uphold its duties to protect victims of trafficking or those assessed to be vulnerable to traffickers. This argument created a special opening for both American and faith-based response to act quickly, effectively, and without bureaucratic oversight in order to make the largest impact on so-called vulnerable populations. This logic resonates with the two organizations described in this book—in China, where an authoritarian government stifles religious and other minority forms of expression, and Thailand, where government and police corruption are reportedly widespread. In these countries, evangelical social justice advocates have found that the state and law enforcement have lost their legitimacy. Thus, Cowboy Rescue and Freedom Unchained activists see themselves as radical grassroots activists working outside the state because they do not believe it is capable of upholding basic human rights.

This belief echoes a widespread global North call for faith-based organizations to step in. World Vision, an international Christian organization that works on anti-trafficking projects in both China and Thailand, includes the following appeal in its mission statement:

> We are members of an international World Vision Partnership that transcends legal, structural and cultural boundaries. . . . We recognise that values cannot be legislated; they must be lived. No document can substitute for the attitudes, decisions and actions that make up the fabric of our life and work. Therefore, we covenant with each other, before God, to do our utmost individually and as corporate entities within the World Vision Partnership to uphold these Core Values, to honor them in our decisions, to express them in our relationships and to act consistently with them wherever World Vision is at work.[20]

Faith-based activism has become an extralegal mode of engagement in situations where government corruption and bureaucracy pose barriers to a swift and effective response. However, while religious organizations have historically enhanced the social welfare activities of the state, in the case of trafficking, many are now also bolstering its criminal justice functions (a topic further explored in chapters 4 and 5).

FAITH AND COMMERCE

While I was selling jewelry alongside Freedom Unchained activists at a secular anti-trafficking conference in Pasadena, California, in 2010, I listened as volunteers boasted about the transformative effects of jewelry making and eagerly shared that "our girls are 'not required' to participate in Bible study." Hearing this, members of the secular audience gladly opened their pocketbooks to "buy for freedom," but what the activist vendors failed to mention is that workers are required to make jewelry for the full hour if they choose to skip Bible study. Many workers told me they choose to attend worship for the break in manual labor it provides—though, at the time, none of the women in China had converted to Christianity and only about one-third of the workers in Thailand had claimed to have converted. Workers suggested that if Bible study were truly "not required," as activist vendors tell customers, "then it would probably be offered after the workday." This convenient and, I argue, strategic obfuscation of religious objectives in front of secular consumers allows evangelical Christian organizations to be indistinguishable from the hundreds of anti-trafficking organizations that frequent monthly anti-trafficking conferences, fairs, and symposiums in the United States. It keeps organizations from dissuading interested consumers who share only part of their agenda.

Such moments of obfuscation happened often, as both Cowboy Rescue and Freedom Unchained needed to navigate a spectrum of anti-trafficking venues from the absolutely secular to the wholly faith-based. The global ubiquity and urgency of the anti-trafficking cause facilitated entry of faith-based organizations to secular and faith-based venues alike. But why might this be a problem? Echoing concerns that workers voice in the following chapter, the dual goals of secular business and religious rehabilitation are problematic when proselytization and daily worship are considered to be calculable measures of wage labor. At secular fairs, organizations were able to cling to a development politics, as distinguished from a politics of salvation. Folded together as they are on the shop floor, this combination becomes confusing for workers. Thai workers say that, were it exclusively a job, as the "economic alter-

FIGURE 5. The author selling jewelry at an anti-trafficking awareness fair in Orange County, California, in 2009. Photo by Tony Ochoa.

native development" frame suggests, they wouldn't feel that the company governed so many aspects of their lives outside work. Were it exclusively about missionary evangelizing, they would not have to work as hard as they do or be subject to such strong production quotas.

Max Weber's foundational treatise *The Protestant Ethic and the Spirit of Capitalism* noted the mutually enforcing modes of capitalist productivity and spirituality. While rooted in the Christian ethics of productivity, redemption has steadily penetrated secular development and criminal justice frameworks in the United States. Additionally, scholars have pointed to the "techno-politics" of development as a strategy by which religious organizations obfuscate religious motives behind secular approaches. In fact, the merits of redemption—secularized through a more familiar politics of rehabilitation—have made redemptive labor a central aspect of correcting social problems far beyond trafficking.

Evangelical Christianity has been a foundational bedrock of the American anti-trafficking movement and has provided ample financial support and human resources to movement causes. As Yvonne Zimmerman has detailed, the 2000 US Trafficking Victims Protection Act (TVPA) and subsequent US anti-trafficking policies were scripted with an explicitly conservative Christian moral framework.[21] Evangelical Christians have established such an active and dominant presence in the movement that, Zimmerman points out, the prominent evangelical leader Chuck Colson even claimed, "Human trafficking was not even 'on the screen' until the tireless work of evangelicals placed it there."[22]

Evangelicals' impact on human trafficking has been widespread. For instance, in 2012, the President's Advisory Council on Faith-Based and Neighborhood Partnerships took up the issue of human trafficking. Religious leaders decided to intervene in human trafficking work because of their underlying conviction that a "religiously based moral certainty that trafficking is wrong . . . automatically translates into effective anti-trafficking strategies and programs."[23] Global efforts to combat human trafficking are remarkable in prioritizing religious interventions in traditionally secular policy realms. For instance, the 2007 UN Global Initiative to Fight Human Trafficking convened a forum of 125 religious leaders to discuss solutions to human trafficking; and, in 2015, Pope Francis declared February 8 an annual International Day of Prayer and Awareness Against Human Trafficking.[24]

As Bernstein and Zimmerman demonstrate, the TVPA reveals the extent to which conservative sexual politics have been folded into US anti-trafficking policy.[25] In particular, the law promoted an anti–sex trafficking agenda by endorsing anti-sex work funding requirements; for example, the "anti-prostitution pledge" prevented any organization that advocates for sex worker rights, health, and safety—as opposed to the abolition and exit from sex work—from receiving financial assistance from the US Agency for International Development (USAID).[26] The conservative posture regarding sex work has prioritized sex trafficking over labor trafficking even though research concludes that cases of non-sexual-labor trafficking far exceed those of sex trafficking.[27] Following extensive critique from researchers, journalists, and US government regulatory mechanisms such as the Government Accountability Office (GAO), TVPA language and practice have shifted over the past decade to focus equally on nonsexual and sex-trafficking forms of labor exploitation.[28]

Across the global anti-trafficking movement, Bernstein has documented how a growing contingent of evangelical Christian organizations has co-opted the anti-trafficking movement to promote the sexual politics of "new abolition"—mounting broad-based political campaigns that target "the linked phenomena of sex, money and migration."[29] Such religious politics align with the politics of radical feminists, challenging a singular "sex-panic frame" by demonstrating how this new sexual politics is an area of convergence for diverse groups—despite their formal identification as religious or secular.

In 2012, I participated in a six-week course on human trafficking offered by a Los Angeles–based evangelical church that saw itself as part of a new brand of social justice evangelical church that sprouted up across the United States in the 2000s.[30] Such anti-trafficking training sessions administered through churches have grown in popularity, and as part of their core mission, they attempt to reconceive Christian citizenship in a global world. Writing about the politically controversial issue of immigration, Matthew Soerens and Jenny Yang, both of whom are affiliated with the global evangelical Christian organization World Relief, explain: "Christians find themselves torn between the desire to uphold laws and the call to minister to the vulnerable."[31] The issue of human trafficking raises contradictory moral and policy stances. Invoking concern for "victims of human trafficking" steers conversations away from the more contentious issues of undocumented immigration and border crossings. To maintain the sanctity of trafficking victimhood—rather than discuss border justice, for instance—Christian anti-trafficking interventions focus on the immorality of sex work, not labor exploitation or undocumented migration more generally.[32]

The unprecedented allocations of US government funding for Christian anti-trafficking NGOs have primarily been aimed at organizations working in the United States, and did not reach Cowboy Rescue's or Freedom Unchained's operations in Asia. Both Freedom Unchained and Cowboy Rescue cover most organizational costs through church donations and missionary support organizations, and they supplement their work through jewelry sales. Turning to the market for funding has allowed them to run their programs free of the administrative and regulatory oversight of secular development guidelines.[33]

MORAL MARKETS TO COMBAT HUMAN TRAFFICKING

In addition to selling jewelry through Christian outlets, American Christian anti-trafficking organizations also began offering opportunities to participate in street outreach, short-term courses to identify victims of human trafficking in the United States, and paid travel opportunities to learn about the topic abroad. Commerce and faith have become mutually reinforcing modes of engagement and celebrate new, secular investments in the idea of social entrepreneurship. They map onto religious commitments in the areas of business-as-mission and the prosperity gospel. The late Thai sociologist Pattana Kitiarsa's edited volume on religious commodification in Asia discusses the diverse ways in which everything from religious experience to sacred artifacts has become an integral part of various political economic markets. Situating these empirical trends within theories of secularization and postsecularization, Kitiarsa and colleagues demonstrate that religious commodification does not necessarily signal a turn to the secular, but rather reflects new, co-constituted modes of religious engagement.[34]

Evangelicals have long relied on the metaphor of the market as a symbolic space in which to practice their faith outside the church. The term "marketplace ministry," for instance, was introduced in the late 1980s to encourage Christians who did not choose full-time ministry to practice religious life in the secular world, away from explicit places of worship.[35] Similarly, the rise of the prosperity gospel in the United States in the 1980s offered promises of abundant financial success along with Christian worship. Alongside the emerging global interest in social entrepreneurship, the category of "business as mission" appeared as a novel concept beginning in the early 2000s.[36] The commitment to business-as-mission and the tenets of the prosperity gospel demonstrate both that spirituality and profit are not opposed to each other and that spirituality may be rewarded with economic success.

Recent scholarship on the growing global Pentecostal movement suggests that a new breed of "progressive Pentecostals" seek a form of social ministry that pursues "economic development rather than individual social assistance."[37] The promotion of a transnational moral economy for goods made by "victims of human trafficking" illustrates how this agenda has bridged secular and sacred development agendas, with good work and faith presented as effecting material and spiritual transformations. The resurgence of evangelical Christian social activism in the realm of secular politics has paralleled an increase in Christian consumption, and the celebration of religious identity *through* consumption. Large cohorts of young, middle-class, "rapture ready" Christians create and consume brands, T-shirts, concerts, and a megaindustry of commodities to demonstrate and exercise their faith.[38] In addition to appearing at secular fairs and shows, these marketplaces serve as ideal sites for Cowboy Rescue and Freedom Unchained to sell their goods, combining concern about human trafficking, explicitly framed as a Christian moral problem, with business interests and aspirations.

Navigating the dual identities of social enterprise, both organizations straddle the line between private enterprise and public service by registering as both nonprofit organizations in the United States and as private corporations in Thailand and China. While dual registration illustrates the tenuous boundaries between profit and charity, this organizational arrangement also points to different state–civil society relationships and the political economies of aid in each place. For instance, the structurally onerous registration requirements for foreign NGOs in China enables government control of social organizations and prohibits nearly all NGOs from formal registration.[39] Thailand does not have a formal legal NGO registration category, and many foreign NGOs choose to register as a local foundation. This process is significantly easier than in China, but does require going through several administrative hoops and making a "charitable donation" of 200,000 baht (US$6,000) in a local Thai bank account.[40] Both Cowboy Rescue and Freedom Unchained often pointed to the complexity of foundation law or the "backward" nonprofit and nongovernmental sectors as evidence of the uphill battles they claimed to face. They also complained that formal private sector rules should not apply to them, as they weren't making as much profit as other entities. In the early years, volunteers in the organizations' offices tried to help evade tax levies by carrying jewelry back and forth in their suitcases. I transported several boxes this way in 2009 from China to the United States, where, upon landing, I mailed the package to the distribution center in the Midwest. However, as both enterprises have grown in the past decade, they now process and distribute orders as private corporations.

ENTREPRENEURIAL GLOBAL SISTERHOOD

The in-home jewelry party model was inspired by the Tupperware parties popular in the 1960s and the proliferation of new, multilevel marketing schemes selling everything from microfiber towels (Norwex) to essential oils (Do-Terra) and makeup (Amway).[41] In supporting cultures of feminine entrepreneurship, organizations suggested an important synergy between the beneficiaries of sales of such products and the entrepreneurial possibilities for hosts. The website for Freedom Unchained celebrates the opportunity to become an "Advocate of Freedom"; at different points in this program's tenure, it has rewarded home party hosts with free jewelry or even a percentage of the proceeds of sales as a commission.

Although most jewelry is sold through church and fair-trade networks in the United States, some is sold at events in China and Thailand. At the fifth anniversary for Freedom Unchained held in Beijing in 2011, jewelry was sold in conjunction with an art exhibition in which several American artists were commissioned to create a series of photographs to commemorate the event. Works were priced competitively, between 600 to 1000 RMB (US$100–150) per photograph, with proceeds donated to the organization. One of photographers took to the microphone to explain the "Before and After Project," as it was named: he said it had been pitched by the organization's directors, who had the idea to ask Freedom Unchained beneficiaries to contribute words describing their feelings before and after becoming involved with the organization. An organization cofounder then welcomed the audience to view the artworks as "a glimpse into the hearts of lives that have been changed by Freedom Unchained."

The event was held at a gallery space in Beijing's famous 798 arts district, where Freedom Unchained housed its production facility. Like other industrial buildings in the former World War II munitions factory compound, the First Sound Gallery is a three-story building with revolutionary slogans preserved on the exterior brick walls, including the obvious "Long live the Chinese Communist Party" and some less legible text about the proletariat. Juxtaposed to these old signs, each photograph was accompanied by wall text. The "Before" and "After" sequence marked the growth, transformation, and progress Freedom Unchained was eager to celebrate. A collection of photographs for sale depicted emotions that the artists claimed workers had shared with them. "Before Freedom Unchained, I felt . . ." "timid," "scared," "strange," as if "I can't speak up" and was "helpless." By contrast, "After" Freedom Unchained, women found an "oasis," "harmony," "acceptance," "flying," "sunshine and rainbows," and "warmth." One said, "My heart is strong." According to wall text, the group offered "counseling" to these women and ensured that 100 percent of the sale proceeds went to the exploited women the organization works with.

The main events over the course of the evening included a live performance by an American expat band, the sale of photography specially commissioned for the event, and a lottery drawing for prizes from the evening's sponsors (Marriott, the Hutong restaurant, and other local restaurants in Beijing). Midway through the entertainment, a Freedom Unchained spokesperson took to the stage. Speaking English, she intro-

FIGURE 6. Guests peruse the art for sale at a 2011 Freedom Unchained fundraiser in Beijing. Photo by Angie Baeker.

duced the project and encouraged audience members to purchase artworks, lottery tickets, and jewelry. In closing, the organizer proudly asserted that some women were present, but explained that they had asked not to be identified and requested the audience's discretion in respecting their privacy. Although the women workers were clearly the organization's raison d'être, they were hidden from view that night, their invisibility justified out of a declared desire to protect them. Angie Baecker, an American art historian who attended the event, explained to me that the announcement was awkward: "This created the effect in which I wondered whether every Asian woman who appeared to be working for Freedom Unchained bore the stigma of sexual exploitation." While it was an "unfair" suspicion to hold, it was one, she believed, that was inevitably colored by the fact that white Christian American women had the mic to speak for the interests of the "underprivileged" Asian women they employ.

Transnational and postcolonial feminist scholars have long cautioned that certain modes of Western liberal feminism reinscribe the power they seek to deconstruct. Using such critical frameworks, they have argued that US anti-trafficking policy relies on a victimizing ideology built around essentializing and nativist discourses. Jo Doezema asserts that anti-trafficking agendas are racialized discourses that all too often portray Asian sex workers as innocent victims; the underlying racism and classism of these portrayals of victimization "refuse to respect the choice of a woman from a developing country."[42] She further argues that US and First World feminists alike still hold moral objections to sex work; however, they use policy as a way to "cloak moral indignation in terms of 'victimization of women.'"[43] This insight draws attention to the ways a feminized victimization can be strategically marketed depending on the specific context.

The success of framing rehabilitation as a development solution also depends on its distance from the American consumer. What transnational social movement scholar Sid Tarrow calls "global framing" in this movement also rests on portraying a marked distance in cultural values and norms between the First and the Third World, a distance that transnational feminist scholars claim others the norms and values of the Third World.[44] These "distance frames" condemn deviant sexuality, victimization, and sexual exploitation as a Third World problem— citing justifications ranging from apathetic governments and corrupt law enforcement, to villainous johns and antiquated cultural norms and family values.

To claim membership in the broader anti-trafficking movement, which defines trafficking in the United Nations' terms of "force, fraud and coercion," these organizations say that their employees are victims of *cultural* coercion.[45] Activists frequently claim that sex workers are drawn to prostitution because of dire economic circumstances *endemic* to specific cultural, religious, and economic constraints in the Third World. For example, Cowboy Rescue activists claim that the origins of gender inequality and the feminization of low-wage migrant labor lie in Buddhism. According to one of Cowboy Rescue's 2008 brochures: "In Thailand, the daughter is culturally obligated to care for her parents once she is of age. The sons fulfill their duty by becoming a monk for a period of time. In doing this they make merit for their parents' next life. Sons are not expected to provide financially for their parents. Daughters, however, take this role very seriously. When they find an opportunity to work in the city they feel relieved that at whatever sacrifice to themselves, they can meet their parents' demands to send money home." When I ran this claim by renowned Southeast Asian Buddhist studies scholar Justin McDaniel, he furrowed his brow and explained that there is considerable evidence for the decline of long-term monkhood for boys in Thailand. He explained that in some cases boys might be ordained for a brief period—as short as just one day—and thus these gendered Buddhist practices are not likely to change entire demographic reliance on girl children to provide for their families "at any cost."[46]

The idea that religious and cultural norms cause women to enter the commercial sex industry suggests that women working in Bangkok's red-light districts are passive victims of bad culture and poor family values. This narrative ultimately obscures the broader role that legacies of militarization and dispossession play in the feminization of labor migration, the structural vulnerability of groups at the margins, and the difficulties women face finding jobs that pay a living wage. Framing migration as forced and victimizing also ignores the pride that many migrants express in making these difficult decisions to support their families.

BY WOMEN, FOR OTHER WOMEN: WHY JEWELRY?

A simple Google search reveals dozens of American organizations that focus on selling goods made by formerly trafficked people or selling conventionally manufactured goods and donating the profits to anti-trafficking organizations. The media have lauded the benefits of such interventions with headlines, such as CNN's "How Jewelry Is Saving Women from Human Trafficking," and the Orange County Register's "Former Sex Slaves Make Jewelry with Orange County Women."[47] Jewelry is a commodity that several organizations have homed in on as part of an effective ethical business model, existing even outside of the anti-trafficking cause. For instance, Mimi Thi Nguyen has masterfully interrogated the parallel marketing and sale of jewelry made by Cambodian landmine victims in humanitarian attempts to redeem their "beauty."[48] When consumers ask why the organizations choose to focus on jewelry making, Cowboy Rescue and Freedom Unchained activists offer a curiously similar answer. During one tour in Thailand, one of the longtime volunteer activists of Cowboy Rescue, the wife of an American pastor who was placed in Bangkok, exclaimed, "The act of making beautiful jewelry restores femininity to where femininity has been lost." In addition to claims that sex-trafficking victims receive therapeutic benefit from jewelry making, activists also said that jewelry was a smart global business decision: raw materials are easy to come by in Asia and the products are lightweight and easy to ship to the United States. Furthermore, they argued, the jewelry business can also be used to teach women a variety of skills, including sourcing raw material, graphic design, production, accounting, and photography.

Celebration of the innately feminine character that jewelry is said to possess emerges from the pitch that jewelry is made *by* women, *for* women. However, the universal bonds of sisterhood extend only so far; rather than celebrate any innate therapy in the creative or artistic process of making jewelry, women workers in both organizations are provided with back issues of American magazines so they can learn about Western women's tastes. In addition to smuggling Bibles into the country, temporary missionary volunteers were also asked to bring back US fashion magazines to "educate workers about the US market." *Vogue* magazines became easy props that allowed activists to claim that "marketing" knowhow was an equal part of the lessons in vocational training.

Consumers also frequently ask whether the women workers design the jewelry themselves, and many activists in both organizations provide similar answers. The response typically includes an eye roll, a chuckle, and an expression of frustration that these workers have not cultivated the aesthetic to understand what "looks good." For example, Jan, an activist who had traveled to Thailand to volunteer, lamented that Thai workers find glass beads prettier than pearls and prefer to create jewelry with glass beads. *Vogue* magazine was offered as a tool of instruction, teaching workers the value of pearls over glass. Jan explained: "We're a business; they need to learn the value of their product; our consumers just aren't going to pay as much for glass beads as they will for pearls." This claim fits with activists' beliefs that lessons about marketing and understanding one's market are vital to vocational training. However, they tend to facilitate imperialist connections and cement only Western feminist aesthetics as desirable.

The sales director at Cowboy Rescue's office in Bangkok offered another example of cultural misunderstanding regarding jewelry design: "Well, we let them dabble in designing some of the jewelry one time, and we ended up with all these pieces that were this ugly combination of yellow and purple. I mean what a truly hideous combination of colors. At the same time, we didn't want to hurt their feelings so I put those pieces to one side and just thought, hmm, maybe I can sell these on the street at a Lakers game once I'm back in LA?" Voicing the frustrations over the logistics of vocational training helped fortify a bond and shared aesthetic sensibility between activists and their consumers.

Not only do these venues for the sale of victim-produced jewelry bring the plight of former sex workers into middle-class American living rooms, but activists also sell the converse idea that Western values and aesthetics are being taught to Asian women. Rarely did activists attempt to understand local aesthetic meanings. For instance, workers shared that they often chose yellow and purple beads because they are patriotic colors, frequently used to portray humility and reverence to the Thai king. Purple and yellow are a perfectly common color combination in Thailand; they're used in the corporate logos of Thai Airways and the prominent Siam Commercial Bank, to name but two examples.[49] Workers' design choices were a nod to a fashion sense so deeply rooted that it was not uncommon for Bangkok residents to wear yellow-colored clothes on Mondays to symbolize affection for the deceased king.[50]

Suggesting that there is an inherent therapeutic reward in jewelry making pushes the bounds of authenticity, creativity, and labor. For workers, however, these programs are squarely about labor. By contrast, for activists, they are often sold as rehabilitative schemes that provide the creative outlets necessary to help fix "broken women." The tensions between these productive and consumptive sentiments, and the fact that the transnational distance prevents them from ever encountering one another, suggest that they cannot be reconciled in a way that supports worker needs.

Finally, while jewelry is celebrated wherever it is sold in North America as a solution to trafficking, the industry also happens to be ensnared in its own troubling labor abuses. In 2018, Human Rights Watch's report "The Hidden Costs of Jewelry" disclosed labor rights abuses that were occurring throughout the supply chain of jewelry production. The demand for gold and precious and semiprecious stones has wrought particular havoc in the mining industries of the global South.[51] Neither organization has discussed the sustainability of sourcing its materials and their related supply chains.

THE MYTH OF VOCATIONAL TRAINING

Rehabilitation and reform are foundational ideas of American social welfare policy, instituted through the modern penal system. Scholarship, including Lynne Haney's ethnography of gendered regimes of rehabilitation in California prisons and Alison McKim's ethnography of drug and mental health addiction and recovery programs have demonstrated how experiments in alternatives to the penal institution still reinscribe different forms of discipline and control.[52] For prostitution-related crimes, law enforcement–assisted diversion programs have emerged as a state-sponsored alternative to misdemeanor-level drug and prostitution crimes, offering community service, job training, and therapy as an alternative to jail time.

The US Trafficking Victims Protection Act (TVPA) established the United States' "comprehensive and integrated" anti-trafficking policy framework. Similar to the international Palermo framework, the US strategy was based on what Americans coined the "three Ps" of anti-trafficking work: prevention, protection, and prosecution. The first P refers to the need to take proactive measures to prevent human trafficking overseas; the second P calls for protection of victims to help them rebuild their lives in the United States with federal and state support; and the last P calls for prosecution of traffickers, including stiff federal penalties. The T-Visa was designed to address both prosecutorial and protective prongs of the "three Ps" approach; the two objectives have been deliberately intertwined because "prosecutions are virtually impossible if trafficked women do not receive protection and support so that they can overcome their legitimate fears and be witnesses."[53] Within the protection imperative, a "three Rs" paradigm also emerged, identifying rescue, rehabilitation, and reintegration as vital components of anti-trafficking work. Within this framework, rehabilitation has involved "efforts to provide emergency assistance and services, effective placement in stable, long-term situations, [and] access to educational, vocational, and economic opportunities for survivors."[54]

Vocational training has thus emerged as a concrete development goal and tool, a vital priority for life after trafficking for its potential to address the economic insecurity that often drives migrants into exploitive working conditions. Rehabilitation through vocational training has become a staple of anti-trafficking work throughout the globe, appearing everywhere from government-run victim shelters to transnational civil society organizations. While the justifications for vocational training reflect logical imperatives for fostering economic security for migrants, their underlying assumption about how the acquisition of manual labor skills unlocks social and economic mobility is questionable given the global precarity of low-wage work.

The fetishization of vocational training as a catchall pathway for social mobility and equality leaves little room for the exploration of larger questions concerning work. Kathi Weeks's seminal insights on the "problem of work" itself suggest that the obsession with meritocracy and the productivity of waged labor creates detrimental forms of women's subjectivity as tied to work.[55] In line with Weeks's arguments, the notion that waged labor can offer sex workers and victims of sex trafficking a form of redemption raises important questions about why work has become the antithesis to exploitation and trauma, when it is precisely paid and unpaid work responsibilities that ensnare Thai and Chinese women subjects into these positions of vulnerability.

This book theorizes rehabilitation by examining how moral concerns and moral panics govern daily life after rescue through the goals of vocational training, rehabilitation, and reintegration into nontrafficking life. Akin to both historical and contemporary forms of rehabilitation through labor—ranging from state-sanctioned reeducation through labor programs under Chinese communism, to forced labor within the American prison industrial complex, and "alternative" prison programs for female offenders—this rehabilitation regime is significant not only for its connections to disciplinary labor but also because it generates a justice-oriented and much celebrated global commodity chain around the products of rehabilitative and "rehabilitated"—though, ultimately, still-low-wage women's work.

BOOTSTRAP MORAL ENTREPRENEURSHIP

Invoking the adage "If you give a man a fish, you feed him for a day; if you teach a man to fish, you feed him for a lifetime," designers and promoters of vocational training programs believe they provide the skills for long-term economic survival. Alongside this ethic, in addition to offering women wage labor, vocational training also aspires to instilling in women a sense of bootstrap moral entrepreneurship. In the early years of Freedom Unchained and Cowboy Rescue's operations, both offered vocational training in trades other than jewelry making, encouraging workers to develop other skills so that they could have additional means to self-sufficiency. Some early challenges led both organizations to question the feasibility of supporting additional vocational training, and at the time of this writing, both have ceased to offer vocational training outside jewelry making.

In the early years of its operation, Cowboy Rescue's director recalled submitting a funding proposal to the USAID in Thailand and expressed frustration over the limited sources of secular and government funding available for the project. Speaking with a former USAID program manager in Bangkok, he explained, "We expect vocational training programs to have a maximum two-year term so that beneficiaries do not become reliant on such programs." Expressing her dismay with this approach, Colleen, the director of Cowboy Rescue, explained, "These grant requirements are unrealistic because they fail to realize that there is no form of vocational training that will give our women better jobs after they leave. These local economies are broken, and I wanted to create a viable alternative to the unsatisfactory low-wage work in this area." After those early years of operation, Colleen's stalwart commitment to jewelry as a long-term profession reflected an intimate understanding of the limits of vocational training in the local Thai economies. She remains committed to creating a lifelong vocation for Cowboy Rescue's jewelry makers.

In addition to the jewelry trade, Freedom Unchained offered formal job training in hotel work, baking, and cosmetology, programs that lasted anywhere from three months to a year and typically cost around US$1,000 per person. Many workers sought such training programs to acquire important credentials in lieu of formal education degrees. As it happens, this belief in vocational training is also widely espoused by the Chinese government, as students can, as early as middle school, elect to pay to attend a second-tier vocational-training middle school to teach them the skills necessary to earn a living wage. At Freedom Unchained, workers who had a genuine interest were encouraged to choose private vocational training programs for nonjewelry trades.

One worker, Nana, explained to me that she chose to go to school for baking. After working a forty-hour week making jewelry, she would attend baking classes for eight hours a day every weekend. Freedom Unchained excused her for one day of work toward the end of her vocational training program when she needed to complete an unpaid internship at a bakery in order to graduate. Nana was placed in a nearby shop in a Western expatriate suburb that sold bagels. She would often talk about the art of making bagels, which were a culinary novelty in Beijing at the time, and at one point began dating a male coworker. The two of them would dream about opening their own bagel business, remarking at how much foreigners seemed to be willing to pay for this curiously small, ring-shaped piece of bread. Ultimately, despite their dreams and carefully laid-out plans, Nana and Zhu never amassed the capital to start a bagel company. The most Nana could earn at the bakery was the minimum wage of 1,200 RMB a month, which was equivalent to her salary at Freedom Unchained at the time, but without the benefits and social capital of working for a foreign company.

Other times, workers were exhausted after finishing their work week and couldn't muster the energy to attend classes. Their motivation decreased further when they realized that these credentials might not offer better economic alternatives to their current jobs. Wu, a Freedom Unchained worker, had been chosen to receive training in business management at Renmin University, widely considered one of the top universities in Beijing. The credential program was filled with those who had completed high school and some who even had college degrees, and Wu constantly felt "*dao mei*," a sense of futility because of her doubt that she, not having finished middle school, would be able to keep up with the program.

To deter such feelings of futility, Freedom Unchained began asking workers to "buy in" by fronting their own money for these programs. If workers completed them and earned a certificate at the end, the organization would reimburse them for the cost of the training. The floor manager, Fu, explained that this was to ensure that workers would adequately apply themselves and weren't simply going along for a free ride: "We will happily pay for vocational training, but they need to be invested."

After this policy was implemented, one younger worker, Shao, quit Freedom Unchained after feeling doubly pressured because she could not meet the requirements to finish the degree in cosmetology. Others explained that there was no way they could front the cost of training. Even though the organization was always understanding and tried to bend the rules or lend workers money, the requirement that workers pay for their own vocational training served as a deterrent, particularly when many of the industries that they would be trained in offered only minimum wages upon graduation. Holding the final degree certificate over the workers' heads as the condition for receiving reimbursement for the training mirrored many of the coercive power dynamics that allow student labor arrangements in China to be so exploitive, as nearly all vocational training programs in China require a mandatory unpaid "internship term."[56] Workers have no ability to contest these conditions during their internships because if they leave, they will not receive their certificates of completion, a problem I examine further when I discuss labor rights challenges later in the book.

The organizations used various methods to shape their workers into what they deemed moral entrepreneurs, espousing a bootstrap model of social mobility that tied freedom to their participation in the formal economy. Vocational training seemed a great strategy for developing the skills necessary for "good work," mirroring state-sponsored vocational training programs for those considered indigent. However, what these attempts revealed is that such rehabilitation programs are markedly vacuous, failing to acknowledge the basic economic and political circumstances facing former sex workers and to bring about positive change in their lives. Workers rarely had the time and energy to devote to these programs after a full workload (as the following chapter shows), and even when they successfully completed the training, they quickly learned that training did not afford them better economic opportunities. For these reasons—the inability to actualize any long-term financial benefits from alternative vocational training and the inability of workers to stay on top of both their jobs as jewelry makers and workforce training in second fields—both organizations have since terminated these supplemental training opportunities.

LEARNING TO DREAM

The tenets of moral bootstrap entrepreneurship also translated into various after-work activities that the organizations planned. During one short visit, Esther, a tourist who worked as a financial analyst in the United States and who had learned about Freedom Unchained from her church in the Bay Area, offered to give workers hourlong "business consultations." As the workers gathered in the living room, the house managers introduced Esther's impressive corporate résumé—including quitting a string of corporate jobs to start her own public relations firm—and invited each worker to talk about their "dreams." The room was silent. With an apologetic chuckle, Manager Fu turned to Esther and offered an explanation in English. "You see. It's a bit of a struggle to help these girls dream. They become so stuck by their reality and the limitations that they faced growing up. We encourage them to dream bigger. We tell them that with prayer, anything is possible. Yet, somehow, they still are stuck."

Guoguo finally broke the silence and offered, in Mandarin, "My dream is to work at KFC." The house manager offered a direct translation, which was met by some surprise. Esther asked Guoguo to elaborate on what appealed to her about KFC. Guoguo shrugged her shoulders and replied that she didn't really know why this job appealed to her, but they seemed to be in high demand, and she thought it'd be a job where she would meet a lot of interesting people. In 1987, KFC was the first fast-food chain to enter the Chinese market. Since then, its explosive dominance in China has made it an indispensable, and arguably luxury, household name.[57] Along with its fame has come the promise of middle-class jobs that pay a living wage and come with the prestige of working for an American fast food empire.

However, the "dream" to work in fast food didn't really fit the kind of entrepreneurship that Freedom Unchained hoped workers would aspire to. Esther adapted her approach and talked Guoguo and the group through the different steps that she might need to be able to secure a job at KFC. Each of the steps she outlined seem to trouble Manager Fu, as they involved Guoguo developing independence from Freedom Unchained. Guoguo's aspirations reflected a tangible objective, though it was difficult to swallow because it didn't necessarily paint the picture of transcendence that Freedom Unchained looked for. This mismatch between the goals and realities of vocational training are abundant in the United States, Thailand, and China.[58]

Rehabilitation alternatives aim to address both the economic and emotional needs of former sex workers and victims of trafficking. Vocational training provides the virtuous labor needed to produce for these social enterprises; it promises economic self-sustainability for workers; and it offers a form of moral rehabilitation through the rote and docile requirements of manual wage labor. This approach underscores a desire to resolve sex work as a condition and job, without understanding the underlying constraints that inform the calculation around all forms of low-wage work.

As further developed in the following chapter, the equation of worship with work that so vividly defines the workday in China and Thailand is invisible across both organization's promotional materials, including their websites and brochures, and at venues in the United States where they sell their jewelry. These obfuscations—between morality and work, between religious and secular, between nonprofit and commercial—succeed because rehabilitation has a far-reaching appeal as a market-based strategy for redemption and reform. The language of self-sustaining economic development has joined the mission of salvific evangelism to herald the merits of vocational training. Obvious to workers on the shop floor but invisible to large parts of the consumer and activist base in the United States, this vision of development invariably relegates women to low-wage work.

Rehabilitation as vocational training takes on new life when it travels to different places. The following chapters reveal the labor relations of vocational training in Beijing and Bangkok, and show what these jobs provide alongside local migrant worker economies and opportunities in sex work as well as nonsexual labor. Whereas this chapter focuses on the moral sentiments of ethical consumption, religious imperatives, and promises of rehabilitation, chapter 2 looks at why and how such promises fail workers. Through the perspective of rescued women workers, I discuss how the American rehabilitation imperative shapes labor processes and moral disciplinary regimes in China and Thailand.

CHAPTER 2

Manufacturing Freedom

Racialized Redemptive Labor and Sex Work

"It's happy hour! Come have a drink."

A woman in a bright-purple triangle bikini top, matching miniskirt, and black patent leather stilettos motioned to our group of eight American women, who had paused outside the Honey Money Bar. It was just after 8 p.m., and the pulse of the Soi Cowboy red-light district on Bangkok's Sukhumvit Road was beginning to intensify. As the night progressed, the street would swell and become saturated with noise, food vendors, alcohol, and sex, as people spilled out of the bars that dotted the narrow alley. Men and women from around the world are drawn to this infamous location every night of the week—a prime tourist destination in central Bangkok, given its name by an American GI who started one of the first bars here in the late 1970s during US military involvement in the Indochina Wars.

On this particular Tuesday night in 2008, during my first summer in Bangkok, I moved through Soi Cowboy with a group of eight Cowboy Rescue volunteers. Every Tuesday and Friday evening, this group of American missionaries embarks on what they call "human trafficking outreach ministry," setting out to identify victims of sex trafficking working in Bangkok's several red-light districts. The group of women includes short-term tourists, longer-term expatriates, and full-time missionaries from the global North drawn together by their shared passion to end sex trafficking.

This evening, outreach teams met for dinner and mapped out the night's approach, which varied weekly, from talking with street-based

53

FIGURE 7. Bangkok's Soi Cowboy red-light district. Photo by author.

sex workers on certain blocks or corners to patronizing go-go bars, beer bars, and "fishbowl"-style commercial sex businesses. Outreach was scheduled from 7 to 9 p.m., during the "quiet hours" each night, before customers began pouring in around 10. Colleen, Cowboy Rescue's executive director, led the weekly outreach and began each evening's outing with group prayer, asking for the Holy Spirit's guidance and for Jesus to "lift the darkness" over Bangkok. The "darkness" she referred to was the undeniable presence of commercial sex in Bangkok's streets, which Colleen claimed intimate familiarity with as a resident of Bangkok for more than two decades. American in nationality, Colleen nevertheless professed to have almost no attachment to the United States, having been raised in a family that did missionary work around the world and having established her own family in Bangkok.

Sex has a front-and-center, highly visible presence in Bangkok, home to one of the largest mass-tourist and sex-tourist industries in the world. Tourist guides harp on this point. The *Berlitz Bangkok Pocket Guide* (2015) describes a district "notorious for its go-go bars and sex shows," while Lonely Planet's 2016 guidebook on Bangkok dedicates several pages to helping travelers understand "the sex industry in Thailand" and pinpointing for its readers the locations of some of the largest commercial red-light districts in the world.[1] Commercial sex in Bangkok, broadcast through tourist networks, now links the city in many minds with human trafficking—following the global tendency to conflate all sex commerce with sex trafficking.

Inside the Honey Money go-go bar, chosen for this evening's outreach, stadium-style seating envelops a stage where Thai women dance on a maze of platforms, adorned in everything from bondage gear to frilly lingerie. The dancers are identifiable to the audience primarily by numbers taped to different parts of their body. Abiding by the outreach manual, I pursue our mandate to purchase one drink for a dancer in order to "buy her time," before engaging her in casual conversations about her work, personal life, and migration history. Each drink buys outreach volunteers fifteen to twenty minutes to converse with workers to gauge their interest in leaving sex work to pursue alternative jobs in jewelry making. For the worker, each purchased drink helps her fill a monthly quota: anywhere from two hundred to three hundred mandatory purchased drinks a month to cover her base salary for working at the bar. In Bangkok, that can range between 6,000 and 10,000 baht (200–300 USD), which grows if the worker is able to transform drinks into outcalls, in which clients pay a bar fee of about 20 USD for the privilege of taking the worker off-site where they independently negotiate sex services.

The first time I participated in outreach, I felt—and presumably looked—awkward and uncomfortable. My legs were covered in sweat from the Bangkok heat, and even in the chilly air-conditioned bar, my bare flesh still stuck to the exposed vinyl seats. I watched this scene of a group of foreigners—all white North American women except for me, an Asian American—calling Thai women offstage with great familiarity and gusto. What was immediately puzzling to me during outreach was how, though our intentions were different, we were asked to interact with women through the exact commercial sex interface that male clients around us were using. Weren't we supposed to somehow be distinguishable in approach, I wondered? If the male clients around us were calling women offstage based on their appearance or dress or the way they danced to certain songs, which characteristics were supposed to inform whom I should call off stage? Seeking advice, I turned to Allison, a recent college graduate from Seattle who was spending her summer as a missionary volunteer with Cowboy Rescue. Ally nonchalantly replied that I should "trust the Holy Spirit to connect with anyone who compels you."

Responding to the pregnant pause that must have evinced my unfamiliarity with the Holy Spirit, Ally offered a bit more specificity. She pointed to a tattoo on the back left shoulder of a worker who was facing away from us. Explaining the symbolism of what appeared to be Thai characters arranged in four straight vertical lines of black text, she remarked: "That tattoo is very popular in these bars, and it's a symbol of demonic possession by satanic forces. We like to engage girls with that tattoo because we find that those girls need us the most." I recognized the tattoo as one that had been made fashionable in the United States a few years earlier by Angelina Jolie, who publicly shared with celebrity gossip magazines that the Buddhist Pali incantation her skin bore represented a religious chant and symbol to dispel bad luck. The deeper meaning behind Ally's explanation of the tattoo would not become evident to me until weeks later when I understood that Christian missionary activists justified their evangelizing objectives by claiming that sex trafficking stems from Buddhist values that subordinate women throughout Thailand.[2]

Against the chorus of Britney Spears's hit song "Toxic," I made eye contact with a dancer with a large, round number 24 pinned to the top of her string bikini. She flashed a smile while swaying her hips to the music, shifting her body to grind against the shiny dance pole. Grateful for the eye contact, I waved my hand to call her over to sit with me in the snug two-person vinyl booth. She hopped off stage and approached with the *wai* gesture, the conventional Thai greeting used to confer respect used throughout the country, a bowed head into two hands pressed together in prayer-like fashion. "Sawasdee Ka," she smiled. "Sawasdee Ka," I uttered and clumsily bowed back, recalling my first-year elementary Thai classes at UCLA. We quickly exchanged our names, and she instructed me to call her by her nickname, "Lek," which she told me means "small."

Lek then subtly signaled to a cocktail waitress to come take our drink order. As the waitress approached, I asked Lek what she would like. She quickly replied to the waitress, "Jack and Coke." I echoed that I would take the same and paid 500 baht (15 USD), for the two drinks, plus a tip for the cocktail waitress.

In the heat of the moment, I had forgotten a key shared principal of outreach and would later be reprimanded by an outreach coordinator for not following the training manual closely enough. Outreach volunteers were to refuse the request of alcoholic drinks from dancers, so as not to contribute to a practice outreach workers felt already led to excessive drinking and drug use. This was an awkward rule to follow in a space where alcoholic drinks were the literal and figurative currencies of exchange, but volunteers were adamant that we stick to the outreach script: "I'm sorry, I'm not able to buy you alcohol, but I can pay for any kind of juice or soda you like, . . . and I will pay the full price of an alcoholic beverage."

Conversations between outreach volunteers and bar workers always followed a similar pattern, negotiating the limited English proficiency of Thai workers and the near nonexistent Thai language skills of volunteers. These exchanges were set against the backdrop of pop music blaring from speakers and dim lighting punctuated by the occasional rogue strobe light flashed on the patrons. It was not unlike trying to strike up an intimate conversation with someone you just met in a nightclub. The dialogue always included the requisite demographic pleasantries one learns in any foreign language: name, age, birthplace, where are you from, when did you come to Bangkok, and how long have you worked here? Synergistically, as most expat volunteers were also migrants to Bangkok, these exchanges could often resemble a conversation despite their masked objectives as preliminary job interviews. Dancers also were well trained in this script because these were the same questions their male clients would frequently pose to them to initiate conversation. Gauging opportunities within each response, outreach workers aimed to identify points of entry to steer the conversation toward workers expressing a desire to leave sex work or job dissatisfaction, critical data points for presenting jewelry making as a better alternative.

While most of Cowboy Rescue's sites of intervention in Bangkok are in the organization's namesake, the Soi Cowboy district, expatriate missionaries in China have identified other venues to initiate encounters with potential "rescues." At Freedom Unchained in Beijing, Chinese and American volunteers visit massage parlors and hair salons in two commercial sex districts and befriend Chinese massage parlor and salon workers through promises of English lessons, health education, and friendship. Using the same methods as in Thailand, sex workers are recruited to become jewelry makers with the offer of a monthly salary in exchange for their manual labor, as well as mandatory shelter housing and spiritual rehabilitation.

In both cities, if a sex worker indicates interest in leaving her job, outreach workers exchange contact information and follow up with text messages or phone calls inviting her to submit a job application. At the time of recruitment, the worker is told the very basics about the job:

you work approximately forty hours a week; receive weekends and Chinese, Thai, and some Christian holidays off; and are paid a salary of 250 to 300 USD a month, just above the minimum wage in Beijing and Bangkok.[3]

As I argue throughout this book, American anti-trafficking rehabilitation organizations in both sites obfuscate the fact that these are minimum-wage jobs that rely on extensive manual labor, thereby generating a transnational moral economy of low-wage women's work.[4] This moral economy is shaped by transnational ethical consumption and anchored in racialized redemptive labor arrangements in production sites in Asia. As this chapter reveals, workers quickly learn that beyond basic manufacturing requirements and production quotas, both organizations include numerous other kinds of *virtuous work* as calculable parts of their salary. In using the term *virtuous* I draw on Kimberly Hoang's notion of "virtuous third world poverty" in describing humanitarian sentimentality regarding Vietnamese sex workers wielded by Western clients and NGOs alike.[5] Such labor is deemed virtuous by white feminist activists only if it fits the inherently extractive forms of low-wage manual labor that drive the global economy.

Worker contracts also include various restrictions on behaviors in and outside the workday. These thus constitute additional forms of *repentant labor,* including church worship and Bible study as components of a worker's salary. Employment contracts also explicitly forbid engaging in sexual commerce or in any social activity that might bring a worker in contact with former coworkers or her old workplace. This duality—of labor's productivity and virtuosity—enables rescue programs to appropriate low-wage women's work at the discursive and labor-process levels.

THE "COMPANY"—FREE-MARKET REHABILITATION IN THAILAND

As sanitation workers sweep up beer bottles and night vendors have just about finished taking down stalls in the Soi Cowboy commercial sex district, Thai workers at Cowboy Rescue begin arriving at work—or what many refer to in English simply as "the Company." Like any workplace, the women who work at Cowboy Rescue each have their morning routines—they grab iced coffee, eat breakfast on the go, some drop their children off at the daycare that the rehabilitation center houses a few blocks away—and all are identified by the distinctly black and yellow form-fitting polo shirts, mandatory uniforms the workers are provided on their first day of work.

Workers huddle around a time-punch clock, eager to check in by 9 a.m., and then hurry over to the nearby church to begin the workday with an hour of Christian worship. Each day begins in song and prayer led by Tim, the in-house pastor, a longtime American missionary and the spouse of the Cowboy Rescue founder and CEO, Colleen. Onstage appear some Thai workers who have become worship leaders and others who share their musical talents by providing accompaniment on the piano or guitar. A single sheet of paper is placed at the back of the worship hall on which workers must sign in if they arrive late. Latecomers log their names and indicate the exact time they arrived at church. Workers are penalized 2 baht (10 cents USD) for each minute they are late, which accounts for the urgency around the punch clock.

At church, Cowboy Rescue's employees, numbering over one hundred, sit in rows of stackable chairs arranged in temporary pews facing the lectern where Pastor Tim delivers daily sermons in fluent Thai, his linguistic mastery accumulated after two decades of missionary work in the country. A handful of veteran Thai workers—the peer worship leaders mentioned earlier—also stand on stage. Embodying their connections to charismatic Christianity, many devotees are often seen with their hands raised, palms facing the sky, gently swaying back and forth, with eyes closed in praise. Other workers sit toward the back of the room; in contrast to the enthusiastic worshippers in the front, some are slouched in their chairs, hunched over their phones checking text messages, Facebook updates, or playing Hay Day—a simulation social network game similar to FarmVille that is popular throughout Asia.

Following the hour-long worship service each morning, workers promptly return to the production building to begin the day's jewelry fabrication. There, eight to ten workers sit around long rectangular tables in the production room, the largest workroom in the facility. Elsewhere, smaller groups of workers package and ship orders or manage inventory and supplies. Lunch is served at noon by rotating groups of workers who are responsible for preparing, cooking, and serving the meals and cleaning dishes. At 1 p.m., employees resume their respective tasks, and each afternoon at around 3, they pause for a rotating schedule of English lessons, games, and Christian life counseling. At the close of the day, at 5 p.m., Cowboy workers clock out and disperse across the vast Bangkok metropolis. Some share rooms in high-rent apartments nearby, while others commute as far as two hours away to more affordable housing. Rather than return home, workers whose Cowboy salaries do not sufficiently cover their living expenses go to part-time jobs in the service or tourist industry to earn additional money.

In 2006, during its first year of operation, Cowboy Rescue recruited forty women, a number that quickly doubled by its third year in business. In April 2009, Cowboy employed eighty women, ages seventeen to fifty-eight, and by 2012 the company's staff had grown to more than one hundred workers. By June 2012, the organization had reached maximum capacity and implemented a "waiting list" of applicants seeking jobs. To date, fundraising emails often point to the waiting list as an indication of the need for more resources to provide more services. The majority (roughly two-thirds) of the women workers are from Thailand's northeastern Isaan province, the largest migrant-sending region in the country. Most of these women migrated to Bangkok through networks of friends and family, and found commercial sex work to be the most lucrative among the limited low-wage job opportunities.

Employees at Cowboy are compensated with both a salary and benefits. The first three months of employment mark a probationary period during which the employee earns a trial salary of 7,500 baht a month (230 USD). Upon completing this probationary period, her salary is raised to the standard 9,000 baht a month (280 USD), which is anywhere from one-fifth to one-third of the salary she formerly earned doing sex work. Workers also receive health insurance, vacation days, and time off for Thai national and some American holidays, as well as Christian religious observance. Formal medical insurance, weekends off, and vacation time are welcome benefits not systematically provided through sex work establishments or in other intimate and informal labor arrangements. Despite the benefits they receive, Cowboy workers who left sex work to become jewelry makers find that they must make significant sacrifices to accept such a considerable salary cut.

As the most important social condition of employment, Cowboy workers must sign a contract agreeing that they will no longer sell sex and will no longer patronize any of the bars where they used to work. The requirement that they no longer see friends or visit environments in which sex is being sold—even if they are not selling it—is intended to prevent the women from, as one activist claimed, "recidiv[ism] into the sex industry." Treating sex and sex work as addictions, activists use rehabilitation strategies based on a transnational moral panic over sex. When pathologized as a disease, sex work is framed as the antithesis of rehabilitation remedies that focus on wage labor, good taste, and appropriate Western femininity.

All workers at Cowboy Rescue understand the contractual obligation against sex work as a condition of employment; however, rumors circulate about certain workers continuing to see clients on the side because their wages as jewelry makers are too low to cover basic living costs. The minimum wage was raised by law in 2012 to 300 baht (10 USD) per day, which meant that the Cowboy salary of 9,000 baht per month was just barely above the national minimum wage, though, unlike most low-wage employees, Cowboy Rescue workers did receive medical insurance and weekends off. In 2010, following rumors about some workers continuing to "work" on the side, Cowboy managers began demanding the Facebook passwords of all their employees to monitor their online activity for any sex work. Workers immediately responded by creating duplicate Facebook accounts, a quick and easy way to subvert such surveillance since they couldn't resist it outright.

While transnational feminist and ethnic studies scholars have charted the transnational racialization of Asian women's errant sexuality, they have not fully documented Western activists' strategies for taming such deviant sexuality.[6] As a tool of both industrial instruction and moral correction, jewelry making is the perfect antidote for "lost women"—a broad label that includes sex workers, the homeless, drug and alcohol addicts, and the indigent. Organizations that claim to "rescue" fallen women inextricably weave their rehabilitation narratives with that of monolithic sexual victimization, a tight subject-spatial positioning that never allows their employees to define for themselves their former jobs as sex workers—whether voluntary or not.

FACTORY OF GOD—SPIRITUAL REHABILITATION UNDER CHINESE AUTHORITARIANISM

The Freedom Unchained project in Beijing was founded in 2005 by two young American women, Sarah, a white woman from the Midwest in her late thirties, and Yves, a Chinese American woman from California in her late twenties. The two met at the Beijing Christian International Fellowship (BCIF), the largest interdenominational Christian church in Beijing. Like Colleen in Thailand, Sarah was a long-term expatriate missionary and had lived for years with her partner and children in China. This long-term presence in the country also meant that, like Colleen, she spoke the country's main language, Mandarin, but relied on Chinese staff to do most of the day-to-day communication with workers. In the early years of their operations, Sarah oversaw daily operations as the executive director, while Yves focused on business development in Los Angeles, where she was earning a graduate degree. As they began their operations, Sarah and Yves volunteered all their time but had a paid staff of three Christian women: a Chinese business director, a Chinese housemom, and an American life counselor. Freedom Unchained was not registered as a nonprofit organization in China or the United States. It receives funding in the form of charitable donations via its fiscal conduit, a registered American Christian charity.

Unlike Thailand, China has outlawed Christian missionary work, which creates an urgency among Freedom Unchained activists to conceal the religious aspect of their work. The Chinese government opposes organized religious activity, and Christian observance is often relegated to private home churches in China. Expats living in Beijing can attend public church services at BCIF, where the Freedom Unchained founders met; however, entry is restricted to foreign-passport holders. While the number of Chinese Christians is unknown, largely because their worship must be clandestine, the World Christian Database estimates that 111 million Chinese are Christian, of whom 90 percent are Protestant.[7]

In addition to being low-key about the faith-based aspect of their work, Freedom Unchained also explains that the Chinese government dislikes that they work on social issues related to sex work. While Bangkok has an established sex tourism sector, with several unofficially recognized red-light districts, female migrant workers in Beijing face a considerably smaller and dispersed commercial sex industry. While many women who migrate to Bangkok take positions working in the red-light district, Quanhe Yang and Fei Guo (1996) found that most Chinese women migrants (63 percent) work in the food and beverage sectors.[8] The Freedom Unchained workers fit this profile, as all of them first took jobs as waitresses and other low-wage service positions before discovering that they could earn significantly more by working in a massage business or hair salon.

Freedom Unchained activists claim that because the commercial sex industry is spatially dispersed in Beijing, the government can turn a blind eye to the problem. They charge the Chinese government with neglecting the prostitution issue out of a need to "save face." As evidence for this assertion, they point to the government's treatment of prostitution during the 2008 Olympics in Beijing. As was the case with other low-wage migrant workers, sex workers were "sent home"; in other words, they were subjected to high levels of surveillance so that they could not continue normal business practices. The Olympic crackdown caused Freedom Unchained to limit its outreach, which usually happened twice a week, and to change its formal mission statement from "rescuing victims of trafficking and sexual exploitation in China" to "rescuing at-risk women in Asia" so as to anonymize its operations during the Olympics.

Government censorship led Freedom Unchained to adopt a strict form of confidentiality in its work—a form of isolation that the organization in turn imposes on workers in dormitories and production rooms alike. Outside the 5th Ring expressway in Beijing, on a dusty road leading to the remote Beijing Capital International Airport, a dozen or so women assemble jewelry around a table in a room with a smoked-glass door that cannot be peered into or looked out of. The sound of beads and metal shuffling around the table are punctuated with small talk as workers make jewelry over the course of an eight-hour workday. To help pass the time, workers used to play music through fuzzy, low-grade speakers on their cell phones, but after concern that too many workers were singing along to popular Chinese love songs with unsavory messages, the Chinese floor manager, Ms. Fu, banned any secular music from being played during the workday, claiming that it led to distraction and decreased productivity.

Like the women workers at Cowboy Rescue, Freedom Unchained workers also start the workday at 9 a.m. by clocking in with an analog time-stamp machine. Employees are paid the equivalent of minimum-wage jobs in Beijing, which in 2010 was 1600 RMB per month (250 USD). They are also eligible to earn a few hundred RMB extra a month if they take on additional responsibilities such as grocery shopping for meals at the shelter, though everyone chips in on a rotating basis to cook the meals. One can also earn a few hundred RMB a month sourcing the raw materials for jewelry design. Sourcing is considered a coveted position because the job is conducted off-site and gives workers the opportunity to shop and show off their bargaining skills. Hunting for good deals and forging relationships with wholesale distributors stirred the excitement and satisfaction that one gets from shopping, a welcome feeling since most workers said they didn't earn enough money to afford much personal leisure shopping.

While workers in Bangkok rent their own apartments, housing in Freedom Unchained's on-site dormitory is mandatory, which to workers initially seems like standard post-socialist "iron rice bowl" provisions,

FIGURE 8. Freedom Unchained employee time cards. Photo by author.

that is, meals and housing that employers provide to all migrant workers, even in some white-collar jobs. This legacy of socialist worker provision is kept alive under explosive industrial-capitalist expansion in China's urban areas and is, some argue, part of a strategy to keep migrant life precarious, with shelter and food explicitly tied to an employer's beneficence.[9] The requisite provision of dorm housing also maintains the transience of the migrant workforce. As Sarah Swider observed of Chinese construction sites, temporary migrant housing is built within the construction site so that the completion of the work project also signals the destruction of the temporary housing.

Freedom Unchained activists reframe the socialist legacy of the iron rice bowl not simply as a benefit of employment but as a mandatory requirement. In the NGO's promotional materials, the dormitory is referred to as a "victim shelter," which satisfies funders who are driven to understand that workers must need a place of sanctuary to escape their brutal experiences in sex work. In these dorms, workers sleep six to eight in a room so that activists and managers may patrol their moral behavior. As in Thailand, workers in China must also sign a behavioral contract, which includes basic rules barring nonviolent behavior and requiring cleanliness and vigilance about turning off the gas valve after cooking. This housing contract also forbids commercial sex work, premarital sex, and abortion—loosely patrolled both by "housemoms," who manage dorm life, and by a system that encourages coworkers to report on one another's infringement of these contracts, as I discuss further in the following chapter.

In Beijing, measures similar to those in Bangkok link manual labor and moral transformation through vocational training; however, in the Chinese context they are justified and amplified through the authoritarian regime's tight control of civil society organizations. In both instances, international religious organizations draw strength from their alignment with state causes against the issue of sexual commerce, which is illegal in both China and Thailand. However, in atheist China, the same authoritarian power that supports the moral grounds for anti-prostitution activities has strict laws against the distribution of religious materials by foreigners, as specifically outlined in the 2000 law "Rules for Religious Activities of Foreigners." Thus, to keep a low profile vis-à-vis government censorship for their evangelical extragovernmental enterprise, the Freedom Unchained office and shelter are geographically remote, in a small Beijing suburb about an hour away from the city's center, where employers can maintain strict control of their workers, both during and after the workday. Freedom Unchained's mandatory shelter marks one of the crucial differences between the under rehabilitation experiences of workers in China and Thailand.

Yanhu, a twenty-nine-year-old mother of one, migrated to Beijing from Zhejiang province in 2002. She is one of eight women whom Freedom Unchained hired as the first group of recruited workers. She came to Beijing seeking employment that would pay her money to send home to her eleven-year-old son and her parents, who help take care of him. However, with only a middle-school education, her opportunities for employment are limited to low-wage service-sector work. She has worked in a variety of jobs in Beijing, including a year and a half as a salesperson for a company that sold construction materials. After discovering that she could make more money working in a massage shop, where her job included offering sexual services to clients, she left the construction job. She worked in the massage shop for several months before being contacted by Freedom Unchained outreach workers.

Yanhu says she was drawn to Freedom Unchained because it sold itself as a temporary "vocational training program." She looks back on her former job in construction sales quite fondly and hopes to open a small

FIGURE 9. A Freedom Unchained
employee threading a piece of jewelry
by hand. Photo by author.

construction materials business in her hometown so she can be closer to her son. During the summer of 2010, I sat in on a "business consulting workshop" held by a group of young Chinese American Christian management consultants who visited Freedom Unchained as part of a weeklong vacation in Beijing. Yanhu explained her future business goals to Christine, who also happened to be twenty-nine and whose expertise as a Google employee suggested that she would have valuable advice to impart. Christine told Yanhu that if she prayed hard enough, God would provide for her business; for Yanhu, who is not Christian, this suggestion was unsatisfying because it did not offer any tangible way to pursue her objective.

Unlike the women workers in Bangkok, who see jewelry making as a permanent form of employment, Freedom Unchained participants claim that jewelry training was advertised as part of a temporary training program teaching valuable skills that would allow them to seek gainful employment outside the sex industry. These workers claimed that they might not have agreed to take such a large pay cut if they had known they would be consigned to making jewelry for an indefinite period of time. Rather, they hoped that through the promised vocational training, they would find jobs that offered compensation close to what they had made as sex workers. As it turns out, they have not been trained in jobs other than jewelry making (due, the administrators say, to financial constraints) and now feel trapped in this liminal employment situation.

Many do not want to return to sex work. Some say they never really wanted to do sex work in the first place. Others say they just weren't good at it. Still others claimed that it wasn't the sexual exchanges that bothered them but that management in the massage businesses frequently withheld owed wages and subjected them to unfair treatment. Each of these perspectives gestures to different reasons for leaving commercial sex, though rehabilitation projects often replayed the narrative of sexual victimization as the animating reason to leave sex work. Freedom Unchained workers like Yanhu choose to stay with the program because they still hope that they might learn something that could eventually lead to better employment opportunities.

QUOTA PRODUCTION

A sign at the front of the jewelry workroom at Freedom Unchained reminds workers of the speed at which they must work. Under this strict quota production system, a worker should produce at least three hundred pairs of earrings per day. Freedom Unchained demands its workers produce jewelry with greater speed and in larger quantities than at Cowboy Rescue because the majority of the Chinese company's distribution occurs through wholesale outlets, a direct result of Chinese impositions on the free market for international companies and NGOs. Whereas sales in Bangkok are driven by a highly sophisticated inventory system that matches individual orders with individual production, online sales are difficult to coordinate behind China's impervious internet firewall. Furthermore, Freedom Unchained faced additional government scrutiny because of its status as a foreign and Christian organization. These disparate forms of government surveillance—actual and perceived—shape the prioritization of mass productivity at Freedom Unchained in Beijing.

In the early years of the organization's operations, a whiteboard at the front of the jewelry production room listed each worker's name along with the number of pieces she completed every hour. Separated and ranked into categories A, B, and C, the workers were paid wages determined by their quotas and speeds of production, with those in productivity category C receiving 200 RMB (35 USD) less per month than those in category A. Speaking to me in Chinese, Manager Fu, a middle-aged Chinese Christian woman with a college degree in the life sciences, explained that the organization developed this strategy because "many of them haven't worked in 'traditional' workplaces, and lack a good work ethic. This board keeps them on track, at least in relation to their coworkers." These visible markers of productivity encouraged the employees to work at an equal pace. While they drew attention to their speed of production, they also encouraged competition and defined individual value based on shop floor output.

The same day in 2009 that the Chinese business manager praised the merits of the white board strategy, she went on to gripe, "Morale has been very low amongst the women. They sometimes taunt or ridicule coworkers who don't work as fast as they do ... this makes certain employees feel bad, and we do not know how to increase morale." Then, switching to English—a strategy she frequently used to demonstrate class distinction from workers who are not bilingual—she posed this problem as part of a broader conversation she and I were having about what activities I could help organize after the workday. During my three summers of participant observation at Freedom Unchained, I tried to make my presence worthwhile by organizing evening activities, but I responded differently to this particular query. Thinking of my own bodily and psychic desires while working as a jewelry maker during participant observation, I suggested taking breaks throughout the day to engage in group icebreakers or movement exercises, but Fu immediately quipped: "Movement games might be a good solution for the evening activities you plan at the shelter; unfortunately, the girls cannot have that kind of distraction during the workday because when we did this in the past, we saw a large decrease in productivity."

It took several years of participant observation before I learned what workers in both sites always know: that any attempt by management to increase worker satisfaction, or to reduce conflict between coworkers, is at its base intended to increase manufacturing productivity. Therefore, rather than turn to management for the alleviation of any problem, workers devise strategies for supporting one another as vital modes of resistance. While some workers are more dexterous with pliers and wires, facilitating greater individual production speed, most of the women workers support one another around the table because they know that there are no rewards to be gained by finishing first. One worker in her late twenties, named Ling, from Fujian province, let me in on a sort of unspoken pact: "If we finish all three hundred earrings before the day is over, we are not allowed to leave early, so there is no incentive to be fast. At the same time, if we don't finish three hundred, then we have to stay late and are not paid overtime. Basically, we don't want to work too hard or too slow; we just want to barely do enough in the time allotted." This creates excitement and frenzy during the last half hour of work, when workers assess how much quicker or slower they must work to just meet the quota. One worker described the most successful employee as the one who produces the closest to three hundred without exceeding her quota, lest the entire group quota be increased in the future.

These are part of a range of strategies that workers employ as resistance on the shop floor. Often they are invisible. As I observe in the following chapter, the more visible the form of resistance, the more likely managers are to co-opt it, framing any women's questioning of labor norms as "acting out"—a symptom of "processing trauma" they endured in sex work. These labor relations embody what Michael Burawoy has described as "manufacturing consent," a co-constitutive process in which employers and employees each carve out logics of work and exploitation.[10] Outright coercion, Burawoy finds, is not necessary when workers internalize management practice. While Manager Fu saw discontent as a case-by-case instance of individual women feeling bad about losing out to their competition, she could not see how group morale is actually tied to the overall group dynamics of allegedly rehabilitative work.

CALLOUSED, VIRTUOUS WORK

The manual labor of making jewelry is difficult and requires technical skill, attention to detail, and enormous patience. Veteran workers teach new recruits how to use pliers in manipulating wires, connecting eyelets, and threading beads and gems at the required speed. Working with small eyelets, and even smaller fasteners as connector pieces, one must acquire agility and precision to work with a set of pliers in each hand. Most of the pieces I made never passed quality control, and I systematically relied on the generosity of someone sitting at my table to fix and improve them for me. Rote and repetitive, the work of jewelry making was not always technically easy and required a work ethic of moral and fiscal sacrifice that proved its worth by its proximity to piety.

In Beijing, I once spent two weeks trying to perfect the art of "wax rope burning," a technique used to prevent a red rope—commonly used in China—from fraying once the bracelets were finished, and the more complicated task of "thinning" the head of the rope so we could thread a tiny bead with it. I considered myself lucky that Jade, the most veteran worker at the time, had the patience to teach me the intricacies of this delicate task. Jade showed me how to hold the rope up to a flame until its waxy exterior melted. She demonstrated how to rub the hot waxy rope between one's fingers to taper it. After just ten tries, I developed boils on my thumb and first-finger pads. I asked if I could use a glove. I asked why we couldn't just use a thinner rope to thread the beads, or just buy a bead with a bigger hole. My tablemates laughed at my questions and protests and explained that it was a delicate task—you needed to have the tactile strength of your fingers to pull at the thread just enough. If you wore a glove, you would inevitably pull too much, causing the rope to disintegrate. They told me to keep at it, promising that eventually callouses would develop on fingertips and numb the pain.

In both cities, my failures to perfect even the most basic of tasks provided a certain comedy relief to my coworkers, though I was keenly aware of the intrusion my presence posed to productivity in both sites. As a volunteer in China, I was never subject to production quotas and would often just pile my scant contributions into the table's output. Much of the ambient noise throughout the workday came from workers laughing, often making jokes at each other's expense, bringing a certain levity to the otherwise bleak work environment. When I was present, conversations and mockery often shifted to me as we discussed everything from the price of the latest Apple product in the United States; gossip and life updates about former American friends and volunteers; disbelief about American consumption of ice water or prescription hormonal birth control; and suggestions for weight loss and skin-lightening techniques.

Workers rarely complained about the technical difficulties or body strains of work—including sore eyes, back and neck pain, and the occasional cut or burn—because they understood these ailments as lying along a continuum of physically taxing work they had done in their lives. Significantly, when talking about prior work life and experiences, none talked explicitly about sex work, preferring instead to reference different kinds of difficult manual labor they had endured, including working twenty-plus-hour days in a fast-fashion garment factory, or as a nurse's aid scrubbing human waste from bedpans, or working at a construction sales company that required hauling 50 kilo bags of cement and tile around the shop, or working in retail customer service where they were frequently degraded by middle-class clientele, or doing domestic work where they also experienced being degraded but in private sites that isolated them from social contact with peers.

Describing some of the natural overlaps between manual labor and sex work, one Chinese worker named Chong Gu once shared her experiences working as a waitress in a Beijing restaurant that catered to a middle-class clientele, including mid-level government officials. "Drunk men screamed at us all the time," she recalled, "and they'd grab you and you wouldn't be able to say anything to them. At least when we worked in the massage shop, it was clear what they were paying for." Chong's point raises an important reality for many workers in low-wage service and manufacturing jobs: sexual abuse in the workplace. Because migrant women workers face some of the highest rates of sexual abuse in the workplace, sex work, some argue, ironically is the most transparent because it places the exchange of sex at the center of the commercial interaction, rather than as an inevitable by-product of poor management. Recent research by Global Labor Justice and the Asia Wage Floor Alliance has demonstrated how intractable gender-based violence in the workplace is throughout manufacturing work.[11] Yet the moral outrage against sex trafficking almost never includes the pervasive issues of sexual assault and sexual harassment throughout low-wage work, again highlighting the discord between the anti-trafficking movement's concern with abolishing sexual labor and its position upholding the decency and dignity inherent in manual labor.

All forms of labor, however, systematically incur physical risk. In Bangkok, a worker was once using a glue gun that malfunctioned and leaked searing hot glue onto her leg. As it dried almost immediately, it plastered some denim onto her leg, which upon being ripped off, took skin with it, creating a raw wound. I immediately thought she would need some sort of advanced skin graft to heal the giant sore. She was simply told to cover it with a gauze pad for several weeks while it healed. I winced every time I saw her change her bandage, frequently necessary in Bangkok's sweltering heat, but she told me empathetically it didn't feel as bad as it looked. Older workers often complained that their eyes couldn't focus on the small beads and hooks, as their eyesight was deteriorating with age. Sometimes these workers were given opportunities to work in packaging and or product quality control. In most cases, those positions were considered promotions and demanded their own set of advanced skills, such as the ability to read English or read and update a Microsoft Excel spreadsheet.

Despite the occasional physical strain of making jewelry, as in much other manufacturing work, women workers preferred to keep the job because it afforded a level of flexibility and certain benefits. The organizations provided a social safety net and access to resources that migrant workers did not otherwise have in the low-wage service and manufacturing industries.

In both China and Thailand, these benefits included weekends off and potential opportunities to increase their income, which also distinguished jewelry making from previous manual labor jobs they had held. Following the end of a particular product line or season, Cowboy Rescue sold leftover unused beads to their workers. During the lunch hour in Thailand, workers would then sell jewelry they had created with these leftover beads. This impromptu marketplace enabled these workers to generate extra income with their jewelry-making skills. Particularly enterprising women would also sell these items on weekends at street fairs and other vending locations. In China, however, this option would be nearly unthinkable, where because of workers' confinement to the remote geographic location, they lacked outlets for basic socializing and life outside work, let alone access to alternative marketplaces to sell their jewelry.

The formalized wage labor of jewelry making created a system of benefits that few other low-wage service sector or manufacturing jobs offered.[12] By mobilizing connections to larger networks of charity and aid—in particular, donations from a global church community—Christian social enterprises could reallocate resources to meet needs that would never be met by local employers. For instance, in Thailand, Cowboy Rescue paid for expensive antiretroviral drugs for HIV-positive workers that would not typically be covered, even under white-collar health insurance plans. In China, the organization once raised funds to pay part of the 20,000 RMB (3,000 USD) penalty incurred by one worker for violating the one-child policy after accidentally becoming pregnant with her second child. It was easy to raise these funds among Christian followers who did not want her to have an abortion. And in both countries, the organizations provided, or found organizational partners to provide, free childcare for infants and toddlers, and sometimes paid for temporary tuition for older children to stay in school in the city. This was especially important in Beijing, where children of migrant workers are not eligible for education in the city. These benefits were incomparable, but they often came at the cost of accepting strict moral limitations and frequently revealed the power of the organization's evangelizing missions.

CURRENCIES OF REFORM: REPENTANT WORK

At the end of one workday in Beijing, I was hanging around the dorm room as we often did. I was sitting in the bottom bunk of a veteran worker, Yin, then twenty-four years old and in her third year at Freedom Unchained. Yin was rifling through her belongings to show me photos of her older brother, whose college tuition in Inner Mongolia she helps pay for through her work as a jewelry maker. Flipping through a small stack of items that she keeps in the single half locker that is her assigned private cubby—the only private space she has in the entire workplace—she came across a large folder and paused. She opened the folder to reveal a "self-assessment form" that workers are required to fill out each year. In addition to evaluating their production, leadership, and teamwork skills, the form also asks workers to gauge—on a scale of zero to five—their commitment to living the teachings of Jesus Christ, as well as their belief in Christ's teachings. Yin had marked a zero for belief in Christ's teachings, but explained that she didn't know how to "rank" her commitment to Christ's teachings. She explained the predicament: "I won't say that I am Christian just so I can get promoted. There are some coworkers here who pretend to believe in Jesus, and they receive all kinds of opportunities. I think the fact that I won't lie to get in good favor with the management is 'living the teachings of Christ.'" Yin eventually decided to leave this question blank, challenging her employers with its ambiguity. Her strategy demonstrates the tremendous insight workers had into the different modes of earning merit and into the ties between moral and financial rewards. Other workers claimed that Christian workers were offered greater opportunity for upward mobility; for instance, extra salary for monitoring dormitory behavior like chores or curfew, or invitations to participate in recruitment, which was limited to those who embraced Christianity because, it was thought, those workers understood the organization's proselytizing goals. Managers justified promotions or financial rewards given to believers through a teleological ethos—that Christ's teachings foster more docile, humble, and productive employees.

The slight monetary incentives for one's own conversion and proselytizing other coworkers make the requirements of redemptive labor difficult for workers living within the rescue industry in China. In Thailand, workers were never asked to rank or quantify their commitment to the teachings of Christ. This may have reflected the relative saturation of foreign religious missionary work in Thailand, which was not only legal but widely accepted as a significant conduit of growth in tourism and the expat population. In short, the religious stakes are simply higher in China. Freedom Unchained activist missionaries are more emphatic about Christianity than their counterparts in Bangkok because missionary activists run greater risks in China. The authorities still consider packing a Bible and "smuggling" it through Chinese customs a subversive religious act—and one that many Unchained volunteers take great pride in doing as they travel between the United States and China. In contrast, Thailand grants more than 150 missionary visas per year and tolerates and permits religious diversity.

Once a year, however, at the annual retreat to a place a few hours outside Bangkok, Cowboy Rescue performs deliverance rituals, which demonstrate to workers, and the larger consumer bases that Cowboy

Rescue advertises to, the number of women who accept God every year. Colleen once shared that about a third of women in Thailand had converted to Christianity, while others remain devout Buddhists, atheists, or animists. Although Cowboy did require an hour of Christian church worship every morning, calculating this as a mandatory part of wages, they also offered a voluntary Sunday church worship that drew a consistent crowd of at least a dozen workers on one of their days off. By contrast, in the Chinese setting, between 2008 and 2012, workers told me that not a single non-Christian worker had converted to Christianity. Still, across both sites, a sense of bitterness often circulated among nonbelievers who pointed out to me that some workers had been promoted after dubiously performing disingenuous religiosity.

Because missionary work is illegal in China, Freedom Unchained activists feel pressure to conceal the religious and proselytizing aspect of their work. Demonstrating its fear and respect for government censorship of its work, the organization produces two identical catalogs, one for in-country distribution and the other for international use. Whereas the international catalog notes that the project works with victims of human trafficking in China, the Chinese-only version merely states that the project works with "exploited women in Asia." These restrictions in sales and marketing suggest just one of the possible reasons why the Beijing organization has grown more slowly as it lacks outlets to the free market due to repression of organized Christianity.

The contrast in religious freedom between China and Thailand suggests that, by formally adopting secularized ideas of a good work ethic and moral reform, Christian missionaries in China have troublingly transplanted the government's authoritarianism to their moral workplace. Freedom Unchained is strategic about managing its fears of government oversight. The organization goes to great lengths to retain anonymity in its operations, as exemplified by its remote location, separate catalogs for in-country and international sales, and reliance on socialist work-unit systems as a way of asserting moral control over its employees. Although Chinese state-owned enterprises have long provided benefits and secure food and housing to workers, Freedom Unchained activists frame these offerings within the contemporary rights-based *rehabilitation regime* for trafficked persons. Secular efforts that claim "rights-based" approaches to seeking justice for trafficked persons call for rehabilitative services that encompass shelters, counseling, and vocational and life skills training. Under the guise of victim protection, or more specifically what Jennifer Musto refers to as "carceral protectionism,"[13] mandatory shelter housing and wage labor are compulsory parts of a sex worker's path to "freedom."

Crying on the Job

Aware of their status in the company above all as workers, employees in both organizations commit to different forms of emotional labor expected of them. This includes knowing exactly how to carve out spaces of freedom and when to demonstrate regret, shame, redemption, and gratitude. One Monday evening in the summer of 2010, I was seated on a couch in the Freedom Unchained shelter living room amid a large circle of about fifteen workers, volunteers, and activists. The mandatory weekly meeting from 7 to 9 p.m. was devoted to "group counseling." Assembling workers usually took some time. Accounting for their tardiness, some said they had to wait for others to finish using the single shower upstairs. Others had taken the bus into town to shop after the workday and returned late. Still others were using the time after work to make phone calls or nap. By the time all staff members were finally assembled in the living room and the program got started, it was usually about 7:30.

On this particular evening, a mysterious roll of toilet paper was passed around the group, and each participant was instructed to tear off a sheet of toilet paper of any length. None of the participants had any idea what activity was about to follow, and each person around the circle pulled sheets of varying lengths. As the roll of toilet paper made its way around the complete circle, we awaited instructions, and Kat, a peppy twenty-four-year-old volunteer from Australia, told us to count the number of squares on our sheet of toilet paper. This number, she exclaimed, would determine how many questions we would each have to answer in front of the group. Participants who pulled particularly long sections gasped, groaned, and sighed in dread of the embarrassment and scrutiny that lay ahead.

I understood this dread-filled response once Kat fired a litany of questions to each person:

(1) What are you most ashamed of in your life?

(2) What is the most important thing that you have lost?

(3) Who has hurt you the most in your life?

(4) What are your dreams?

(5) What do you give thanks for?

Kat delivered these queries to each worker without ever losing her peppy demeanor and smile. Using a rehearsed Mandarin in awkwardly formal phrasing, she sounded as if she was celebrating the new vocabulary words she must have just memorized from her Mandarin language class earlier in the day. The robotic but enthusiastic delivery of the questions grated against the awkward reticence of those who were supposed to answer them. Most responses were met with a stony silence, avoidance of eye contact, or a simple "I don't know" or "I don't remember." Kat's interrogation gently probed a little further using another set of basic Mandarin prompts. When these probes failed, Manager Fu intervened with a more aggressive approach, speaking in Mandarin to bring up detailed parts she knew of someone's past or personal information to jar their memories. Pushed to the brink, many participants ended up crying, which seemed to me to be the ultimate goal of the exercise—or the only possible result of the palpably thick tension that coated the room. Only after a woman was brought to the point of tears did Kat or Fu agree to move on to the next person. Explained within their model of psychological counseling, which focused on resolving "sin," crying indicated to activists that workers were coming to terms with their sins, and only after they "willingly addressed the shame of their past" could they truly receive moral transformation.

I drew only two toilet paper squares myself, and Jade quickly grabbed the piece out of my hand and replaced it with the much longer roll that Li, the youngest worker, sitting on the other side of her, had grabbed. I understood this quick, nearly invisible swap as one of the numerous ways Jade tried to take care of younger workers. At the time, at age thirty-three, Jade was one of Freedom Unchained's oldest employees, and she assumed a natural leadership role over the younger participants, offering advice on everything from jewelry making to food preparation to budgeting their money. She was keenly aware of Freedom Unchained's strategies for moral reform and, while resentful of them, knew when and how to perform redemption, because such demonstrations of emotional labor were an inseparable part of her wage. After the toilet paper activity, she told me: "Everyone hates the Monday night group sessions because they always ask weird questions, and it's as if they're not satisfied until you cry. Only after you cry do they think you are really doing something good for yourself. I know this makes them happy, so sometimes I just cry to make it end quicker." Managers and activists across both workplaces understood crying as a form of redemption in which women confront their past as sex workers. This mirrored the Christian tradition of testimonials, according to which American visitors to the jewelry-making facility were often invited to share their own tales of hardship, faith, and ultimate redemption. Jade, like some other workers, often strategically performed such visible acts of redemption as a calculated part of earning her wage.

Crying was meaningful to activists, who interpreted tears as signifying everything from repentance to guilt to honest testimonial. When participants cried, movement activists believed they were coming to terms with their sins and, in addressing the shame of having been a sex worker, were truly accepting moral transformation. However, just as workers learned to cry on demand, they also learned to withhold tears at other moments. One evening in the shelter, I heard of an argument between workers and their housemom, a Chinese Christian woman just barely twenty years old. Spats were frequent because workers had a hard time understanding why they had to abide by so many rules after the workday. Furthermore, they found it difficult to accept that the shelter manager was just twenty, younger than almost all of them. Why, they wondered, should she have a say in how we live our lives after the workday?

When I asked managers about the housemom, they assured me that "Li Yan is a hard-working Christian girl. Since she is close in age, she can relate to the girls and teach them something." Li Yan often confided in me that she found her position nearly impossible. The women in the shelter didn't respect her authority. She chalked it up to their "situation": they were emerging from a past so dark, she assumed, that it would be difficult to abide by such strict rules.

One early evening in the shelter, residents had a particularly intense argument with Li Yan. Ling had been assigned bathroom duty—one of a rotating set of household chores that included sweeping the bedrooms, mopping the living room, cleaning the kitchen, washing the dishes, and cleaning the bathroom. Common in many middle-class apartments in Beijing, the small bathroom had no shower stall or tub. This meant that no matter how diligent you were after showering, the floor would be covered with water. Ling claimed that she had already mopped the bathroom, but that someone else must have showered after her. I was not present for this particular fight, but when Ling reported back to me, she said, "I didn't want to clean the bathroom again," and recalled that after she continued to protest, Li Yan tried to reason with her and dismissively said, "You are so uneducated, this is why Freedom Unchained enforces rules around you." This created an uproar among the seven Freedom Unchained workers who heard the argument, who frequently felt that activists looked down upon their lack of formal education, despite how often they brought it up as a testament to how they needed to be reformed by the organization. I understood these chores and their regulation as pressure points within the shelter where seemingly small and inconsequential conflicts could occur that had the potential to explode.

When we arrived at work the next morning, Manager Fu had already heard about this fight and started the day with a lecture, delivered from the front of the workroom. She told everyone that such fights would not be allowed. She asked the group to recount what had happened the night before, and all were tight-lipped. She then decided that she would call each of the women one by one into the main administrative office to hear their account and figure out what had happened. The first woman to be called was the youngest, Li. No one knew what would happen behind the closed door, but the tension grew once we all could hear Li crying. She emerged from the office about five minutes later and told the group of us making jewelry that both directors were in the room with Li Yan, the housemom. Li said that each worker was supposed to go inside and apologize to Li Yan, and to accept Li Yan's apology in return.

Jade corralled all the remaining women together and instructed them not to apologize and certainly not to cry: "We didn't do anything wrong, so don't apologize to her." The remaining six women emerged united, and Manager Fu frowned in disapproval: "You all need to learn that grace and forgiveness are important virtues." The women rolled their eyes at one another, discretely signaling their pleasure with Fu's disappointment.

Contesting Trafficking

Most Chinese and Thai workers understood jewelry making as hourly wage labor. They regarded some forms of redemptive labor introduced throughout the workday as advantageous, allowing them to take a break from hours of sitting and making jewelry. Workers didn't mind participating in these redemptive exercises as long as they were calculated into their wage. But the Monday-night mandatory group counseling sessions trespassed on workers' social life, time after work that they didn't believe they were being compensated for. In both cities, workers were consistently caught between performing redemption and doing manual labor because they did not share activists' insistence on the meaning of their own past trauma.

This discord between how workers and activists understood their life struggles came across most shockingly when I asked workers to describe how they understood the term *trafficking,* which appears throughout the marketing material for their crafts.[14] In Chinese, this is officially translated as "*guai mai,*" literally meaning "kidnapped and sold." The four women workers I sat with were shocked to learn that this term was being used to describe their lives. As Chinese workers told me more about the various reasons they came to Beijing, I learned that they had all voluntarily migrated to the city seeking different forms of low-wage employment. Many had started off working as restaurant employees and later learned that they could earn significantly more money working at hair salons or massage parlors, where they would provide sexual services. They insisted that no one had forced them into those situations and that though they could have left whenever they wanted, they chose to stay because of a self-imposed sense of responsibility to send money home to their families, and job opportunities were limited.

The most troubling paradox is that most women begin sex work after—and alongside—doing many other forms of low-wage manufacturing work. One Thai worker kept breaking the rules and was dismissed from Cowboy Rescue several times. Each time she returned, the organization welcomed her back. When I asked why she returned despite feeling frustrated with the work at Cowboy, she replied simply that during her time away, the easiest job to find was garment factory work, which she considered worse because she often worked ten- to fourteen-hour days for the same pay that she could earn making jewelry. Migrant workers are all too familiar with the parallels between minimum-wage garment factory work and sex work, but narratives of sexual slavery that consider sex work to be distinct from nonsexual labors do not capture this fluidity.[15]

While many commercial sex workers recognize their labor as "hard work"—including one thirty-something Cowboy Rescue worker named Kao, who showed me scars on her forearms from years of self-cutting as a means of coping with on-the-job sexual abuse and violence—they see their new position as jewelry makers as just another low-wage job in an economy with limited job prospects. Jewelry making, I was once told, also comes with its own scars—calloused fingers and burns, eye strain, back pain, all of which accrue value because they at least fit the bill for appropriate female labor. In fact, many consider the job of lesser status, finding the rote character of wage labor and the consistent monitoring of social behavior considerably less dignified and autonomous than their experiences with sex work.[16] They regard the decision to be jewelry makers as a calculated move that benefits them to the extent that wage labor can be easier under certain circumstances—when a sex worker, for example, grows older, becomes pregnant, is newer and "unskilled," or enters a long-term relationship with a client.[17]

Some workers profess they enjoy the social capital and prestige that come with working for a foreign American company. Across the board, making jewelry for an American company was much more socially acceptable than sex work as one's employment to share with Chinese and Thai friends and family. For many, jewelry making was the first job that they didn't lie about to protect worried parents who waited in the countryside. Affixing price tags to jewelry every day, workers also see how much money individual jewelry pieces sell for, and unlike corporate-owned factories where an assembly line separates different parts of the manufacturing process, the jewelry-making shop had workers often creating, packaging, and pricing finished products. Because the organization markets to customers *and* workers as a social enterprise, workers hold onto hope that they may benefit from profits as the organizations grow—a opportunity for profit sharing unavailable to most low-wage factory workers throughout the world. Workers who are proud of their decision to leave the commercial sex industry point to the choice they made for themselves more than the abstract concepts that activists' promotional materials celebrate, such as freedom or dignity.

Justifications about the morality of humanitarian intervention go beyond the regimes of authority on the jewelry shop floors at both Cowboy Rescue and Freedom Unchained. These contemporary efforts have predecessors in the attempts at "imperialist motherhood" in various colonial and postcolonial contexts that historians have documented extensively. For example, Angelina Chin's work on colonial charity and social control in Hong Kong in the 1930s discusses the work of the Po Leung Kuk (PLK), a rescue institution and women and children's shelter founded by local Chinese middle- and upper-class men.[18] By producing categories of disempowered and dangerous women, the PLK became an institutional tool for the colonial state in dealing with the contradictions between emancipation and immorality. Similarly, Nancy Rose Hunt's work on Belgian women's intervention into the practices of breastfeeding and milk distribution in Belgian Congo in the 1910s examines colonial reproductive and care work. Hunt writes that "these colonial initiatives were linked to a discourse which viewed African birth spacing customs as insidious and saw a solution in European women."[19] Discussing antislavery activism among Progressive-era whites in the Chinese community in San Francisco, historian Peggy Pascoe noted racist relations of rescue in which "a group of protestant women in San Francisco used the rescue work of Chinese prostitutes to establish their own moral authority, inculcate Chinese women with Anglo-Victorian gender values, and promote Christian marriage within the Chinese American community." Similarly, writing about white rescuers in New York City's Chinatowns, Mary Lui has documented how the efforts of white Protestant reformers overshadowed the efforts of Moy Gum and other Chinese residents of Chinatown to provide support to Chinese migrant women seeking assistance. Commenting on the historical projects of racialized rescue in anti-slavery movements of the nineteenth century, Jessica Pliley has noted that the "activities rescuing 'enslaved' Chinese prostitutes constituted an important antecedent to anti-white slavery work."[20]

The historical antecedents of both religious and racially motivated reform are abundant, and the policing of deviance has been documented across a wide range of offenders—substance abusers, single mothers, alcoholics, homosexuals, and transgender individuals, to name only a few—but arguably what makes the human trafficking rescue industry distinct from earlier forms of deviant reformation is its profit from the work of prior offenders. As a result, the activists' claims to rescue and protect women, claims rooted largely in sexist and gendered notions of submissiveness and victimhood, go largely uncontested by funders, donors, and jewelry consumers.

THE RACIAL WAGES OF RESCUE

Vocational training and rehabilitation projects for sex workers aim to address human trafficking by generating attractive economic alternatives to sex work. This is the ultimate promise recruiters make when presenting alternative employment to sex work. What they do not disclose, however, is the focus on moral transformation through vocational training. The fixation on forms of virtuous and repentant labor as the main drivers of social mobility ignores the complex racialized hierarchies that exist within the low-wage workforce and the ways minimum-wage manual labor is systematically exploited to advance profit and global business interests. Interventions in China and Thailand relegate migrant sex workers to low-wage work while maximizing profits and consolidating social capital for the actors who design and consume them. These blueprints for life after trafficking do not redistribute capital or enhance the work and economic prospects of migrant workers. Rather, they maximize a rehabilitation regime of expertise from which migrants themselves may rarely benefit.

This chapter argues that US evangelical-Christian anti-trafficking vocational training centers in both countries mobilize resources through the church and market to construct a moral economy of low-wage women's work. This moral economy is anchored by racialized redemptive labor that allows activists to sell jewelry as a proxy commodity for virtuosity and repentance. These anti-trafficking programs ostensibly revise but actually reproduce low-wage women's work in the market processes of production and consumption, obfuscating the exchanges of sex, labor, and capital. By transforming the sale of their sexual labor into the sale of their manual labor, these social entrepreneurs inculcate Third World women workers into another orbit of capitalist production. While the market may provide an alternative to state intervention, it survives only by imbuing the movement with its own Western, Orientalist and feminist morality that profits from the reformed deviance and difference of the Asian sex worker. Participants in these programs often said that their freedom and empowerment are restricted by rescue projects through different means of coercive discipline. Further, most participants in these rescue projects did not even consider themselves to have been "trafficked." Instead, they continually spoke with dignity of their experiences as commercial sex workers and as the proud choices of women workers living within the limits of their local economies and global capitalism.

These novel forms of racialized redemptive labor provide an important framework for understanding how contemporary humanitarianism, particularly as it responds to problems of gender, migration, and development, reinstalls new rescue regimes that mirror the humanitarian objectives of US empire. They not only map difference between the global North and the global South, or colonial relationships between the colony and metropolis, but also repeat recurrent racial scripts about white saviors and Asian sex slaves who need rescue not only from the brutal conditions of sexual exploitation but also intractably backward family values. As the following chapter discusses, activists often draw on the metaphor of the family to naturalize the need for racialized redemptive labor arrangements. However, workers have begun to contest these rehabilitation frameworks. On the shop floor, workers persistently find that an hour of manual labor is worth the same as an hour of worship: both are mandatory, and both are paid at just the minimum wage. Furthermore, the coercive practices of social and moral control, along with the discipline of the industrial production of jewelry, mirror prevailing practices in factories in these same countries and largely contradict stated norms of labor and gender rights promoted in anti-trafficking fairs in the United States.

CHAPTER 3

Bad Rehab

*House Moms, Shelters, and Maternalist
Rehabilitation*

Oh-oh-oh-oh-oh-oh-oh
I was in bad rehab;
Oh-oh-oh-oh-oh-oh-oh
Kept in a bad rehab.

Ra Ra-ah-ah-ah Somaly ah ah,
Want an escape plan.
You think I'm ugly,
You think I'm diseased.
You took everything.
You know I'm not free.

I want to leave,
Leave leave leave.
I want to leave.

I hate your drama,
The touch of your hand.
They said they rescue,
they said they save me.

I want to leave,
Leave leave leave.
I want to leave.

FIGURE 10. Title card for "Bad Rehab" music video. Video still from Asia Pacific Network of Sex Workers.

Rape is not rescue.
I want my life back.
I want to go home to be on the street,
With family and get ART.

It's not rescue:
They cut my hair.
They push me on the ground,
send me to jail.
Sex work is work, we have our rights.

Don't want your bad rehab.[1]

Sung to the tune of Lady Gaga's multiplatinum pop anthem "Bad Romance," the lyrics quoted above, written by the Asia Pacific Network of Sex Workers (APNSW) in 2010 for a parody music video, highlight sex workers' concerns about systemic abuse in both state-run and nongovernmental rehabilitation programs. Articulating grievances from Cambodian sex workers, the music video employs Barbie dolls to enact different scenes that sex workers have recalled while serving mandatory "sentences"[2] in rehabilitation centers, revealing a sharp dichotomy between the public face of rehabilitation programs and the private experience of those participating in them. Photos of lavish anti-trafficking galas attended by Hollywood celebrities and snapshots of various commercial products sold in the name of raising funds for victims of sex trafficking are juxtaposed with scenes of rape committed against detained sex workers by police officers or prison guards. The glamour of the rescue industry thus comes into close visual contact with the realities of those supposedly being saved, illustrating the moral tensions between the traditional axes of "good" and "bad" and the sentimentality of these polarized portrayals.

The video's narrative features Somaly Mam, a prominent Cambodian anti-trafficking activist. Mam became mired in scandal following a 2014 *Time* Magazine exposé revealing that she and her organization, Acting for Women in Distressing Situations (AFESIP), had coached beneficiaries to lie about being survivors of trafficking and had perhaps even lied about her own history as a survivor of human trafficking in order to align herself with the emotional sentiments and funding priorities of the global North. The video places in stark contrast images of Mam dressed in formal wear and flanked by A-list celebrities-turned-activists—including Susan Sarandon and Demi Moore—against photos, graphics, and text evoking sobering realities; for instance, a clip that reads: "Somaly earned over $1 MILLION dollars at one dinner—but still says not enough money for rice and medicine at her rehab center." Another frame presents a product sold by international cosmetic company The Body Shop for its "Stop Sex Trafficking" fundraising campaign. Next to the "Soft Hands Kind Heart" hand cream, proceeds from which The Body Shop promises to donate to "victims of sex trafficking," the video places in bold red text: "To Be Kind Hands Off from Arresting Sex Workers" and "Save us from our Saviors."[3]

Such stark juxtapositions expose one of the main tensions described in this book: the tangled juncture between the unbridled optimism and funding that the anti-trafficking movement has garnered in the global North and the universal ignorance of the harrowing accounts of the movement's impacts in the global South. This chapter turns to the provocative framework of "Bad Rehab" to look past the veil of virtuosity donned by the rescue industry and investigate further the underlying practices of social and moral control that that make those who have experienced anti-trafficking rehabilitation programs consider them "bad."

Sex worker rights organizations such as the APNSW have astutely pointed out that popular interventions centered on the rescue and

FIGURE 11. "Bad Rehab" video frame centering sex worker voices in anti-trafficking efforts. Video still from Asia Pacific Network of Sex Workers.

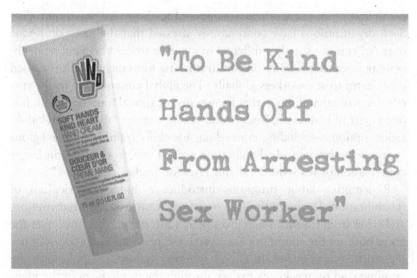

FIGURE 12. "Bad Rehab" video frame critiquing The Body Shop's Soft Hands Kind Hearts hand cream fundraiser. Video still from Asia Pacific Network of Sex Workers.

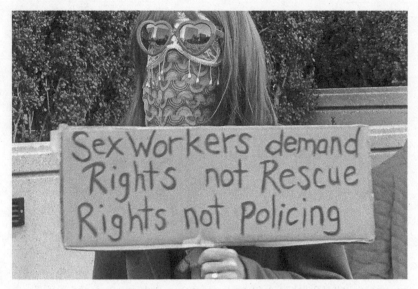

FIGURE 13. Sex workers take part in the International Women's Strike on March 8, 2017, demanding "Rights not Rescue" and "Rights not Policing." Photo by Carol Leigh.

rehabilitation of sex workers are opposed to those that focus on rights. Such organizations have continuously stressed that the focus on rescue over rights is not simply a different orientation toward help but an deliberate political decision by the anti-trafficking movement that has caused great harm to sex workers globally. The global commitment to the specific form of rehabilitation that focuses on vocational training reveals just one aspect of bad rehab. Understood within a larger "menu" of rehabilitation options—including counseling, life-skills training, and religious conversion—rescue and rehabilitation are just two programs in the larger conversation of sex worker rallying cries for "rights, not rescue."[4]

Redemptive labor programs introduce a hidden curriculum of rehabilitation—including moral transformation, spiritual redemption, and relief from trauma—that gives them tools of social control over the poor, both on the shop floor (as seen in the previous chapter) and once the workday has ended. In China, workers' behavior is policed in the evenings and on weekends mainly through the mechanism of the mandatory on-site shelter, and in Thailand, workers rent their own apartments, but their labor contract limits how they may spend their time after work. Even so, workers resist by carving out spaces for autonomy in each realm.

Despite differences in housing requirements, rehabilitation takes on a maternal character in both settings, often framing labor relations in terms of familial relationships. The focus on maternal forms of repair stem from the desire to correct the perceived moral problems with sex work at an individual level, while ignoring political economic factors that shape migrant workers' decision to choose sex work or other kinds of informal or underpaid labor. The unique mandates of rehabilitation are shaped by implicit Western feminist illusions about what decent work and a dignified life entail. These largely hetero-patriarchal and capitalist ideas of aspiration clash with the realities that exist for workers before, during, and after they choose sex work. In sum, workers and activists have suggested that rehabilitation becomes "bad" when the false equation of liberation with vocation justifies maternalist forms of social control and co-opts worker resistance in each place.

THE NGO SHELTER AS SITE FOR MATERNALIST CONTROL IN CHINA

"It's prison visiting hours!" Yin squealed, referring to the few hours each Saturday and Sunday afternoon when outside friends and family members could visit and spend time in the Freedom Unchained shelter. The lack of private gathering spaces because of Freedom Unchained's practice of bunking six to eight women together in each dormitory room, combined with the shelter's remote location, meant that visitors seldom came to spend time there. However, on weekends, workers were allowed to leave the premises and sleep elsewhere as long as they returned before the 10 p.m. curfew on Sunday night to begin the work week on Monday morning. Yet, for many women, their friends were also migrant workers with similar living conditions and couldn't host overnight guests in their equally crowded dormitories.

Sitting on her bottom bunk, Yin and I talked about what we would do this particular weekend in early September 2010. She told me that she wanted to introduce me to a guy she had just started dating, but that we would have to meet him outside the shelter because visitation was strictly limited to female guests. Freedom Unchained forbade men from visiting the shelter, because it claimed that they posed a dangerous emotional trigger for shelter residents who were recovering from experiences of sexual exploitation endured at the hands of men. Workers understood this restriction in a different way. They shrugged it off and explained that the organization just didn't want to deal with them possibly having sex in the dorms. The rules didn't seem out of the ordinary to the workers, because they were the same ones that Chinese employers enforced in dormitory housing for many other low-wage jobs. Across the board, rules like these caused workers to feel that management simply didn't understand intimacy: how, or why, would I have sex with my boyfriend in a bottom bunk with six other people in the same room? It was just one more rule that didn't necessarily have a logical explanation but upheld the scaffolding of authoritarian supervision after the workday had ended.

Yin decided that we should visit her boyfriend at the bakery where he worked. We planned to arrive there around 4 p.m., when his shift was scheduled to end, and help him finish his work if the manager wasn't around. We headed downstairs to the living room, where three other workers, Li Yan, Chong Gu, and Bing, were seated on the couch, and asked them if they wanted to join. They were lounging comfortably in their pajamas, their attention split between watching a Chinese soap opera on the television and texting and playing games on their phones. None of them looked up from their screens, but offered groggy responses expressing noninterest. Sensing the commotion, Xiao Hua, a middle-aged Chinese Christian designated as housemom at the time, popped her head out of her single private room on the first floor. She chided the three workers, expressing her disappointment at their behavior: "Aiya," she sighed deeply. "You have this volunteer here—from America!— who wants to take you out to see things in the world and learn new things, and open your eyes to things you don't know, and all you want to do is sit inside and play on your phones."

She then turned squarely to face me and, as a gesture of her own social mobility, deftly switched to English. "See, it really takes a lot to move people beyond brokenness and help them dream beyond their current situation." I winced, stunned at how quickly seemingly inconsequential weekend plans were reframed as opportunities for discipline, shame, and transformation, all under the pretense of reform. But worse was how my presence as an outsider—and a middle-class, educated Chinese American—was used as one more tool of domination over workers. I tried to protest and reason with Xiao Hua. I explained to her that Yin and I really weren't planning to go anywhere particular. I also worried that my plans had excluded others. It took three years before I accepted the fact that workers were content to stay in the house on the weekends, with no particular urgency to make extracurricular plans following a week of hard work.

In both Beijing and Bangkok, "weekends" were a foreign concept and commodity for low-wage migrant workers, who typically get only two days off per month in most low-wage service sector and manufacturing jobs. The autonomy of sex work—more so in Thailand than in China—presented an alternative that offered a bit more liberty. Thus, one of the most tangible benefits of working as jewelry makers in both Beijing and Bangkok was the free time on weekends, though the imperatives of redemptive labor and rehabilitation meant that each social enterprise imposed an invisible hand through various restrictions. Anti-trafficking shelters are an important feature of rehabilitation programs in that they provide safe places for victims to live and heal after being trafficked. Yet, despite their portrayal as neutral spaces for living and sleeping, shelters often play a distinct role in the project of rehabilitation that extends far beyond the simple function of residential assistance. Mandatory residence at the Freedom Unchained shelter outside Beijing enabled the sweeping project of moral and social control over worker's lives and behavior after the workday ended.

According to a blog entry on the organization's website, "A typical day at the Freedom Unchained shelter includes everyone waking up and getting ready to go to work. Some people will eat breakfast at the shelter while others will buy something on their way to the office. Upon completing their work day, the women living in the shelter may run personal errands or enjoy an activity outside of the shelter or return home. At the shelter women can be seen cooking, working out, studying, or watching TV together, before going to bed." This description seems a transparent account of daily life in the shelter. Yet important details are conveniently omitted, reflecting a disturbing pattern I found throughout my research. Most notably, this account leaves out the shelter's governing structure. It suggests that the women living in the shelter are at complete liberty to organize their day as they like. In reality, the activities and behavior of the workers in the shelter are strictly supervised.

Life in the Beijing shelter is managed by housemoms who, like Xiao Hua, are typically Chinese Christians with at least a high school education. The housemoms are paid only several hundred RMB more than the rescued workers they patrol, a low salary that they accept as a testament to their sacrifice and as a result of the limited job opportunities for Christian workers under China's intolerant religious environment. The house moms enforce rules such as nightly curfews and visiting hours, monitor the behavior of the residents, and provide moral guidance. This distinctly maternalist philosophy of governance, assigning Chinese

Christian "moms" to supervise the behavior of rescued workers, suggests a distinctly moral project of reforming supposedly licentious women, one that envelops all aspects of the shelter residents' lives. Even the simple, innocuous decision to spend a Saturday afternoon watching TV could be criticized as idle and unproductive and as indicating a lack of motivation to improve one's life. The shelter thus enables the constant moral supervision and reform of rescued workers' behaviors and life decisions, allowing for the establishment of new, "proper" rules, habits, and ethics for former sex workers. Based on a commonly rehearsed narrative that poor family values and cultural beliefs were common causes of trafficking in China, the shelter reconstitutes an artificial family governed by a traditionally virtuous Christian "mom" in order to instill specific principles, values, and behaviors.

As noted earlier, shelter rules prohibit male visitors out of a professed concern that "residents have already endured significant trauma at the hands of a man." This narrative of monolithic sexual victimization demonizes men of color from the global South and upholds chastity as one of the key objectives of moral freedom and salvation.[5] However, this rule often confuses and raises tension among workers, who are often single young women seeking not only financial security but also the formation of new romantic partnerships and emotional connections with friends and family. The participants in these programs, even those who have experienced violence from male clients in sex work, still seek friendship, intimacy, and romantic relationships. Yet the shelter moms dissuade workers from entering into such relationships, not trusting women to create intimate relationships with men and implicitly suggesting that romantic relationships are inherently morally deviant.

Such rules at the Freedom Unchained shelter are strictly enforced. Workers are penalized 1 RMB (15 cents in USD) of their salary for each minute they are late for their nightly 10 p.m. curfew. In fact, all infractions are assigned monetary fines, and those concerning behavior are punishable by termination from the program. There is, of course, no clear way to patrol the private and personal activities of workers during their free time on weekends; thus, workers are encouraged to contact staff and directors if they learn of contractual trespasses committed by any of their peers. Such reporting is unofficially rewarded through an opaque bonus structure, which one participant described as reminiscent of Cultural Revolution–era Red Guard policies that encouraged children to "expose their parents for anti-communist thoughts" to gain favor with the Communist Party. Our conversations revealed that workers were aware of a distinct moralizing project at the shelter, entrenched in both a strict punitive regime and a culture of constant monitoring. This structure of stringent governance sought to guide and reform workers based on a specific idea of morality, embodied in the figure of the Christian "mom."

FROM INCARCERATION TO HOUSING: THE CARCERAL LEGACY OF SHELTERS

The culture of governance and project of moral rehabilitation present in the Freedom Unchained shelter can be understood in the light of prior sociological research on shelters. Described by Erving Goffman as a "totalizing institution," shelters have been widely studied for the ways they isolate their residents from external social forces, dictating a resident's sense of self and moral worth entirely according to the ethos of shelter management.[6] Anthropologist Rebecca Surtees has done groundbreaking empirical research on shelter programs for victims of trafficking and has raised specific critical concerns about shelter housing as residential assistance.[7] This scholarship explains why some victims decline assistance, and further problematizes how state-sanctioned rehabilitation in government shelters often denies victims the right to refuse assistance by framing it as "rehabilitative."[8]

Government shelters in China and Thailand reproduced many of the maternalist power dynamics identified in the Freedom Unchained shelter. In 2012, the Thai sex workers' rights organization Empower Foundation published the report *Hit and Run,* which detailed the experiences of sex workers who had been detained in Thai government shelters following rescue and raid efforts.[9] Like all of Empower's work, this report was researched and written by a team of sex workers. It documented, in extraordinary rigor, numerous human rights abuses that occur in government-run shelters. To facilitate the accessibility of the report by its primary beneficiaries—which include non-Thai-speaking and nonliterate sex workers—Empower also created a 200-square-meter tapestry that illustrates the research findings via embroidery.

Corroborating some of Empower's findings with research in the Indian context, Vibhuti Ramachandran and Kimberly Walters have pointed to the ways anti-trafficking shelters often fail to provide basic food and medicine and offer only scant legal counsel in the face of sentences often of indeterminate length.[10] Writing about state-run anti-trafficking shelters that collaborate with NGOs in Bangladesh, Diya

FIGURE 14. The Mida Tapestry, embroidered by migrant sex workers to document the impact police raids have on their lives. A companion to the 2012 Empower Foundation report *Hit and Run*, it has made the report's findings legible to workers across different languages. Photo by Empower Studio Bad Girls Films.

Bose has similarly argued that as paternalist projects in "protective custody," institutions follow disciplinary practices that model those of state prisons. In fact, several of the women at the Dhaka shelter also refer to the shelter as a "prison," as does Freedom Unchained worker Yin at the beginning of this chapter.[11] Across each of the aforementioned examples, rehabilitation through vocational training persistently emerges as an offering by government and NGO shelters alike.

During my own visit to the government-run human trafficking shelter for boys in Bangkok, many of the findings present in Empower's *Hit and Run* report would not have been immediately evident in a tour of the premises. For years, the primary government shelter for women and girls, Baan Kredtrakarn, was heralded as a model by the Ministry of Human Development and Security and allowed a steady stream of foreign volunteers and international visitors. Responding to a rash of criticism, however, the shelter has since closed its doors to public visitors. I gained access to Baan Phumvet, the shelter for boys, after meeting the shelter manager at a United Nations training session on human trafficking in South Korea's Jeju Island. This two-day training course convened several members of civil society to discuss strategies for dealing with human trafficking.

As a formal visitor to Baan Phumvet, I was taken on a tour of manicured shelter grounds in a five-building compound, its periphery defined by a twenty-foot white steel fence. Prior to my visit, a friend and astute researcher, Rebecca Napier-Moore, had warned me to "pay attention to which direction the spokes in the fence face." Without Rebecca's ominous prompting, I certainly would not have seen that they curved inward, suggesting that the fence was there not to protect workers, as shelters often claimed, but to prevent them from escaping. The shelter was located about one hour from downtown Bangkok via public transportation. The street it was on featured a large portrait of the queen and various placards touting the Ministry of Social Development and Human Security's numerous shelters, including those for the blind, the deaf, infants born with mental and physical disabilities, and orphans. The director told me about different programs the shelter provided, including food, counseling, and daily education. Residents included Thai boys under the age of eighteen, as well as undocumented immigrants from neighboring countries, most of whom were victims of labor exploitation or child begging. Baan Phumvet typically holds ten to fifty residents at a time. I asked if education was offered in all the languages shelter residents speak, and the director explained that they did not have the resources to do that. She noted that this was not a cause of concern, because those who cannot attend school due to language barriers are given vocational training in different crafts.

Similarly, in China, shelters descend from a long history of Chinese government-run punitive institutions. In China, victims of human trafficking were merely absorbed into existing institutions of government-run shelters, due to a combination of factors including lack of funding, low political will, and a mistaken belief that these populations shared roughly the same needs for control, protection, and punishment. These shelters typically serve indigent populations, including victims of domestic violence, migrants, and youth requiring punitive detention centers. Noting the lack of government-run anti-trafficking shelters, Freedom Unchained saw an opportunity to create a shelter specifically for victims of trafficking. However, as in the case of the Freedom Unchained shelter, these NGO-run institutions often partnered with government-run shelters or reproduced many of the same effects of punitive regimes.

Responding to the substantive global concerns regarding shelters, the China office of the United Nations Inter-Agency Project on Human Trafficking (UNIAP China) launched a shelter improvement project in 2012, cofunded by UNIAP and the Chinese government's Ministry of

Civil Affairs (MOCA). The project focused on three government-run shelters in the Kunming, Guangxi, and Guangdong provinces that, like most de facto shelters throughout the country, have long histories as penal institutions, functioning as alternatives to prison for a range of indigent populations including the homeless, the mentally ill, and victims of domestic violence. Research on the experiences of shelter residents who use these services is still scant under a political regime that holds tight control over research and publication.[12]

The shelter improvement project brought international consultants to the three shelters to develop tools for the identification and care of victims of human trafficking and train local shelter staff on the special needs and vulnerabilities of trafficked persons. My interviews with shelter coordinators and staff revealed that most were unsure what constituted a victim of trafficking. When asked about "human trafficking," they preferred to explain that many of their residents had experienced different forms of poverty, violence, exploitation, and vulnerability. To the dismay of the international expert trainers, each of the three shelters also claimed that it took no measures to separate "trafficked populations" from the rest of their residents, because it lacked the staff to do so and because identifying and differentiating victims of human trafficking was difficult. Such ambiguity around the needs and experiences of trafficked persons and what specific services they might require reveals the challenges of mobilizing new international victim categories within existing penal institutions. The attempt to transform shelters for indigent populations into rehabilitative institutions marks a significant feature of the Chinese state-led anti-trafficking efforts—not just initiated by the Ministry of Public Security but also filtered through government institutions that have traditionally emphasized incarceration and confinement as opposed to rehabilitation.

Reconciling Christian Values in Residential Assistance

The challenges with managing shelters and reconciling Christian values and development principles has been explored by a Cambodian-based coalition of more than fifty Christian anti-trafficking organizations that signed onto the Chab Dai Charter. Chab Dai, an organization founded in 2005 to build partnerships within the anti-trafficking movement, created a universally chartered coalition in 2010 in response to the vast and disparate landscape of accountability and practice among faith-based organizations working in Cambodia. In signing the Charter, faith-based organizations committed to a rights-based and culturally sensitive approach to anti-trafficking work along the lines of (1) protection, (2) collaboration, (3) participation, and (4) transparency. Underlying each of these four "Pillars" was a biblical foundation that unified the organizations' missions; however, the uppermost commitment to the broad category of "excellence" responded to some challenges that faith-based organizations had faced regarding organizational inconsistency.[13]

Reflecting differing degrees of openness in their missionary work, foreign religious organizations have often skirted oversight from government agencies, claiming that it impedes their ability to execute faith-based missions. Under the Chab Dai Charter, organizations pledged to respect the registration requirements of their respective governments and not to go rogue. Religious social enterprises, however, including both Cowboy Rescue and Freedom Unchained, can register as businesses, which allows for a greater degree of liberty. Private sector registration doesn't require enterprises to state the nature of religious practice as clearly as public sector registration, since the legal codes pertaining to private organizations deal primarily with transparency around profit and management.

While neither Freedom Unchained nor Cowboy Rescue has signed the Chab Dai Charter, it demonstrates efforts to reconcile faith-based with development-based prerogatives.[14] Though not inherently incompatible—and as mentioned in chapter 1, many Christian anti-trafficking activists assert that faith is an asset to development work—issues emerge when religious imperatives undercut a rights-based framework. As seen in the previous chapter, this rights infringement happens on the shop floor in the ambiguity over how embracing Christianity can change promotion prospects and how church worship figures into the calculation of wages.

My research straddled both the troubling shelter dynamics at the NGO shelters and the larger state and civil society efforts to improve shelters at UNIAP. Seeing the possibilities for connection, I asked my colleagues who were working on the shelter improvement project at UNIAP China if we could share the shelter improvement tools with the Freedom Unchained shelter. But, by 2012, I was visiting the Freedom Unchained shelter only occasionally, as I felt my presence wasn't improving working conditions on the shop floor. UNIAP China agreed, and I was thrilled when the director of Freedom Unchained was open to the idea, saying that she thought it could certainly help since they had experienced a few incidents of conflict at the shelter.

The shelter self-improvement toolkit that I introduced to the managers of Freedom Unchained aimed to build the capacity of managers of government shelters to maintain standards for victim care and support, a significant section of which involved assessing and developing plans for "victim empowerment." As a central assessment area, the toolkit posed the following question: "Is the overall environment and philosophy behind case management one of client empowerment, choice, and confidentiality? Are economic and legal needs recognized, as well as psychosocial and safety? Having support providers with an empowering attitude is critical for victims of trafficking, at every step along the way."

The manager of Freedom Unchained seemed to embrace this toolkit and was eager for official UN guidance on some problems her shelter was facing. After a reevaluation of the shelter's values, philosophy, and rules based on the checklists and assessment tools I provided, Freedom Unchained released new guidelines for residents and employees. However, I was disappointed to see that the new guidelines merely reinstitutionalized existing restrictive and punitive policies, without any fundamental change to workers' empowerment and autonomy. The guidelines forbade residents from having sexual relationships even outside the shelter; violators of this rule would be punished by eviction without a housing subsidy. In addition, internet access remained restricted to set "communal use periods," and residents were not allowed to browse the internet unaccompanied. A strict 11 p.m. curfew remained in place, and violations of other rules were designated with new, specific fines ranging from 30 to 100 RMB (5–15 USD).

Essentially, the shelter disregarded the policies of victim empowerment and failed to set up a system of discipline based on "constructive measures and positive reinforcement" as suggested by the UNIAP shelter toolkit. Freedom Unchained reinforced its punitive structure of governance, using the fact of having nominally reviewed its programs through the UNIAP toolkit to legitimize and further institutionalize existing rules. My attempt to introduce a global governance toolkit to reform the shelter was not met with genuine reflection and consideration; instead, it was absorbed into the organization's strategy of enforcing its self-righteous program of moral rehabilitation through strict control and governance. I was steamrolled just as forcefully as the workers had been when they protested the factory visits. Neither of us was powerful enough to resist an organization that believed firmly in its policies, governance, and methods. Nearly every attempt to contest workplace surveillance has been met by some form of co-optation.

The rehabilitation programs studied here clearly enacted an extensive system of social and moral control of rescued workers that pushed the boundaries of "assistance." Workers were given little room to exercise their personal autonomy, were restricted to a specific framework of moral reformation, and were left with no real options for redress of their working conditions.

SEEKING AUTONOMY AFTER THE WORKDAY IN THAILAND

Whereas the Freedom Unchained shelter provides a built-in mechanism for policing moral behavior, Cowboy Rescue employees in Thailand all live in and pay for independent housing. Around 4:30 every afternoon, the workday at Cowboy Rescue draws to a close and workers begin adjusting their pace of production. They finish the pieces of jewelry they have started and are careful not to begin any new pieces that would require them to work past 5 p.m. sharp, when the workday ends. This is just one of many strategies workers use to control their own labor output. Across the table of six workers where I sat one afternoon, there was the usual discussion about what everyone was doing after work. Moe was headed back to her apartment to make dinner for her brother, age nineteen, who had recently arrived in Bangkok from her hometown to work at a job organized through their church. Kao was headed to her part-time job at MK Gold, the popular shabu-shabu restaurant at Central Paragon Mall where she worked five days a week after leaving her job as a jewelry maker. In a rather anomalous arrangement, another worker, Pong, kept a full-time night job for almost two years of her employment at Cowboy Rescue. Pong worked at the customer service counter in the Thonburi train station from 11 p.m. to 5 a.m. I was amazed that she maintained her schedule making jewelry for the entire day, then headed for her second shift at the railroad station. There wasn't enough time for her to return home, because the room she rented was almost an hour and a half away by public bus. Rather than go there, she would swing by her friend's clothing shop every day to nap for a few hours on a stool in the small three-by-three-foot fitting room.

When the clock strikes 5:00 at Cowboy Rescue, workers clock out, and the scene looks like almost any other factory. After leaving the workplace, workers walk down different streets and alleys, inevitably passing by beer halls, go-go dance clubs, and different entertainment venues where many other people work. As Cowboy Rescue workers finish their day, these workers are just starting to prepare for the night ahead. This early in the evening, they are dressed in plain clothes but sit on benches outside the clubs, applying makeup and doing each other's hair. Cowboy Rescue workers and I would often wave in familiarity as we walked by, each wearing a different uniform—one starting their evening, the other ending their workday.

Even though the Cowboy Rescue workers are technically off the clock in the evening, they do not have full autonomy over their personal time. The employment contract forbidding commercial sex also bans workers from patronizing any bars where they used to work. After the workday, they are expected to travel home and are discouraged from engaging in additional paid work. A list of prohibitions restricts how they should spend leisure time and defines what constitutes inappropriate use of income. The fact that Cowboy Rescue workers do not live in a shelter under constant supervision grants them more autonomy over their time and personal activities than workers in Beijing enjoy, but their employment contract still strictly defines permissible behavior. The threat of losing one's job carries enormous weight and is a highly effective deterrent. Even in this case, where workers have independent housing and a clear demarcation between their work and personal lives, the anti-trafficking rehabilitation program effectively governs private aspects of workers' lives to ensure that they do not engage in what the organization deems "immoral" behavior.

After work, I usually spent a few hours every day with the worker named Ploy, who is mentioned in the book's introduction. One afternoon, as Ploy had just finished clocking out, she suggested we forgo our typical stroll around Chuvit Park and instead grab a drink at a bar, since she had something she wanted to talk about. Only then did it dawn on me that she had been unusually silent, solemn, and snippy all day. I readily agreed, understanding that there was something on her mind. A drink in an air-conditioned bar was a luxurious respite from our usual after-work routine of strolling the crowded Bangkok streets during rush-hour traffic, eating street food, visiting her street vendor friends, and taking speed-walking laps around a small park.

We turned onto the major thoroughfare, and rather than walk in the direction of our usual street-food stalls or the park, Ploy continued toward Soi Cowboy. She seemed to have a clear sense of where she was going. I asked her what our destination was, and she told me, "I want to go somewhere I have never taken you. I want to go to the bar where I used to work." We had talked about her former work in the beer bar on occasion, when it came up naturally. I didn't push her to share her experiences with sex work as much as I tried to understand her experiences as a jewelry maker—and I never asked to go to the bar where she had done sex work for fifteen years.

We approached the bar, whose entrance was marked by an open façade like an open garage door with a wooden bar perched across, looking out onto the street. As we entered, the smile on Ploy's face was met by familiar shouts and greetings from former coworkers. Some came over and asked how she was doing, others screamed out to her across a hallway as they applied makeup, curled or straightened their hair, affixed fake eyelashes, or ate dinner in preparation for the evening ahead. She introduced me as her American friend. Ploy and her former coworkers went back to making small talk. After being served two Heinekens, we took a seat at the wooden bar, which perfectly framed the bustling red-light district in front of us.

As the night progressed and workers slipped away to sit with male patrons who had begun entering the establishment, we continued to sip the beers alone and Ploy adopted a more serious tone. She began to tell me about her youngest sister, whom I knew of vaguely. Every time I visited Ploy at the small room she occupied on a month-to-month basis in Sukhumvit Road's Paradiso Hotel, I would see half of the small six-by-nine-foot quarters filled with another person's belongings, including hair-dressing tools, fashion magazines, and clothes. I had never seen her sister, a masseuse, because she worked a late shift; by the time Ploy and I left work around 5 p.m., she was usually gone. The arrangement, I thought, worked perfectly to provide privacy for each sister, though their housing situation provided little of that commodity.

Presently, Ploy dove right in and told me that her sister had been arrested the previous weekend and was in jail. It was the third time she had been arrested for selling ice (crystal meth), and Ploy said the government had a three-strikes rule, which meant that her sister would be in jail for a while, though she wasn't sure how long. The sentence was for three years, but she thought it could be shortened. Her family needed to raise money for various penalties and legal fees. I sat, mostly silent, as Ploy unloaded all of this. She told me about the pressure she felt to hide this news from her mother and father, who lived in Udon Thani in the northeast, a twelve-hour bus ride from Bangkok. She said she felt an even greater obligation to send money home, as her sister wouldn't be able to contribute to the amount they usually sent to their parents, and in fact would require an additional few hundred baht per month for her living expenses in jail. Ploy thought her sister had been innocent the first couple of times this happened, but that this last arrest over the weekend had made her think her sister was lying. Ploy also acknowledged that this might not entirely be her sister's fault, but a result of being wrapped up with bad coworkers and friends. She shared her feelings of guilt for thinking that jail could potentially be good for her sister as a way of extricating her from those circles. I was silent through most of the conversation, nodding, not really knowing what to say and unable to offer much except more beers, which I was buying, and lighting her cigarette when she reached for one.

After about an hour and a half, the sun set and the street became animated with the neon glow of go-go bars. Ploy and I let her sister's predicament linger and returned to normal postwork gossip. The street began to flood with the evening's patrons, the majority of whom were white men, some in groups, others alone—a diverse group of customers ranging from young backpackers to old expatriate retirees who lived in Bangkok full-time. Suddenly, I saw Ploy's face darken again as she stared down the street past me. Ploy abruptly stamped out her cigarette and flicked it toward the bar behind us. She shot me a quick warning: "Colleen [the director] is coming this way; I think she saw us." I panicked and froze in my tracks, not knowing what to do. Should I hide the beer I'm drinking? Is there some way I can hide the fact that I, a volunteer, have joined a worker at Soi Cowboy? Should I duck? Do I hide Ploy? These impulses arose because I knew that as a Cowboy Rescue employee, Ploy had signed a contract forbidding her from patronizing the bars where she used to work. Because jewelry making was intended to be an alternative to sex work and a remedy for human trafficking, one of the key features of its labor contracts is that "rehabilitated victims of sex trafficking" are no longer allowed to visit the spaces they used to occupy as sex workers.

The next morning, I was called into the director's office. In a firm, reprimanding tone, Colleen told me that I was not to socialize with workers because it would encourage them to "triangulate resources." She asked if Ploy asked me for money. No, I replied quickly, though it certainly was implied that it would help. She said the managers were concerned that helping her financially would only enable her sister. With a continued stern demeanor, Colleen continued, "We are also concerned that Ploy has all these people outside of Cowboy Rescue that she is turning to. You and this American boyfriend named Frances, whom we have heard of."

In other words, the organization interpreted the friendships I had been building as a liability. Rescue organizations worried that if workers developed friendships with me, they might seek me out as a resource instead of turning to the NGO's maternal embrace. Yet this thinking was deeply counterproductive to rehabilitation and ignored how all people need vast community networks and support systems to thrive. Rather than foster a sense of independence, Cowboy Rescue adopted the strategy of collapsing employment and social support into its rescue projects to create a singular dependence on the NGO. While workers told me time and time again how much they needed to rely on personal social networks, in addition to their jobs, for economic and social security, rescue organizations strenuously sought to limit reliance on those outside the organization. I could understand the employers' point of view to a certain degree. My presence at each site was limited and temporary. I would soon return to the United States, and it was Cowboy Rescue that would continue to be there as a long-term employer and one of few available safety nets.

THE PARADOXICAL PRISM OF REHAB

Despite the multiple ways the rehabilitation programs of Cowboy Rescue and Freedom Unchained restricted worker autonomy, both organizations actively capitalized on their narrative of moral rescue and development. In addition to marketing workers' personal stories through social media and sales venues, both organizations invited visitors to Beijing and Bangkok to tour the shop floor of jewelry production. These guests included a wide variety of individuals, ranging from college students studying abroad to tourists, missionaries, and global buyers. In China, where I was fluently bilingual, I was sometimes given the task of translating for tourists who came through. In Thailand, where I had only basic Thai-language skills, I sat in the production room, likely indistinguishable from the other Asian workers around me. Experiencing both sides of what anthropologist John Urry called the "tourist gaze" allowed me to understand how workers, employers, and visitors understood and experienced these site visits.[15]

On one occasion, I met a couple from Florida who came to conduct a "site visit" at Freedom Unchained because they planned to sell the jewelry at a fair trade marketplace in the United States. They explained that their company supplied fairly traded products for school fundraisers: "You remember those chocolate bars you used to sell to raise money for class trips? We do that, but with ethical fair trade goods." This white couple in their late thirties told me that they traveled the world sourcing ethically traded goods to add to the catalog, and that this trip was their first to China. They had learned about Freedom Unchained jewelry from a friend, and as they did with all their producers, they wanted to visit the organization and speak with some of the workers. While they didn't have a formal accrediting standard by which to ascertain if a product was fairly traded, they took it upon themselves to make these assessments by visiting and talking with participants in these social enterprises.

Their visit was brief, lasting only one afternoon, but it was packed with the intensity typical of site visits. The assistant manager, Eunice, was assigned as their translator and took them around the premises. I was working on the jewelry tables that afternoon and wanted so badly to hear what was being said behind closed doors. I imagined it followed the typical script of dramatized narratives involving the rescue and moral rehabilitation of abused sex workers, girls who suffered from poverty, trauma, and misguided values. The American couple were also assigned two workers to talk to. The other workers pointed this out as unfair because the same people were always chosen. It's not a bad gig, they joked, because it gets you off the shop floor.

On the work floor, visits were disruptive. In Bangkok, where English fluency was rare among workers, I thought it strange that activists and visitors spoke so fluently about the worker's life stories in a language foreign to the subjects of their conversation. Activist tour guides would make deliberate attempts not to point out or make eye contact with certain workers, despite the fact that they were offering intimately personal details about their lives. A standard roster of jokes, stories, and pleas for support accompanied each site visit. One Thai worker confided in me that she actually understood much more English than she let on during the workday, and thought it satisfying power to be able to understand what was being said about her when her bosses thought she couldn't understand them.

Journalists often visited the workplace in Thailand. One summer, I met two sisters, Christians visiting from Canada, who shared accommodations with me in the volunteer house. They had come to Cowboy Rescue because they wished to write a story about the organization and asked if they could interview some workers. The organizers consistently chose Lee, a woman who had become pregnant by a Japanese client who took no responsibility for their child. Cowboy Rescue became a safe haven for this mother, who could no longer work in the bars later in her pregnancy and just after the child was born. The organization not only provided a job with maternity leave but also paid for the child's medical expenses and, later, built a thriving day care facility around this child. The day care enabled some other employees to bring their children from their hometowns to live in Bangkok, though most chose not to because of the exorbitant housing costs.

Lee set up a time to meet with the Canadian sisters at a Starbucks outside working hours. The interview lasted roughly two hours, and, as was often the case, she was not offered an honorarium for her time. Journalists sometimes offered, but the organization accepted a donation rather than an individual honorarium. Logically, this solution sought to ensure that benefits could be spread throughout the organization, but it didn't seem to mitigate the additional time imposition employees had to bear when being interviewed.

Workers sometimes contested these practices of exploitation. In one of the more formal protests I witnessed against these visits, Chinese workers got together in early 2009 and announced they were tired of foreigners coming in, watching the workers through a glass window, and talking about them in English when they couldn't understand what was being said. Intended to throw a wrench into the spinning wheels of anti-trafficking commerce, the workers told their boss that they would no longer tolerate the site visits in which strangers looked in on their work as if it were a zoo. I couldn't disagree with the sentiment. The visits seemed as though they were taking place behind a one-way mirror; workers couldn't stop what they were doing and had to look happy making their jewelry—a performance implied in their job description.

Activists deftly manipulated this request to their economic advantage, telling visitors that they were no longer able to provide tours of the factory out of protection for the workers. Rather than respect the workers' desires to keep their personal lives out of the profit-making arm of the organization, Freedom Unchained merely added the workers' resistance to their larger overarching story of rescue. The lack of access only helped bolster a narrative of vulnerability that secured more sales, contrary to the workers' goal of preventing the organization from profiting from their stories and visibility.

TRAFFICKERS, "MOLES," AND "AT-RISK WOMEN"

When workers reflected about the many paradoxes of their lives in rehab, they frequently spoke of the hypocrisy and fluidity of the trafficking label. In both China and Thailand, many workers had endured considerable strain in precarious jobs and suffered abuses that might meet the legal threshold of trafficking. However, they often rebuked the trafficking victim label because its local meanings were stigmatized and carried moral, cultural, and social burdens. Yet the same social stigma around trafficking that leads to workers' hesitancy to embrace the term is perhaps the same force that makes the trafficking label such a compelling policy discourse and marketing ploy, for it provides a social and moral story that can be used to appeal to a diverse audience.

The "victim of human trafficking" designation was often used by Freedom Unchained and Cowboy Rescue to boost their programs in various ways, as by including it in their narratives of moral rescue to sell their products to consumers in the global North, and as a way to control who was admitted to the rehabilitation program. During one anomalous instance in China, this included the short-lived incorporation of an older woman named Big Sister Luo onto the shop floor. We were told that she had been recruited by a Christian colleague of Freedom Unchained through outreach at a prison, where the colleague learned of Big Sister Luo's complete transformation of faith while incarcerated. Workers eventually learned Luo had been convicted of trafficking and served a two-year prison sentence. Luo explained to others that she was victimized by ring leaders and that she was punished as a scapegoat for the trafficking crimes of others.

I found it difficult to wrap my head around this situation. Disregarding potential concerns about trauma for former victims of human trafficking, who were the main subjects of Freedom Unchained's rehabilitation program, the organization actively recruited a former trafficker to work alongside victims in the factory. Workers distanced themselves from Luo, not because they feared her as a trafficker but because they found her to be disingenuous in her proclamation of reformation through Christian conversion. Freedom Unchained activists saw an entirely different image, one of transformative justice and the powers of redemption. Big Sister Luo's presence showed that if formerly trafficked persons and former traffickers could come together and accept Jesus, there would be no greater testament to his love.

In Thailand, Cowboy Rescue accepted the application of a young woman who had heard about the job of making jewelry and was drawn to the opportunity to work for an American firm. Her friend, a current employee, coached her to say that she had worked in a commercial sex bar but that she didn't want to discuss details. Rumors soon floated around the shop floor that the young woman had never been a sex worker. After her employment at Cowboy Rescue, the woman went on to graduate from college, which Cowboy Rescue celebrated among its consumers as one of the organization's success stories. All the while, other workers claimed that the graduate had always been on the path to college and that the organization shouldn't take credit for her story to funders.

In China, after workers banded together in attempts to resist and reform certain policies, Freedom Unchained used the fluidity of the trafficking victim label to plant an individual to keep an eye on worker activity. Women commonly rotated in and out of employment, and when I returned to Freedom Unchained my third summer, I noticed a new worker named Charlotte who spoke excellent English and had an especially cheery disposition. Her Bible was always in plain sight on her bunk bed, and she read it religiously every night. When I asked veteran employees about Charlotte, they just said, "She's not like us; she works alongside us but she's not like us." Later, when we went off-site to buy groceries for dinner, Yin explained to me that Charlotte just showed up one day and was assigned to make jewelry with the team. The workers didn't think she had been recruited from street outreach. No one explained to the workers where Charlotte had come from, but they pieced things together, and the most logical guess was that Charlotte was a young parishioner at their employers' church who was interested in being involved in anti-trafficking work.

As the days went on, it became clear that Charlotte was exempt from certain mandatory activities. She was allowed to skip group counseling on Wednesday nights, because she led outreach with one of the American volunteers. The workers firmly believed that Charlotte was there to "maintain harmony"—jokingly referencing a Chinese government euphemism for quelling dissent. In other words, they were calling her a spy. This ironic language resonated with stories I had heard about the regime of government surveillance in China, with plainclothes police embedded everywhere from NGOs to art gallery openings. Around the same time, the legal aid organization I had worked with since 2004 had been dealing with intense government scrutiny of its operations, including interactions with plainclothes police officers. I saw a clear parallel between Charlotte and the plainclothes policemen assigned to deliver messages from the state. The organization thus used the fluidity of the trafficking label to uphold an apparatus of governance and control eerily similar to China's authoritarian regime.

Whenever the trafficking label didn't serve the specific goals and objectives of the organization, it could be easily discarded. As noted earlier, prior to the 2008 Olympic Games hosted in Beijing, Freedom Unchained changed the language on its marketing brochures from "trafficked" women to "at-risk" women in response to perceived pressures from the Chinese government. Sarah, Freedom Unchained's director, explained to me that "during the months leading up to the Olympics, the Chinese government has been cracking down on migrants in the city, forcing them to go home." This policy, widely reported in the media, suggested that the Chinese government was taking action to clean the streets of Beijing before the Olympics. Rumors also circulated that police were closing down sex shops and would send home any migrant worker who could not produce a Beijing *hukou*, or residency permit. Sarah changed the brochure's wording to reflect governmental interest in "pretending that prostitution doesn't happen in Beijing." As a result, the organization reprinted its promotional literature to paint itself as a protector of "at-risk" women. These two sets of essentially identical brochures, with two separate discursive strategies to advertise the project at hand, underscore how the framing of trafficking is based more on an organization's marketing and operational decisions than on the lived realities of its participants. Whereas workers reject the "trafficking" label, activists, governments, and international organizations alike freely use the term, or not, depending on how useful it is for sustaining their cause.

While I certainly do not intend to adjudicate who is accurately designated a victim of trafficking, my aim in sharing these quotidian confusions is merely to show how fraught the term currently is as it is used and misused in practice. It is indeed so flexible that Pardis Mahdavi has likened the term to a "rubber band," expanding enough to include most forms of suffering but often contracting around moral ideas of sex and migration.[16] As I discuss in the following chapter, "trafficking" has become so emotive a term and has come to be used so colloquially that it frequently stands in for everything from rape and sexual assault to undocumented migration and poverty. Such malleability has enabled the facile marketability of trafficking, despite the fact that most workers at Cowboy Rescue and Freedom Unchained do not consider themselves victims of trafficking. As further demonstrated in chapter 5, workers all over the world have pushed back against the idea that there is something truly exceptional about the exploitation of trafficking, echoing Janie Chuang's argument that the search for the most exceptional forms of abuse has created an "exploitation creep" in which the mundane aspects of labor abuse are easily ignored.[17] This criticism prompts a serious call to pause, reflect, and reformulate how we define trafficking and what the goals of rehabilitation should be.

The phrase "Bad Rehab" provides a novel and important framework for understanding how contemporary humanitarianism, particularly as it responds to problems of gender, migration, and development, reinstalls rescue regimes that are grounded in the power and force of US empire. Bad Rehab not only maps differences between the global North and the global South but also repeats recurrent racial scripts about white saviors and Asian sex slaves who need rescue from both the brutal conditions of sexual exploitation and intractably backwards family values.

Freedom Unchained and Cowboy Rescue have established narratives of rehabilitation that cast rescued workers as "lost *girls*" in need of support, guidance, and moral reformation in all aspects of their lives. The programs have thus developed systems of governance and moral guidance with strict rules that reach far into the personal lives of these women, regulating everything from their personal relationships to the places they frequent and how they spend their disposable income. This maternalism in which anti-trafficking rehabilitation activists emerge as parental figures responsible for the moral behavior of their "girls," not only heavily restricts the autonomy of rescued workers but also effectively delegitimizes their existing family structures as well as their individual attempts to achieve economic independence and personal self-determination.[18]

For managers and activists, the maternalist character of stringent monitoring and control during and after the workday is believed to heal and correct the trauma endured during trafficking. However, rehab is bad for workers, I argue, when it allows moral notions of redemption to do the work of justice. Ultimately, workers have asserted, rehab is bad for the same reasons that low-wage jobs are bad in certain instances: there are limited feedback mechanisms or modes of remediation for worker grievances. This means that attempts at reform and resistance are ignored or, worse, co-opted by the institution to further justify its presence.

Workers frequently spoke to me about their actual families, not their symbolic NGO ones. I often listened to them talk about the pressures they faced that revealed they weren't so much preoccupied with sexual victimization as with the typical problems that come along with low-wage work. Workers under rehabilitation have very few outlets for expressing grievances about their work conditions; the very framework of rehabilitative labor suggests that workers need to be reformed out of a particular mindset that entraps them, binding any expression of discontent to moral tenets of gratitude, faith, and indebtedness. Because these programs suggest that virtuous labor provides a pathway to redemption, other forms of release and reprieve were framed as further delays and hindrances to the process.

The call to amplify workers' voices and support their resistance aims to highlight the various power structures that keep these perspectives silent. Notably, for instance, the music video by the Asia Pacific Network of Sex Worker mentioned at the outset of this chapter was launched six years before the *Time* article that ultimately led Somaly Mam to resign from her organization. *Time*'s findings of Mam's fraudulent trafficking claims validated what many sex worker activists in Asia had argued for years, often to deaf ears. And despite the widespread media exposé, Acting for Women in Distressing Situations (AFESIP) continues to run its programs at this writing.

Because rehabilitation programs pitch themselves as exit strategies from sex work, they do nothing to improve the working conditions present in sex work or the other precarious service jobs that people navigate between. However, the labor regimes of sex work can illuminate characteristics of working conditions across all forms of labor. The following chapter shows how anti-trafficking can easily betray and work against labor rights in the Chinese context.

CHAPTER 4

Trafficking Benevolent Authoritarianism in China

Just before the Lunar New Year celebrations each year, Freedom Unchained workers are awarded annual bonuses based on their performance reviews. In January 2011, one by one, workers were called into the manager's office to receive their bonuses. As they sat eagerly anticipating the announcements, I spoke with Ling, who had just exited her meeting. As the oldest at the time, and one of the most veteran participants in the program, Ling was surprised to receive only 300 RMB (45 USD), which was not enough to pay for a round-trip train ticket to her home province of Fujian for the Chinese New Year celebration. With only $45 in hand—which, she pointed out, was less than the price of a single bracelet that she makes, and she can make about four of them in an hour—she quickly calculated that rather than travel home for the new year, she would remit all the money back to her nine-year-old son, whom she had left behind when he was an infant. Leaving children in the care of grandparents and other family members is a decision that most Chinese migrant laborers make.[1] Due to prohibitive *hukou* requirements, which attach social services like school to residency status assigned by birthplace, it was often impossible for children to attend local school when they migrated with their parents. While there were some schools for migrant workers' children in migrant-dense communities on the outskirts of Beijing, these were anomalies. Furthermore, the fact that dormitory housing was included as part of nearly all salaries also meant that migrants could not afford to rent housing independently in order to live with their children.[2]

As with other employees, the manager instructed Ling not to tell other workers about the amount that she had received for her bonus, so as not to create "sinful" sentiments of envy or greed. However, rumors naturally circulated among the small staff, and it soon came out that many of the newer participants had received bonuses of up to 600 RMB (90 USD), similar to what Ling had received when she first arrived at Freedom Unchained four years earlier.

Ling and I sat in the inventory room, where she had been promoted to a quality-control position. The space was a converted walk-in closet that had been outfitted with floor-to-ceiling shelves, each stacked with bins filled with finished pieces of jewelry. The promotion took her off the jewelry shop floor and into a space with more autonomy, though it was so cramped that two people at most could fit. She spent most of the day alone here without oversight. She closed the door and sat on a small red plastic stool rubbing her temples with the heels of her hands. After a few minutes, she broke the silence and vocalized her brewing speculation. "My bonus has nothing to do with my production or performance, but with my hesitance to embrace Christianity." As she continued, her voice got louder, and she strung a set of expletives together cursing her patience for "stupid fucking activities." I recognized this tone, one for which she was often scolded when she used it to defend herself in the shelter or on the shop floor. Her rage seemed always to be brewing beneath the surface, and Xiao Hua, one of the house moms, once shared with me that this was a symptom of the trauma Ling had experienced in her former work.

Ling shifted from rage and paused for a serious moment. Turning to me, she asked if I had heard about the Foxconn workers who had figured prominently in the media for protesting workplace abuses—including twelve workers who died by suicide to draw attention to poor working conditions.[3] I told her that I had, and without skipping a beat, she replied, "Sometimes, I also think about jumping off this building." Ling elaborated that she shared the same sense of futility as workers who had so valiantly asked for better working conditions but were continually ignored. She felt trapped in this moment, frustrated with a coercive bonus system that was responsible for "luring" newer workers to stay at Freedom Unchained while refusing to reward older employees who had fewer employment alternatives.

Noting the quiver and hesitation in my voice, she assured me that she had just been exaggerating and had too many responsibilities to *tiao lou* or "jump off a building." She stressed that she was just using the example of Foxconn workers to claim solidarity with a struggle that had reached a global scale. Indeed, earlier that year, Foxconn workers had received recognition in international news outlets ranging from *The Guardian* to the *New York Times,* and Ling understood that her claims of feeling cheated at Freedom Unchained might be considered legitimate only if compared to other prominent labor abuses that had reached global notoriety. I sensed an irony that while activists sought a resonant frame in the anti-trafficking movement, Ling sought solidarity with migrant workers in China's southern manufacturing hub.

What continues to haunt me about hearing Ling profess suicidal thoughts is the cool and flippant way she expressed them. In a workplace lacking venues for processing grievances, as described in the previous chapter, such drastic complaints were commonplace, and as a researcher—not a shop-floor manager—I became a repository for them. When I relayed these complaints to managers in both cities, they disagreed with workers' interpretations of their own situations—often citing a sense of "brokenness" that prevented them from comprehending their own responsibility. I was also frequently told that I didn't see the full story, because my presence was short-term. And, given my lack of personal conviction in the power of Christ to heal, activists in both organizations grew frustrated at my siding with workers, which they saw as interferences with the larger project of spiritual conversion. As these tensions around my personal belief system and presence as an ethnographer grew, I reconsidered the ethics of my daily presence in each organization. After three years, this was also about the time that I reached a point of ethnographic saturation, where I began to see the same patterns emerge day in and day out. Hoping to further understand the anti-trafficking movement in China and Thailand, in 2011, I expanded my research to state and secular, civil society projects.

Ling's invocation of the Foxconn worker suicides helps guide this chapter, which seeks to understand how global anti-trafficking policy imperatives collide with Chinese struggles over workers' rights. The anti-trafficking social enterprises I discuss in previous chapters largely ignore the vast differences in political and legal frameworks specific to each place because a flattened narrative often best fits marketing strategies aimed at American consumers. Equally important, they avoid discussing the particularities of each nation-state because they have sought out the market as a strategy to escape state control and oversight of their work. However, the distinctions between migrant-sending and destination states must be carefully considered in order to understand the different challenges migrants face in each place. In the cases of faith-based social enterprises that sell "slave-free jewelry," the labor relations of production are bound by the specific features of neoliberal global capitalism and local politics around gender, labor, and migrant rights.

Thus, I now turn to state and civil society organizing in China, where an aggressive state has co-opted the anti-trafficking agenda to craft a government policy agenda that still staunchly opposes labor rights. Driven by Ling's serious contemplation of solidarity, the chapter thinks through how the institutional characteristics of anti-trafficking have fostered, to borrow Shen Yuan and Ching Kwan Lee's term, an "anti-solidarity machine." The mobilization and institutionalization of global anti-trafficking efforts in China mirror what Shen and Lee have argued is characteristic of labor rights NGOs in China: "Rather than cultivating workers' collective power, many labor NGOs have an anti-solidarity tendency."[4] In the case of China, state power itself is reproduced and legitimated through its engagement with the global anti-trafficking apparatus. By comparing anti-trafficking work to labor-organizing efforts, I bring the larger consideration of labor rights in the Chinese context into discussion of anti-trafficking rehabilitation programs and the transnational social movement. Zooming out to the macro-level state and civil society relationships also helps us understand how workers' concerns raised in two American anti-trafficking programs—of paternalism, misplaced feminism, white saviorism, moralism, and market fetishization—are not unique to faith-based organizations but endemic to the question of labor relations under a globalized racial capitalism.

MORE ANTI-TRAFFICKING SONGS

On a bright Sunday afternoon in December 2012, an audience of nearly five hundred men, women, and children gathered on a cement basketball court in a large migrant-worker community on the outskirts of Kunming City, the capital of Yunnan province. Residents of Fude, primarily low-wage workers in Kunming's construction, garment, and service sectors, curiously awaited a rock concert focused on "human trafficking." Audience members squeezed into the community gathering space in front of a makeshift stage across which stretched a large banner announcing the concert's agenda: "Returning Home: New Migrant Worker's Band Anti-

FIGURE 15. 2012 Anti-Trafficking concert in Kunming featuring a rainbow arched banner with the words "Prevent Labor Exploitation, Achieve Safe Migration." Photo by author.

trafficking Concert." Front and center, amid the growing audience, some of which had scaled fences at the court's periphery to get a better view of the commotion, proudly sat two middle-aged Communist Party representatives from the All-China Women's Federation (ACWF), a government entity in charge of women and children's welfare. During the concert, the two sang along, pounding their fists in the air, to lyrics that called for increased protection of worker safety and rights. Backstage, coordinating the event, was a remarkable group of Chinese and international civil society cosponsors: the United Nations Inter-agency Project to Combat Human Trafficking (UNIAP), the International Labor Organization (ILO), and the international Christian organization World Vision.

This idyllic scene of transnational solidarity around the theme of "combating human trafficking," and in particular *labor* trafficking, was unprecedented and unexpected in authoritarian China, particularly in light of the Chinese government's crackdown on labor-rights NGOs in the years following the concert. In December 2015, Guangzhou police detained seven labor activists because, according to the state media, they "incited workers to go on strike," accepted foreign funding, and "disturbed social order." The following month, on January 10, 2016, Chinese authorities arrested four labor activists on charges of "disturbing social order." One of them, Zeng Feiyang, was, and as of this writing still is, the director of the Panyu Migrant Workers Center in Guangzhou and is considered one of China's most prominent labor activists. These arrests and media campaigns were and still are emblematic developments in an ongoing labor crackdown under President Xi Jinping.[5] In many of these cases, and specifically in that of Zeng, activists have reported that the detained are held overnight in a police station without charges and, after their release, are often followed, beaten, and sometimes simply disappeared. In

2015, Chen Huihai, the director of worker training at Laowei, a law firm specializing in labor disputes, warned, "The crackdown last year [2014] was the toughest in history. 2015 is going to be even tougher."[6] This is not the first central-government crackdown in the twenty-first century; in May 2012, the Beijing government launched a "100-day campaign to crack down on illegal foreigners."[7] The campaign increased Public Security Bureau oversight of migrant populations and lashed out at undocumented migrants as part of the state's increased monitoring of foreigners.

These crackdowns were seen as a response to rising labor unrest following the slowdown of the Chinese economy, especially in the manufacturing coastal province of Guangdong; however, they are part of an enduring history of labor repression in China. According to the *China Labor Bulletin,* the number of strikes in China more than doubled in 2014 to 1,378, from 656 the year before.[8] Pun Ngai and Sam Austin explained that the crackdown appeared designed to warn workers that unrest would not be tolerated at a time when many factories were either closing as a result of China's slowing economy or relocating to parts of South and Southeast Asia where costs were lower.[9]

The anti-trafficking activism that has burgeoned since the mid-2000s, unperturbed by the ongoing aggressive crackdowns on labor unrest in China, poses a critical paradox. China's anti-trafficking response—largely motivated and often funded by international global governance agencies and moral imperatives—creates new and exceptional categories of victimization that allow the state to criminalize ethnic and sexual minorities and migrant workers. Similar to the way in which Shen and Lee have argued that regressive Chinese labor politics have foreclosed opportunities for worker organizing, the case of trafficking reveals that the fortification of a government-led anti-trafficking stance paves the way for greater restrictions on migrant mobility and on gender and labor rights. The state has manufactured new gestures of anti-trafficking engagement that gain it favor on the international scene. This perceived goodwill then carves out space for the Chinese state to continue to aggressively stymie activism on behalf of worker rights. Interactions between the authoritarian state and transnational civil society reveal how the state has co-opted the global anti-trafficking movement to establish new forms of social control and state legitimacy. In global terms, this co-optation is one way the global anti-trafficking movement has displaced worker organizing.[10]

THE MALLEABILITY OF LABOR TRAFFICKING
DISCOURSE

Although China ratified the UN Palermo Protocol in 2010, it has yet to adopt the international definition of human trafficking in its National Plan of Action (NPA). The initial, 2008–2012 plan recognized only the trafficking of women and children (excluding men as victims) and refused to define *forced labor* as a form of trafficking; the government claimed that forced labor is adequately addressed under Chinese labor law.[11] The particular form of state-led capitalism in China, which Yasheng Huang has termed "capitalism with Chinese characteristics," is protective of employers' interests, rather than the labor rights of employees.[12] Thus, excluding labor exploitation from the national definition of human trafficking is part of a longer tradition of securing employer impunity and thwarting labor unrest of any kind.

The subsequent National Plan of Action, issued in 2013, reflected changes in the Chinese government's approach to trafficking between 2013 and 2020. Significantly, the plan changed its focus from the "combating trafficking of women and children" to combatting "trafficking in persons," thus broadening the scope beyond women and children. The name change seems largely symbolic, however, as the overwhelming focus on women and children remains. Bonny Ling's thorough analysis of the 2013–20 National Plan of Action revamp finds that government anti-trafficking rhetoric was still being carcerally deployed to eradicate prostitution.[13] Most news articles about trafficking in China have continued to focus on cases involving kidnapping of women and children. Many also cite law enforcement statistics; for example: "Official figures show that police across the country rescued 8,660 abducted children and 15,458 women, while breaking up 3,195 criminal circles engaged in human trafficking in 2011."[14]

In this crucial way, the state has, to borrow Ching Kwan Lee and Yonghong Zhang's term, "absorbed" the anti-trafficking movement: selectively defining trafficking using exceptionally narrow categories. In China, the exclusion of labor from its trafficking definition is rooted in a contentious history of state control and negotiation of labor rights.[15] The Chinese Communist Party's resistance to adopting the transnational definition of human trafficking is characteristic of China's resistance to global human rights norms. The Chinese state protects capital interests in labor; thus, excluding labor exploitation from the national definition of human trafficking is part of a longer tradition of stymying labor unrest of any kind.

Another main way the state has harnessed this movement for its own ends is by placing its hub of countertrafficking work in the Ministry of Public Security's Inter-Ministerial Office Against Trafficking (IMOAT), which, according to the mandates of the "Public Security" department, focuses primarily on prosecuting and policing trafficking, rather than victim protection or prevention.[16] In many other states, anti-trafficking operations are monitored through the equivalent of the Chinese Ministry of Civil Affairs; for instance, in the United States, through the Department of Health and Human Services and, in Thailand, through the Ministry of Human Development and Social Security—entities that at least nominally focus on the social welfare needs of trafficking victims. China's strategic framing of human trafficking within the purview of the Ministry of Public Security has allowed the state to prioritize criminal justice over social welfare in its responses to trafficking.

Between 2008 and 2014, the government's Inter-Ministerial Office Against Trafficking worked exclusively with the UN Inter-Agency Project on Human Trafficking office in China to administer counter-trafficking work domestically and control the information flows between China and the UNIAP Regional Management Office in Bangkok. The Chinese IMOAT allowed anti-trafficking projects to be conducted only if they had a government partner; for example, UNIAP was required to partner with a government-approved researcher to conduct trafficking research of any kind, and research findings were reported straight to IMOAT, before they could be disseminated. Information flow was a big part of my daily tasks working as a researcher at the UNIAP office, entering data into endless Excel spreadsheets, work so tedious that it often took longer to report the research findings than to conduct the research itself. Such vertical relationships between sponsoring institution and researcher skew research questions and data collection toward the state agenda, and alienate a number of civil society organizations that conduct anti-trafficking work, by giving the government exclusive control over the movement's access to resources. While these mechanisms of global governance intend to hold states accountable to the United Nations, they simultaneously create channels for the UN and other interagency partners to be accountable to and be scrutinized by the state—inadvertently carving out mechanisms that *strengthen* governmental oversight of countertrafficking activities.

By this mechanism, state efforts to "combat human trafficking" have had the effect—intended or not—of criminalizing already-marginalized populations, in particular, undocumented migrant workers and sex workers. In the past two decades, anti-trafficking media reporting has focused on the forced selling of brides from Myanmar into China, a phenomenon often attributed to a gender imbalance stemming from the one-child policy, and resulting high rates of female infanticide in the 1980s and '90s. When local Chinese police discover cases of forced marriage, they fail to protect the rights of Burmese victims, choosing instead to deport marriage migrants under the anti-trafficking framework of "repatriation"—even if the women have children in China. Fear of such systematic deportation has made stateless and Burmese victims of forced marriage less likely to seek assistance after they are trafficked.[17]

In addition, because prostitution is illegal in China, efforts to rescue victims of forced prostitution under the trafficking law have resulted in the heightened surveillance of voluntary sex workers. Thus, the emphasis on "forced" prostitution as a category of victimization is rarely relevant, because the police have just cause to arrest anyone found engaging in commercial sex. What is notable about sex workers arrested under the purview of the human trafficking law is that Chinese sex workers are sentenced to mandatory "reeducation through labor," in which they serve jail time by learning skills like sewing and jewelry making—something that, as discussed in the previous chapter, happens throughout the world in anti-trafficking shelters.[18] Further, sex-worker participant research coordinated with the Asia Pacific Network of Sex Workers has found some cases in which part of a detained sex worker's reeducation involved memorizing some of the country's new anti-trafficking laws and the UN Palermo Protocol.[19] Programs like Freedom Unchained and Cowboy Rescue are intended to be a better alternative to this reeducation, but in the Chinese context, they fall short of their goals when they focus on the aforementioned maternalist modes of reeducation.

Alongside these more punitive ways the state has used the anti-trafficking movement to promote carceral agendas and curb migration, it has also unveiled a set of anti-trafficking programs that, I argue, can be read as gestures of benevolent authoritarianism. Here, I build on Lee and Zhang's theory that contemporary Chinese state power is maintained through the rote process of "bureaucratic absorption," whereby state entities formalize power through putative collaborations with aggrieved populations. Lee and Zhang argue that repressing social protest can be facilitated only through the state's absorption of protests. Going further, I argue that in the case of its anti-trafficking response, the state has "absorbed" the anti-trafficking movement in order to create new spaces of state legitimacy and justify old tactics of repression and state control.[20]

LABOR TRAFFICKING AND LABOR TRANSNATIONALISM

During the active years of UNIAP, the Chinese anti-trafficking ministerial office joined ministers from six countries in the Greater Mekong Subregion for the Senior Officials Meeting (SOM) on Human Trafficking, organized by UNIAP. At this conference, convened in early 2013 at a luxury, five-star hotel overlooking Bangkok's Chao Praya River, I interviewed a senior official of the Chinese Ministry of Public Security. When I asked him why labor trafficking is still not included in the country's human trafficking definition, he replied: "The international community insists that labor exploitation is a problem; I guarantee you that labor is not a problem. What people outside China don't understand is exactly how strong Chinese workers are. We have a kind of culture of work here—as such, it's not likely that a case of trafficking will involve labor." This reasoning, which embeds nationalist logics and gendered assumptions about the strength and virility of a masculine Chinese labor, allows Chinese state actors to align themselves with the transnational anti-trafficking movement by discursively shaping transnational rights in the interests of the nation-state. This state agenda stems from a highly organized central government that prioritizes maintaining "harmony," quelling civil society unrest, and developing its national economy. Following economic reform in the 1980s, undocumented migration, human rights protests, and ethnic-minority disturbances have increased, but public security forces have swiftly stifled them. The senior official's rhetoric also reflects a socialist legacy in which the state has exalted the working class as the primary engine of growth.[21]

During a lunch break at the meeting, over an elaborate buffet-style meal in the hotel's banquet hall, documentary filmmakers from MTV's project "End Exploitation and Trafficking" (known as MTV EXIT) requested that I translate an interview between MTV and the high-ranking official from the ministry's anti-trafficking office. In an email before the meeting, an MTV EXIT project manager told me that they regretted not having a Chinese-speaking staff member on their team of filmmakers from the United States and United Kingdom. As we sat down for the interview, the team explained to the senior official that they were working on a multicountry documentary series called "Enslaved" and were eager to highlight one case of cross-border labor trafficking from

China. The official listened intently and was startled. "Labor exploitation!?" He furrowed his brow, sternly shook his head, and uttered with the utmost conviction: "It's unlikely that we have any cases of labor exploitation; my office certainly has not heard of any of these. Maybe in brick kilns with physically and mentally disabled workers. But it would not be advisable to film a case of labor exploitation, because this would not give a very complete picture of trafficking in China."

The emphatic assertion that labor exploitation happens only to workers who are physically or mentally disabled in their capacity to fight for their rights confirms his earlier assertion that able-bodied workers, and particularly male laborers, ought by nature to exemplify *good*, strong workers—as an extension of the Chinese state. The official's assertion that the strength and virility of Chinese labor prevents workers from being exploitable stymies efforts to address the systemic infringement of labor rights. It further justifies the widespread quashing of labor organizing.

MTV EXIT, an independent foundation affiliated with MTV Europe, was founded to raise awareness about human trafficking across the Asia-Pacific region. It hired popular regional bands to perform concerts at shopping malls in what it claimed were "second-tier cities," where crowds of young people gathered to raise awareness about human trafficking. At a 2010 concert I attended at the SM Mall in Cebu City, Philippines, I noticed that most of the young attendees were more interested in MTV's branding and performances (projected on screens) by The Hills and Punk'd than in the message against human trafficking. Reflecting on these concerts, the anthropologists and cultural activists Heather Peters and David Feingold shared the skepticism that it was unclear how effective this program was in achieving anything other than increasing MTV's presence in its "emerging markets" in Southeast Asia.[22] MTV EXIT's efforts remained well funded through a combination of individual and foundation grants until the project ended in 2014. The fact that I, then a research intern at UNIAP China, was asked to provide services as an interpreter points to critical structural characteristics of the transnational anti-trafficking movement in the region: that few staff of the transnational movement organizations speak the local languages of the areas in which they work, and that UNIAP and other international organizations are frequently called upon to serve as the literal translators between transnational civil society and the state.

Marina Zaloznaya and John Hagan's work on the governance of anti-human trafficking efforts in Belarus theorizes a model of "selective compliance" whereby "selective tight coupling rather than decoupling from on-the-ground policies enables the simultaneous compliance and worsening of authoritarian repression."[23] They argue that the Belarussian government pursues certain social protection policies in the name of ending human trafficking to gain merit on the transnational stage but that this form of legitimation affords greater authoritarian power over subjects of human trafficking. As in the Belarus case, and as this chapter illustrates, the transnational pressure to engage in "interagency" efforts to combat human trafficking offers the Chinese state an opportunity to monitor and oversee all labor-trafficking efforts—even though it excludes labor exploitation from its own definition of human trafficking.

MULTISECTOR COLLABORATION

In 2010, UNIAP regional management officers from Bangkok decided to fund the China office's "Migrant Worker Band Project," which would hire a well-known migrant worker band to write and perform songs about human trafficking. They hoped this creative strategy—organized around the innocuous songs—would be the least likely to offend their government partners. Cosponsored by the multinational Christian foundation World Vision and the United Nations, this project first needed to instruct the band about the definition of human trafficking, as it had oriented its activism and organizing previously around frameworks of migrant and labor rights. The discourse of "human trafficking" was, thus, relatively new to the band, and organizers felt a training session would be necessary to clarify the word's specific policy meanings.

Founded in 2004, the Migrant Worker's Home, a local NGO that emerged from the New Workers' Artist Troupe, established an increasingly distinct profile in the NGO community in Beijing.[24] Known for performing concerts about migrant pride before migrant worker communities throughout the country, the band had well-established formulas for delivering messages about safe labor practices. While its concerts are largely uncontested by the government, the NGO's work in convening an annual conference of labor NGOs at its headquarters in Beijing often raised alarms among government censors. Activists told me that in 2012, they deliberately changed the focus of their annual conference from "labor strategizing" to "celebrating labor culture." The UNIAP China office, aware of the band's seemingly benign, yet powerful previous concerts, was hopeful to pursue collaboration with the New Workers' Artist Troupe.

The eighteen-month project was funded at over 100,000 USD by UNIAP and World Vision, one of the primary international NGO actors in China's limited anti-trafficking movement. The multinational Christian foundation collects money from Christians in the global North to promote "rights and democracy in the developing world." As one of the larger anti-trafficking funders in China, World Vision should be an unlikely partner in staunchly secular China. Political scientist Timothy Hildebrandt has written about the unexpected social movement–promoting coalitions between the Chinese government and faith-based organizations.[25] One significant reason for World Vision's robust participation may be that its financial contributions to government anti-trafficking efforts come with very few stipulations. In addition to paying for various anti-trafficking programs that gain it merit among its global funders, it also endears itself to the government by paying for things like the minister's first-class airplane upgrades to attend UN meetings, a cost that neither UN nor Chinese government budgets will cover.[26]

World Vision was likely motivated by the promise of *guanxi,* a system of relationships and reciprocity regarded as necessary in Chinese social, economic, and secular political arrangements.[27] Following a lunch meeting at the UNIAP office, I observed how remarkable it was for World Vision to have a seat at the table during government-led anti-trafficking conversations in China. The director told me that World Vision has been operating in China for over a decade and that its success is due to "prioritizing cooperation opportunities." The organization has chosen to mask its Christian priorities, evidenced by different verbiage in the international versus Chinese versions of its website. While the Chinese version states, "World Vision is a relief, development, and advocacy nongovernmental organization," the World Vision International page describes World Vision as "an international partnership of Christians whose mission is to follow our Lord and Saviour Jesus Christ in working with the poor and oppressed to promote human transformation, seek justice and bear witness to the good news of the Kingdom of God."[28] Hints of Christianity are also apparent or buried in other parts of the website; for example, the English-language version requests a church affiliation in a job application cover letter, while the Chinese-language version omits the request, though World Vision workers in China are mostly Christians, as the office requires staff to engage in daily group prayer.

World Vision created a favorable relationship with the Chinese government through its generous funding and cosponsorship of government anti-trafficking projects. This connection has paved the way for it to run its own projects with relatively little oversight. For instance, the organization runs a children's shelter in the suburbs of Kunming City that houses more than one hundred homeless, orphaned, disabled, and runaway street youth. In addition to anti-trafficking, World Vision's other projects focus on poverty alleviation, education, and children's rights. The organization claims no proselytization of its beneficiary populations; however, its offices hold Christian worship every day, and employees consider faith an important motivation for their professional endeavors. Reflecting the organization's international stature as a large, global Christian nonprofit organization at the helm of Christian anti-trafficking efforts, World Vision has a page of its website devoted to its anti-trafficking projects. In addition, it calls on supporters to engage in global prayer to end human trafficking.[29]

In addition to UNIAP and World Vision, the project required a government partner to comply with government requirements for oversight. The All-China Women's Federation filled this role; this governmental organ occupies an interesting position in China because it is not housed within the government ministerial infrastructure, but serves as a liaison between civil society and the government, a particular category that has been labeled a "Government Organized NGO" (GONGO) in China.[30] The regional UN inter-agency focus is easily adopted to accommodate the Chinese government's model of "partnership" as oversight in all non-governmental work. Such mandatory and often stifling governmental oversight is considered a serious a hurdle for many non-profit organizations and foundations in China, which persistently struggle with government compliance and censorship. Many non-governmental organizations, like Freedom Unchained evade these requirements by registering as for-profit entities, as social enterprises, or through a fiscal conduit.[31]

CONTENTION, CONVERGENCE, AND COOPERATION

The Migrant Worker Band Project kicked off in 2012 with a three-day "concept training workshop," held in the UNIAP Beijing offices, designed to train the band about human trafficking so that it could compose effective lyrics on the topic. Seated in a small conference room in a high-rise building in a diplomatic compound in Beijing (entry to which is granted without question to foreign passport holders, but to Chinese nationals only after an extensive registration process), eight members of the band were seated around a table where they listened to presentations from UNIAP, the International Labor Organization, and the All-China Women's Federation. The national project coordinator of the UNIAP China office, a charismatic, forty-something former government employee and member of the elite Communist Youth League, gave a formal presentation about the Chinese government's stance on human trafficking and on four select cases of trafficking that have occurred—though not one was a case of labor trafficking.

Although the phrase "labor exploitation" floated across numerous PowerPoint slides, not one of the "expert trainers" articulated the specific kinds of labor exploitation that may be considered human trafficking offenses in China. This gap exists because China does not recognize labor trafficking; these trainers nevertheless included discussions of labor exploitation because they are constantly negotiating the gaps between international and Chinese working definitions of human trafficking, and because this meeting's implicit agenda was to train a labor rights band/NGO on the issue of human trafficking as a way of merging the labor and trafficking frameworks.

Curiosity, confusion, exasperation, and sheer boredom by turns washed over the band members as many whispered comments about the unnecessary formality of the training. On about the fifth PowerPoint slide, which ceremoniously flashed the words "labor exploitation" on the screen (the slide was about how the UN Palermo Protocol includes labor exploitation as one type of human trafficking), the founder of the band raised his hand.

Band Member 1: I don't understand what you mean by "labor exploitation." Our [labor rights] NGO and community center meets clients on a daily basis who have many different kinds of problems, from unpaid wages, bad working conditions, [to] faulty contracts, so you are saying that we can file these as human-trafficking cases?

UNIAP Representative: Not really. This protocol is really talking about *extreme* cases of labor exploitation.

Band Member 2: Well, then the word "labor exploitation" is unclear. This is a concept that we really need to understand if we are to write songs about it, and if workers are supposed to be able to understand these songs.

Band Member 3: [interrupts] Yeah, I mean, we all know that we are essentially all exploited as workers . . . [chuckles] . . . I mean, some could say that you, the UN, is exploiting us right now. Or that you, too, are being exploited.

ILO Representative: [intervenes] It's basically to say, the *worst* forms of labor abuse that occur.

Band Member 2: What would that entail? Does that include what is going on at Foxconn right now?

ILO Representative: If those cases deal with children under the age of sixteen, then yes.

UNIAP Representative: That's right! China has a child labor law which prohibits any child under the age of sixteen from working—any child who works is a victim of human trafficking.

ILO Representative: I also want to let you know that ILO takes this problem very seriously and is beginning a baseline study into the student labor problem next year.

Bang Member 3: OK, so I want to write one of these human-trafficking songs about the serious problem of student labor abuses that are happening at Foxconn as a problem of human trafficking.

UNIAP Representative: OK . . . but you need to make sure it is clear in the lyrics that it's about children under the age of sixteen.

As Freedom Unchained worker Ling noted, Foxconn is a Taiwan-based electronics-manufacturing company that employs thousands of workers in factories throughout China, with its largest factories located in southern China's Guangdong province. It recently came under global scrutiny after over a dozen workers died by suicide, and over one hundred and fifty workers threatened suicide in protest over the factory's maltreatment of its workers, hazardous working conditions, and exploitation of student labor. Though certainly not the only factory guilty of such labor abuses, it has gained the most international notoriety because of its connection to American suppliers. The concern over worker's rights reached US shores when activists and journalists revealed that Foxconn is one of the largest manufacturers of Apple, Dell, and Hewlett Packard products, and asked consumers to put pressure on these popular brands to address labor exploitation in their supply chains.[32]

Noticing that the problem of exploited student labor might gain some traction with the trafficking community, the youngest band member was excited to have found a concrete point of overlap between the labor- and human-trafficking agendas. She was quickly told, however, that only student workers under sixteen could be considered victims of trafficking. The actual mechanics of exploitation, or what Yihui Su has called the "dual commodification of education and labor"[33]—including the mandatory completion of unpaid, unsafe, and extensive hours of work at the behest of "vocational training schools" that withhold identity cards and diploma certificates until the "internship" period is complete—

are not considered trafficking, despite the extreme exploitation of such vocational training programs. In the interaction above, and at other points during the training, band members showed uneasiness with the UNIAP and ILO representatives' quick dismissal of the widely publicized incidents of labor abuse at Foxconn and cases of labor abuse that they manage daily. UNIAP and ILO staff members took this position on labor abuse because, as members of global governance agencies working closely with the Chinese government, their priority is the government's definition of trafficking. Any flexibility in interpretation would challenge the future of their work and collaboration with the government.[34]

The Foxconn labor crisis offers a compelling case with which to explore why certain forms of labor exploitation fall outside the purview of China's anti-trafficking response. The case brought to light the pervasive exploitation of student workers who took on unpaid internships in order to receive credentials and graduate from vocational schools. It also exposes some of the false promises of vocational training, misleading precisely because private corporations benefit from the unpaid labor they receive from student labor so arranged. The UNIAP office generally ignored this labor crisis because China's National Plan of Action did not encompass nonsexual forms of labor exploitation, and the office assumed these problems were managed exclusively by the Ministry of Labor. That the band would recognize an opportunity to advocate for student workers is a clever interpretation of the UN human trafficking protocol. Advocating for the inclusion of labor rights in human trafficking activism certainly mirrors the United States' and United Nations' interest in pressuring the Chinese government to recognize labor trafficking; however, as this chapter demonstrates, authoritarian state interests can easily co-opt and absorb the transnational human trafficking protocols used to mobilize labor activism.

When I interviewed Chinese labor rights activists, lawyers, and NGOs about their thoughts regarding the mobilization of labor rights in anti-trafficking activism, respondents where either confused or agnostic on the matter. Many did not know the definition of human trafficking, and my attempts to explain the differences between the Chinese and UN definitions often devolved into a confusing and ineffective dialogue similar to the interaction I recount above. Debby Chan, the director of Students and Scholars Against Corporate Misbehavior (SACOM), a Hong Kong–based labor rights and advocacy NGO that has fiercely advocated for Foxconn workers' rights, explained that labor activists were already embroiled in a decades-long battle to enforce labor law and ensure supply chain accountability. Chan explained, "We have not worked with the anti-trafficking protocols because they don't seem to be very strong in China. We have a difficult enough time enforcing the provisions of a labor law that have been around for decades. To derail such efforts doesn't make sense with our advocacy strategies, and we already don't have enough manpower." Chan's response was neutral; she did not necessarily see a problem with using the anti-trafficking protocols, but she and other labor activists did not see the connection between the glossiness of the global agenda on human trafficking—which predominantly represented it as a problem of *sex*—and, to a certain extent, she did not trust its newness.[35]

In his ethnography of the World Bank, Michael Goldman uncovers how this global governance institution generates expertise concerning economic development in the Third World. Relying on the testimony of international experts (frequently this refers to English-speaking consultants who have completed schooling in Western countries), international organizations and policy makers ignore local and Indigenous knowledge.[36] Similarly, the training of the migrant band should have been an opportunity for exchange given the band's decade-long experience operating a community center for migrant laborers living outside Beijing. In addition to their direct service to migrant populations, in 2008, the organization opened the Migrant Worker Culture and Art Museum, the first of its kind in China, with plans to take a traveling exhibition to the Museum of the Chinese in America in New York.[37] The group's experience with the changing concerns and composition of migrant labor in China is invaluable for informing songs about labor exploitation, yet this firsthand knowledge went unrecognized throughout the training.

Rather than use their own on-the-ground experience as a resource, transnational actors—in partnership with the Chinese government—asked the labor rights NGO to redefine labor within the rather distorted interests of trafficking. Shaped by the Chinese state, this definition labels only the "most severe" instances of labor exploitation as labor trafficking, which ends up defining human trafficking offenses by their *exceptionalism,* thereby marginalizing widespread, everyday labor abuses. Rarely have such transnational efforts, even in other contexts, looked to existing labor rights organizations and activism; instead they found new organizations or co-opt existing ones to address the newer issue of labor trafficking.

PERFORMING TRANSNATIONAL AMBIGUITY

Setting aside the difficulties and discrepancies of working through competing definitions of human trafficking, and of what makes labor trafficking distinct according to Chinese definitions of trafficking, the band composed ten songs in the assigned six-month period. UNIAP and World Vision planned concerts in five cities throughout China, including Beijing, Guangzhou, Suzhou, Jiangsu, and Kunming and produced around five hundred copies of the band's CD to distribute. The Kunming site was selected because, since 2004, the ACWF has worked with the ILO to support a local NGO that provides services to migrant workers in the community. This NGO's modest community station in Fude has a staff of about ten and works on issues such as health, education, and legal rights and houses a library and drop-in center for young children.

Throughout their performance, band members narrated the concert and explained the meaning behind the different songs, often linking lyrics to concrete laws intended to protect migrant workers. During the introduction, the band leader commanded the audience's attention in the style of an emcee: "You may have heard of trafficking, and you may have heard that this is a problem relegated to women and children, but the United Nations has just noted that trafficking can include labor exploitation." Throughout the concert, they maintained a consistent labor rights message, mentioning brick kiln workers and underage child labor—pointing primarily to the exceptional cases that the Chinese government has deemed trafficking.

Just as it was not entirely clear what the practical and material message of "labor trafficking" was during the band's training, it was not clear to the audience how the human-trafficking framework the band presented would address the attendees' day-to-day labor grievances. Alongside the band's focus on labor abuse and other forms of trafficking, one song highlighted a missing girl who had been kidnapped on her way back from school. During this song, a local resident of Fude, a middle-aged woman dressed in clothes whose colors were muted by what appeared to be excessive wear, dust, and sun, approached a volunteer. With tears streaming down her face, the woman clutched a photograph, explaining that her eight-year-old daughter had not returned home from school two weeks prior. The volunteer pushed through the crowd and brought the audience member to the organizers, who recorded the general information about the case and photographed the image of the missing child. Later on during the concert, the emcee, a full-time staff member at the local partner organization, came onstage to report the missing-child case. As the audience hushed and the mood significantly dampened, the emcee quickly assured the audience that a song later in the program would be sung in honor of this lost child. UNIAP staff later jumped in and announced that they had just posted the girl's photo on the IMOAT director's microblog site about human trafficking, proudly adding that the site has over 500,000 followers.[38]

For the audience, the messages about labor trafficking were just as confusing to the public as they were in the UNIAP conference room during the band's training. Without regard to the needs of the local population, the purpose of the concert was not to learn about the unique problems different migrant communities faced but rather to teach communities about international understandings of human trafficking, and the conceptual move to include labor trafficking in China's definition of trafficking.[39] For the audience, however, the most powerful and resonant part of the concert was the firsthand testimony of child kidnapping—a phenomenon that community members agreed occurs far too often because of long parental working hours, absence of community and educational resources for migrant youth, and lack of political will on the part of police to track down lost children.

Earlier scholarship examining the incompatibility of transnational mobilization with local circumstances found that transnational policy agendas receive more visibility because of unevenly distributed resources and power.[40] As Joe Bandy and Jackie Smith argue, "Centralized circumstances with greater resources tend to reinforce power imbalances among organizational participants, such as those occurring between men and women, racial groups, or national organizations."[41] The anti-trafficking movement has proven to mirror such a "centralized circumstance" as it attracts significant funding from states, global governance institutions, and NGOs, while reproducing inequalities based on nation, gender, and class. Similarly, Ethel Brooks's study of the transnational movement against child labor in Pakistan finds numerous disconnections between the transnational and local social fields of understanding:

> The core failing of the transnational campaign against child labor was the continued exclusion of disempowered workers from dialogues about what policy changes would improve their living conditions. By viewing children as outside of power, US activists and politicians framed the debate as one among adult, white people about children in the developing world. The debate as it is currently framed precludes a discussion of the challenges faced

by entire urban communities in the Global South, and of the communities' own responses to challenges. The child-labor focus of the campaign also downplayed the very real and systemic economic deprivation faced by the families that are forced to send their kids off to work in the first place.[42]

Ghanaian British sociologist and ethnographer Samuel Okyere has shown how the anti-trafficking movement's essentialized focus on child victims obscures larger calls for greater justice for children and adults alike. Drawing on ethnographic participant observation with youth who work in Ghanaian copper mines, Okyere argues that global anti-trafficking efforts that demand the abolition of all forms of child labor fail to acknowledge that child labor stems from developmental and infrastructural inequities resulting from colonial conquest in Ghana.[43] These calls for a development- and colonial-contextual understanding of child rights are frequently ignored, particularly by anti-trafficking NGOs that stand to earn a great sum by claiming to unilaterally abolish child labor.

The anti-trafficking concert in Fude, and Fude residents' responses to it, illustrates grave incompatibilities between transnational agendas and local realities. By addressing only the most extreme cases of labor exploitation or child kidnapping, concerts that focus on human trafficking largely ignore the diverse forms of migrant exploitation and the decision making that leads to migrant laborers' choices, and scarcely acknowledge the lack of community resources in migrant communities to promote child safety. It is this same narrow focus on transforming sexual into manual labor that causes vocational training and rehabilitation programs to fail to address systemic problems with the current menu of low-wage jobs.

THE BLOODY HIGH HEEL AT A TRUMP SHOE FACTORY

Six months following the concert described above, the US State Department, in its annual June 2013 *Trafficking in Persons Report* (*TIP Report*), demoted China to the lowest tier, Tier 3, for the first time in the report's decade-long history. Before receiving the damning Tier 3 ranking in 2013, China had spent two years on the Tier 2 "Watch List," a ranking given to countries as a "warning" of their pending downgrade to the third tier if their interventions do not align with US protocol.[44] China remains in Tier 3 at this writing, most recently codified in the June 2022 report. The *TIP Report* has criticized the Chinese government's lack of attention to labor trafficking and refusal to recognize the trafficking of men. This is particularly significant given the scale of labor protest in China's manufacturing hubs. Traditionally unrelated to anti-human trafficking advocacy, in the past decade—a period of heightened labor unrest—worker rights organizations have vociferously argued for increased attention to worker safety and rights recognition.

In explaining its rationale for China's downgrade to the third tier, the US State Department has cited lack of Chinese government transparency, limited government cooperation with interagency commitments, and foremost, China's reluctance to address labor trafficking in its National Human Trafficking Plan of Action. The *TIP Report*'s comments on China's lack of accountability for labor trafficking follows a general shift in focus of US anti-trafficking engagement from a highly criticized, sensational focus on sex trafficking to a more sustained engagement with the broader issues of labor trafficking. The international community has followed this shift, increasingly using the language of "modern-day slavery" to apply to a range of labor exploitation cases.[45]

During the Trump presidency, labor rights groups pointed out the US inconsistency between standing behind an elaborate anti-trafficking framework and supporting systemic exploitation. When the 2019 *TIP Report* was issued, Ivanka Trump, Trump's daughter and a senior advisor in his administration, was the White House's face of anti-trafficking, and published an op-ed in the *Washington Post* about the importance of modern-day abolition.[46] Her self-congratulatory editorial was surprising in that it was published amid a great scandal involving labor disputes with workers at the Ivanka Trump brand's shoe factories in southern China.[47] Labor activists with the nonprofit organization China Labor Watch who worked undercover at several of Ivanka Trump's shoe factories, including Huajian Ganzhou, which produces just the heels of Ivanka's branded shoes, obtained evidence of substandard pay ($1 an hour), forced overtime, and fears of retaliation for expressing grievance.[48] Workers in these factories were also subject to brutal violence, as proved by a video showing a manager berating a worker for arranging shoes in the wrong order, and by eyewitness testimony of a manager causing a worker to bleed after striking him in the face with the sharp edge of a high heeled shoe. Shortly after sharing these findings, the three undercover labor activists were detained. They claimed that such government oversight of their work reflected increasing government censorship of labor rights groups, as described in this chapter, but also to their investigation of a Trump manufacturer. Pointing to the curious simultaneity of the Trump family being at the helm of the US anti-trafficking project while ignoring labor abuses within its own businesses, the activists aimed to illustrate once more the hypocrisy in much anti-trafficking bravado.

The global governance of human trafficking in China reveals how global countertrafficking movement goals are reciprocally shaped by distinct state interests—in China, the prevention of labor unrest in one of the largest migrant workforces in the world and, in the United States, the corporate- and consumption-driven desires to export manufacturing to countries with cheap labor. Global anti-trafficking social policy is actively constructed and contested locally vis-à-vis national anti-trafficking laws, government ministries, bilateral and regional memorandums of understanding, and collusion with or exclusion from peripheral movements related to gender, sexuality, and labor, migrant, and human rights. Under Chinese authoritarianism, new mechanisms of rights censorship—including the creation of a government ministry to address human trafficking—have secured the government institutional space for policing and deporting undocumented migrants and for allowing the ongoing exploitation of migrant workers.[49]

My glimpse of the anti-trafficking movement in China reveals instances of solidarity and co-option in which global governance institutions, the state, and NGOs each follow their own motives and interests. As international resources fund the fight against labor trafficking in China, they also ignore ongoing local labor mobilization, as so clearly demonstrated by the jarring dissonance in Ivanka Trump's posture at the helm of the Trump administration's anti-trafficking team while ignoring labor criticisms launched at her shoe company. The case of the Migrant Worker Band Project reveals how the transnational move toward recognizing labor trafficking can have detrimental consequences for local organizations and local labor solidarity. It is a cautionary tale of how global solidarity can sometimes create spaces of local exclusion, both for labor organizations that find the definitions of human trafficking too narrow to include the vast majority of commonplace labor grievances and for those organizations that find the abundant resources available for "human trafficking" to represent a gross misallocation. The recent turn to a framework of labor trafficking in China occurred without recognition of local labor politics and organizing; these transnational frameworks were mobilized by a mutually complicit network of actors with their own motivations and interests, ultimately demonstrating a unique case of transnationalism without local solidarity for labor rights. This chapter reveals how, by ignoring labor organizing in order to promote the anti-trafficking agenda, government and civil society in China mirror many of the same complications seen in American social enterprises.

The following chapter turns to Thailand to reveal how transnational social movements are reciprocally shaped by Thai politics around gender, labor, and migrant rights. In Thailand, an aggressive rescue industry has inculcated global civil society members in national policing efforts—offering evidence of how the global anti-trafficking movement has fortified the carceral state and nonprofit repression. The repeated turn to forms of carceral control in these state and secular contexts mirrors the dynamics that we have witnessed through both Cowboy Rescue's and Freedom Unchained's rehabilitative practices.

CHAPTER 5

Vigilante Humanitarianism in Thailand

In early 2017, American political commentator Glenn Beck traveled to Thailand with the American nonprofit organization Operation Underground Railroad (OUR) and its founder, Tim Ballard, and his wife, Katherine. Describing the trip on his radio show, Beck professed an admiration for the organization's work, specifically praising the relationship OUR had developed with Thailand's Department of Special Investigations (DSI)—often described for American audiences as "Thailand's FBI"—and the Royal Thai Police. Beck described the privilege of meeting the DSI director, whom, he claimed, thanked him for the generosity of the American people who fund OUR's work through private donations. Since its founding in 2013, OUR has amassed a 44 million USD budget, once again demonstrating the fundability of the anti-trafficking cause. Nearly all of the organization's donations come from American corporate sponsors, private foundations, organizational fundraisers, and individual donors. The absence of government-sponsored funding is notable given OUR's mission of amplifying foreign state capacity to govern trafficking. Furthermore, its lack of US funding does not diminish its close collaborations with the US government. In 2017, OUR was one of the only anti-trafficking organizations in the country invited to the White House to speak with Ivanka Trump's anti-trafficking task force.

In Thailand, OUR focuses on expanding state policing forces through training, donation of tech surveillance infrastructure, and manpower to assist with rescue and raid operations for sex workers. Since 2013, OUR has brought in former US Army and Navy enlistees and former Seals, FBI agents, police officers, and special-operations military personnel to conduct civilian-led raid-and-rescue efforts around the world, including in Haiti, Nicaragua, Ghana, and Thailand. Ballard's experience as a former US special agent for the Department of Homeland Security has added to the organization's allure and credibility, both in recognition of his sacrifice for leaving his career in the US intelligence community and for the technical know-how needed to deploy US military resources abroad. Through numerous news outlets and in fundraising pitches that narrate the organization's founding, Ballard often recalls his investigative work as part of a government anti–child trafficking unit, which, he claims, helped infiltrate and dismantle dozens of trafficking organizations that kidnapped children and forced them into the sex industry. Ballard often bemoans the incapacity, while working as government agent, to "rescue children if their cases lacked a US nexus or if the case could not be tried in a US court."[1] Echoing a similar claim of North American jewelry anti-trafficking organizations, OUR's founding marked a distinct turn away from state-driven efforts toward civilian forms of vigilantism that are not beholden to state accountability.[2] OUR claims that "by mentoring law enforcement agencies through the entire process—from investigation techniques, to gathering evidence for offender prosecution, to executing a rescue—local authorities are empowered to more aggressively fight trafficking within their jurisdiction."[3]

Despite Glenn Beck's ultra-conservative political leaning, his interest and participation in a human-trafficking tour of OUR's work reflects a wide-ranging interest in human trafficking among widely diverse groups. Like Beck, I also traveled to Thailand, in my case in 2012 with a group of nineteen American tourists interested in learning more about human trafficking in Thailand. Along with one of my dissertation advisors, Elizabeth Bernstein, we paid a fee of $1,300 to enroll in a week-long tourist experience labeled a "human trafficking reality tour."

I had learned of the availability of such tours because several anti-trafficking jewelry organizations had begun offering annual trips for their customers who wished to "see and experience first-hand" the lived realities of jewelry makers. At the time, Bernstein and I chose from a roster of a half-dozen tourist packages. In recent years, these trips have become so popular that a 2017 New York Times travel section featured an enthusiastic profile of them: "A Vacation with Purpose: Fighting Trafficking in Thailand."[4] Participants in these diverse forms of travel

Glenn Beck and Tim Ballard team up in Operation Underground Railroad video in Thailand

By Trent Toone | ttoone@deseretnews.com | May 9, 2017, 3:18pm EDT

f 🐦 ⤴ SHARE

FIGURE 16. Glenn Beck and Tim Ballard during their 2017 trip to Thailand with Operation Underground Railroad. Photo from Toone 2017.

often explained to me one common motivation at their core: the desire to see what human trafficking looks like firsthand. What the tours deliver, I argue, is slightly different: a glimpse into the world of anti-trafficking work refracted through the very organizations that stand to benefit financially from American funding of this work.[5]

This chapter examines why and how Thailand functions as a pivotal destination for American human-trafficking raid-and-rescue projects. It also situates transnational anti-trafficking endeavors within Thailand's political and economic history and the legacy of US militarism in the region. The transnational anti–human trafficking movement in Thailand has created new forms of market-based and vigilante humanitarianism that extend far beyond the grassroots religious social entrepreneurship of organizations like Cowboy Rescue. Yet it is vital to understand Cowboy Rescue in the context of the expanding *vigilante humanitarian* efforts encompassing both human trafficking reality tourism and paramilitary rescue operations. I use the term "vigilante" to qualify the "humanitarian" objectives, because they are new modes of extranational surveillance and policing that once again gain legitimacy and support from market forces.

Underneath the broad umbrella of these international actors' aspirations, from wanting to see trafficking to wanting to stop it, little is known about the consequences of such short-term engagements with trafficking in Thailand—be it reality tourism or OUR's renegade forms of law enforcement. As with the "slave-free good," the hope and optimism that anti-trafficking interventions do good often override questions about the underlying systems of power and inequality that facilitate them. This chapter digs into this discomfort, arguing that tourist enterprises selling packaged narratives of trafficking victimhood encourage a global racial vigilantism around anti-trafficking. Emboldened by moral conviction and a strong profit motive, such programs have enabled transnational civil society to ally with local police forces in establishing a network of transnational paramilitary engagement fortifying an apparatus of security that, in practice, rarely protects rights or provides assistance to trafficking victims. Classifying such operations as "paramilitary" points to their extralegal institutional affiliation, though they draw on state-sanctioned military expertise. It suggests, again, that such rescue imperatives actively displace the health, safety, and advocacy efforts of local sex workers and sex worker rights organizations. Detailing the consequences of Western-led humanitarian efforts in Thailand and outlining the relationship between sex tourism, anti-trafficking reality tourism, and paramilitary anti-trafficking operations, this chapter reveals the adverse political, economic, and cultural dynamics such enterprises reproduce.

THAI POLITICAL ECONOMY

Global interest in the problem of human trafficking in Thailand is expansive. The country has received more dedicated chapters in monographs on trafficking than any other country in the world, including Kevin Bales's *Disposable People* (2004 [1999]), David Batsone's *Not For Sale* (2010), and Siddharth Kara's *Sex Trafficking* (2017). In 2019, the pope used the opportunity of his visit to Thailand to join a global chorus of voices arguing against pervasive sex trafficking in the country. This demand is so ubiquitous among the self-proclaimed "abolitionists of modern-day slavery" that in 2018, the NFL's Pittsburgh Steelers invited Operation Underground Railroad to its summer training camp to tell the team about its work in Thailand.[67]

Each of these accounts focuses almost exclusively on the prevalence of *sex* trafficking in Thailand. Bales's celebrated *Disposable People,* first published in 1999, calls readers to action through his depiction of rampant sexual slavery in Thailand, a form of "modern-day slavery" that Bales obliquely links to the nation's values: "Thailand is a country sick with an addiction to slavery. From village to city and back, the profits of slavery flow. Once authorities and businesspeople become accustomed to this outpouring of money, once any moral objection has been drowned in it, a justification of slavery is easy to mount, and Thai culture and religion stand ready to do so."[8] Bales's comments and those of other authors who have echoed similarly essentialist sentiments about the Thai character of slavery reference economic inequality, rural-to-urban migration, government corruption, and corporate labor exploitation—features that are hardly peculiar to Thailand.

What, then, explains the American anti-trafficking movement's persistent preoccupation with Thailand? I suggest that this global commitment has been facilitated by a hospitable mass tourist destination, the legacy of the American military's enjoyment of sexual services, the visibility of commercial sex in red-light districts as a proxy for sex trafficking, and the government's acquiescence to transnational treaties and welcoming of foreign capital. This American fascination illustrates how mass tourism and commerce fuel the global concern about sex trafficking in Thailand while also serving as vital facilitators of anti-trafficking humanitarian efforts in the country. Thailand's vibrant transnational civil society and booming global tourism industry are both legacies of military imperialism, Western-led development schemes, and contentious and violent struggles for state power situated between state sovereignty and market governance.

To understand why the global anti-trafficking rescue industry has found such a thriving host in Thailand, we can visit the work of Thai economist Pasuk Phongpaichit, who argues that Thailand's economic policies in the past two decades exemplify "neoliberal populism," in which market-driven policies that favor the rural masses form the foundation of Thailand's economic development and its democracy.[9] Large wealth disparities have persisted between Bangkok and the country's seventy-six provinces. Currently, most of the nation's wealth is concentrated in the nation's capital, and Bangkok alone accounts for

47.5 percent of gross domestic product (GDP).[10] The political struggles of the past decade have oscillated between populist strategies to win over the rural majority and Bangkok-centered development schemes that appeal to the urban elite, further exacerbating a deep-seated division between the "country's northern rice bowl and the entrenched urban elites."[11] Market-driven development and persistent rural poverty thus set the stage for transnational market-based anti-trafficking efforts that bind the state, private sector, nonprofit organizations, and migrant workers.

Market-based governance under both administrations of Prime Minister Thaksin Shinawatra provides context for the Thai government's response to human trafficking, as well as the transnational anti-trafficking movement and American rescue industry interests in Thailand. An influx of foreign capital, both from private corporations and in the form of development assistance, reached record-high levels after the Asian financial crisis in 1997, and has helped Thailand ascend as one of the strongest economies in Southeast Asia. Since then, Thailand's rapidly escalating GDP and foreign direct investment have transformed the country from an aid-recipient country to a donor country in the Asia-Pacific region.[12] Sharing a physical border with several nations that report a much lower GDP—in particular, Cambodia, Laos, and Myanmar—Thailand is also the recipient of significant flows of migrant workers and refugees from throughout the region.[13]

Thailand was a central destination for military R and R during the Indochina Wars in the late 1960s and early 1970s. The market for intimacy in these "pleasure belts" generated a new moniker among the many American military servicemen who frequented the areas; rather than "rest and recreation," many used the alternate "I and I" (intoxication and intercourse) to more precisely describe their activities there. After the formal exit of US military troops from Southeast Asia in the early 1970s, the commercial sex industry remained central to the Thai tourist industry's expansion.[14]

State interests in Thailand have prioritized business-friendly economic development as a primary path to providing social welfare. Thailand's export-driven economy—planned and funded by the International Monetary Fund and World Bank following the 1997 financial crisis—privileges exports, tourism, and corporate expansion, primarily in Bangkok. As anthropologist Ara Wilson has demonstrated, the market has penetrated most aspects of Thai life, and the merging of markets and intimacy is evident everywhere, from mass retail to medical tourism and from private homes to public go-go bars.[15] The prevalence and visibility of sex work—which many faith-based and abolitionist groups argue are the primary source of demand for human trafficking—illustrates the relationship between human security and economic development in Thailand. While the sale of sexual services is currently illegal there, the Thai government does little to curb the sex tourism industry aside from raiding sexual entertainment establishments to nominally enforce the law and meet police quotas. In fact, the government has historically supported sex tourism because of the industry's contribution to the Thai economy. For many of the same reasons that it is hospitable to tourism, Thailand has succeeded in attracting foreign direct investment and is the regional hub of numerous global governance and humanitarian aid organizations, including the United Nations, the International Labor Organization (ILO), the Asia Foundation, the International Organization for Migration (IOM), the Red Cross, Save the Children, and the Global Alliance Against the Traffic in Women.

GLOBAL SHERIFFS OF THE THAI STATE

These powerful narratives have fueled the international community's unflappable concern with human trafficking in Thailand, which has united global governance institutions such as the United Nations and ILO with state and nonstate actors in Thailand, the United States, Western Europe, Australia, and New Zealand. In 2013, the Global Slavery Index ranked Thailand as the twenty-sixth worst offender regarding slavery—earning it a spot in the top 10 percent globally—reporting that in a country of nearly 67,000,000 residents, an estimated 472,811 were victims of modern-day slavery.[16] A global ranking mechanism first published in 2013, funded by an Australian NGO, and partnered with the ILO and IOM, the Walk Free Foundation's Global Slavery Report makes explicit the alliances between global governance institutions and certain Western state and nonstate actors.

This global ranking system shares a great deal in common with the US State Department's *Trafficking in Persons Report,* which, since 2000, has been criticized for playing the role of "global sheriff" whose claims of "global governance" have come to represent the interests of Western economic powers.[17] In the early years of the *TIP Report,* 2003–9, Thailand was consistently ranked as a Tier 2 country, the middle-tier status assigned to the majority of countries on the list. Beginning in

2010, Thailand received a sudden downgrade to the Tier 2 Watch List, a special category for countries that do not comply with anti-trafficking efforts as outlined by the US State Department. After being on the Watch List for two years, the nation faced an automatic downgrade to Tier 3, which would be matched by economic sanctions. The 2013 *TIP Report* stressed that despite an increase in trafficking investigations (83 in 2011 and 305 in 2012), Thailand did not prosecute enough cases, with just 27 prosecutions in 2012, compared with 67 the year prior.

Anticipating the threat of a downgrade to Tier 3 in 2014, the Office of Commercial Affairs in the Thai embassy in Washington, DC, hired DC-based law firm Holland and Knight (H&K) to assist with a legal public relations campaign regarding Thailand's anti-trafficking efforts and rankings. The eight-month program cost $408,000, and though little public information has been made available about the partnership, the Thai government seemed to rely on the firm's legal expertise and political clout in Washington, DC. H&K provided press releases, public comments, lobbied on Capitol Hill, and provided testimony in congressional hearings on behalf of Thailand's government.[18] Despite these efforts, in the June 2014 *Report,* the US State Department demoted Thailand to the lowest, Tier 3 ranking, citing its lack of attention to cases of labor trafficking in the deep-sea fishing industries and to the rights of Rohingya refugees from Myanmar.[19] As a Tier 3 nation, Thailand risked loss of development aid, economic sanctions, and potential ostracization by other countries that do not want to do business with noncompliant governments.

The Thai government's countertrafficking efforts are led by the Ministry of Human Development and Social Welfare and coordinated among numerous other government entities. Compared to other countries in the Asia-Pacific region, the Thai governmental response is robust, well prioritized, and autonomous in that it does not *need* to partner with the international agencies present in Thailand for financial support. Its national human trafficking shelters, for example, are fully run and funded by the Ministry of Social Development and Human Security. Shortly after their inception, these shelters were upheld for following best practices in the region, in part because few governments around the world had shelters devoted exclusively to assisting trafficked persons. Despite their novelty globally, however, Thai government shelters have been heavily criticized as the site of numerous documented rights violations, creating new tensions between the Thai government and global governance institutions working in Thailand.[20]

TRAFFICKING AMERICAN INTERESTS IN THAILAND

Thailand is home to more than thirty different nongovernmental and global governance projects listed on End Slavery Now's public directory of anti-trafficking organizations, with dozens more grassroots organizations claiming to work on the issue.[21] These organizations span a range of functions from advocacy, awareness, and fundraising to direct service. Because Bangkok is considered a regional NGO hub, many anti-trafficking programs that work in other East and Southeast Asian countries choose to have their regional headquarters in Bangkok. For instance, two organizations whose China operations were discussed in the prior chapter, MTV Exit and UNIAP, both chose to have regional management offices in Bangkok during their years of operation. Equally important, the global secretariats of the Global Alliance Against Traffic in Women (GAATW) and End Child Prostitution and Trafficking (ECPAT) direct their regional operations from Bangkok.

Anti-trafficking programs in Thailand have become so popular—and arguably profitable—that a curious slew of fraudulent anti-trafficking schemes have also emerged. In 2012, an Australian organization founded under the name "The Grey Man" was exposed for its fraudulent claims concerning trafficking. Founded by a former military special operations officer and funded by donations from Australian citizens, The Grey Man facilitated the missions of former Australian soldiers and policemen to rescue victims of sex trafficking in Thailand. The organization claimed to work with the Royal Thai Police; however, a journalist discovered that none of the organization's claims of rescuing Akha-ethnicity children were true. The Thai Department of Special Investigations later found that the organization had in fact posted "false rescues" online to generate financial support for the organization, and its operations in Thailand have been suspended.[22]

A 2016 film, *The Wrong Light,* takes its audience on an journey through what happens when the anti-trafficking story falls apart. The documentary reflects on the filmmakers' own motives for coming to Thailand to make a film about "girls who are sold into sex slavery." Their primary contact, and the subject of the film, is COSA, an NGO founded in 2005 by Mickey Chootesa, who spent years raising money by promising that COSA would provide rescue and rehabilitation services to Thai victims of child trafficking. As they filmed the documentary, the filmmakers were surprised to find a different set of unexpected "truths" while interviewing former victims and their families. These episodes of anti-trafficking fraud resonate with the issues raised in the Somaly Mam scandal of 2014, discussed in chapter 3: the profitability of the anti-trafficking cause has become has led many organizations to spuriously use the term to gain funding.

SEX TOURISM AND ANTI–SEX TRAFFICKING REALITY TOURISM

In addition to the multitude of anti-trafficking organizations that run rescue and rehabilitation operations within the country, Thailand's thriving sex tourism sector has also evoked a strong response from many commercial tour outlets seeking to educate global citizens about the issue of human trafficking through the experience of prepackaged mass tourism. Promising a firsthand look at modern-day slavery, such tours focus primarily on painting a picture of rampant sexual slavery and the heroic campaigns that aim to curtail them. Multiple tours are offered by diverse outlets, ranging from churches to adventure expedition companies and educational institutions. These offerings tap into generalist hobby arenas; for instance, an organization that taught photography skills promised an insider's glimpse at human trafficking—as an ideal subject with which to practice the craft. Others fall into the category of "voluntourism," a large genre of unpaid temporary volunteer stints with NGOs in Thailand. In some cases, volunteers pay for placement, housing, and administrative costs. Many others are part of university-led study-abroad experiences that include human trafficking as one object of study.

The seven-day human-trafficking reality tour that Elizabeth Bernstein and I attended was cohosted by two nonprofit organizations, one that sponsors such tours to destinations throughout the world and the other, which focuses on advocacy and awareness of human trafficking. The trip cost 1,300 USD, not including airfare. That fee promised three-star hotel accommodation, ground transportation within Thailand, "expert" tour leaders and guides, meals, donations to organizations, meetings with different anti-trafficking activists and NGOs, and, finally, "learning effective strategies for undermining slave rings, and experiencing first-hand how victims rebuild their lives."[23]

Nearly all participants in this reality tour expressed an interest in sex trafficking as their core motivation for attending the tour. When, on the second day of the seven-day trip, we received our itineraries,[24] we saw that we would visit only one anti–sex trafficking organization. This organization, City Light, in Chiang Mai, was founded by a young American woman who claimed to rescue young men—whom the organization's activists universally refer to as "boys," though they are over the age of eighteen—from sex work in Chiang Mai. The itinerary also included visits to a home for orphaned and runaway youth (cosponsored by the American NGO that organized the trip); a Thai migrant-worker organization that provided services for Burmese and Cambodian male victims of extreme labor exploitation in the deep-sea fishing industry; and an Australian government–funded project that provided human trafficking identification training to Thai law enforcement officials.

Such reality tours can be found in Thailand because its free-market economy is fertile ground for multiple forms of tourism: sex tourism, mass tourism, medical tourism, ecotourism, ethnic minority–hill tribe tourism, volunteer tourism, and reality tourism.[25] Illustrating the opportunities that the Thai market and civil society make available, the director of the reality tour's sponsoring company contacted me to ask for advice on how one would go about setting up a reality tour in China, as his preliminary efforts seemed to be meeting with skepticism by local NGO partners and travel agents in China's authoritarian political environment, which offers limited opportunities for small American enterprises. In our ensuing discussion, I asked the director if the company's operations had needed to secure the support of the Thai government. The director responded with relief that they had not needed to register, because the Thai tourist sector is "so large in Thailand." The fact that there are nearly ten other educational or recreational tours concerned with human trafficking demonstrates the country's possibilities as a site of international humanitarian action and commerce. It also suggests the limited accountability these programs have.

Our primary tour guide, a Cambodian American expat living in Phnom Penh with ten year's experience as a consultant for USAID, UN organizations, a large American anti-trafficking NGO, and several other development projects, said he hoped to deliver a balanced portrait of human trafficking. The resulting itinerary included visits to organizations that dealt with a range of important development issues, though links between such issues and human trafficking were never clearly articulated. The series of sites, seen primarily through the lenses of poverty, ethnic-minority disenfranchisement, and nonprofit intervention strategies, produced a general feeling among the group members of the country's vulnerability to trafficking. When visiting the sponsoring organization's flagship project in northern Thailand, we were told tragic stories of stateless mothers from Myanmar who were addicted to drugs. While mothers were detoxing,[26] a large group home for youth provided housing for their children, "saving them from begging on the streets." During their residence with the respective care programs, the organization's director shared that both children and adults were taught jewelry making, so they could earn supplemental income and generate revenue to support the organization.

On a different visit, to the Echo Foundation in Northern Thailand, we were taken to an Akha-ethnicity village, the destination of numerous popular "hill tribe trekking ecotours," and spoke with the village chief. Through an interpreter hired by the organization, eager tour participants asked the village head about the presence of human trafficking. He said repeatedly that trafficking was not an issue, precisely because the village's location near a prominent national park created job opportunities close to home.

Although formal visits to sex worker rights organizations were not included, the sample itinerary promised a "visit to nightclubs and bars to observe activities." Our guide provided our tour group with two opportunities to participate in evening walkthroughs of red-light districts in Bangkok and Chiang Mai. The guide explained that these areas were quite busy and dangerous, so there would be no formal tour or commentary; rather, it was important we make our own observations as we walked through. Several people voiced concern over the safety and ethics of walking in the red-light district. They expressed discomfort with being near the sale of commercial sex, perhaps in that way condoning it. In response, the guide simply remarked: "In order to understand human trafficking here, you really need to just see the red-light districts." Consistently speaking in such abstract and elusive ways about commercial sex did maintain its allure; yet the commentary never provided reality tourists with the contemporary or historical context of sex work or sex tourism in Thailand. It is this perpetual seduction surrounding the exploitive aspects of commercial sex in Thailand—allegedly so ubiquitous and monolithic in character that it obliterates sex workers' diverse experiences—that makes it such an ideal destination for reality tourists.

In addition to two primary guides and talks arranged with "anti-trafficking experts," the tour employed one local Thai guide who was accredited by the national tourist agency. This individual, the only

Thai-speaking guide on the entire trip, translated for all twenty tourists in the group. For his work, our Thai guide was paid 1,000 baht (30 USD) per day, a sum less than the 3,000 baht (100 USD) donations that the tour agency gave to a select three of the NGOs we visited. Interviews with this guide and staff at local tour outlets revealed that this salary was the average market rate for local Thai tour agents. When Elizabeth and I publicly probed into the question of our tour guide's salaries, tour participants discouraged us; in their minds, any accusation of underpaying the guides would spoil a trip sponsored by a nonprofit organization they felt was "just trying to do good."

Our local tour guide shared that he was able to offset a lower salary with the sizable tips he earned from tourists on commercial expeditions. It is worth noting, then, that *reality* tourists did not feel obligated to tip, since they believed the nonprofit organization organizing the tour would engage in fair wage practices and did not want to mar their relationship with their local guide with cash—many considered him "like family" by the end of the travel. This powerful emotional connection to the proclaimed beneficence of reality tourism reflected a powerful disconnect with the material reality of the project as a commercial undertaking.

THE LAST REALITY TOUR OF SIAM

While the human-trafficking reality tour did not arrange visits to any sex-worker rights organizations, some other American tourist groups have tried to contact them during their travels in human-trafficking education. When my ethnographic fieldwork took me to the Empower Foundation in Chiang Mai for several months between 2012 and 2014, I witnessed between ten and twenty groups visiting per month; these included journalists, researchers, and students—mainly from Western Europe and North America, though some were from Japan, Australia, and New Zealand. For nearly all of these visitors, curiosity about human trafficking drove their inquiry. A distinct other set of visitors included sex workers and their allies from around the world who facilitated various workshops ranging from belly dancing to massage. Their visits were typically oriented around sex worker organizing strategies, and they often discussed the harm that the anti-trafficking movement had brought to their working lives in different places around the world.

Founded in 1985, Empower was operating long before the global anti-trafficking movement so robustly descended upon the Thai political

FIGURE 17. Empower's Can-Do Bar and Museum in Chiang Mai. Photo by Empower Foundation.

and legal infrastructure. The foundation provides a range of community support services to sex workers throughout the country and helps coordinate the Sex Workers of ASEAN (SWASEAN) meetings, an annual gathering of sex workers from the ten ASEAN member countries that has cleverly appropriated the ASEAN model of political economic cooperation and fashioned it into a platform for regional solidarity among sex workers. Despite the organization's unparalleled firsthand experience in providing outreach, direct service, and advocacy to and by sex workers for nearly thirty years, it frequently finds itself as the "last stop" on study tours of human trafficking. Groups usually arrive armed with skepticism and curiosity as they attempt to reconcile the grave tales of sexual slavery that other organizations have reported to them with the contrasting accounts that Empower workers share.

In spring 2013, I watched as a group of twenty undergraduate students from a small liberal arts college in South Dakota arrived at the Can-Do Bar, the Empower Foundation's sex worker–owned and –operated bar in Chiang Mai. The group was led by two middle-aged white American men, one a professor from their home university in South Dakota and the other the director of foreign-exchange programs at Chiang Mai University, a longtime expatriate who organizes such visits for numerous student groups. The group of thirty juniors and seniors was winding up a two-week journey to understand human trafficking in Thailand: basically an extended spring break for the students as part of their semester-long course on human trafficking. In the days leading up to their visit to Empower, the students visited a variety of anti-trafficking organizations, including the Not For Sale project and other American abolitionist organizations fighting sex trafficking. The visit to Empower was their last NGO visit before they wrapped up their spring break with a weekend on the Krabi islands, one of Thailand's famous beach resort destinations in the south.

The Empower Foundation fields daily requests from visitors—journalists, researchers, students seeking internships, and college classes—most of whom express an interest in learning about "human trafficking." During the visit I observed, four Empower employees joined the group to share their experiences with sex work and sex worker activism, and they encouraged the students to ask whatever questions they had. As an example of one of their advocacy tools, and as a product of their research on the anti-trafficking movement, they screened a film, *The Last Rescue in Siam*,[27] a satirical recounting of common injustices experienced during a police raid at a beer bar.

The film opens in a bar on a normal day at work there. A woman and her male client, who happens to be a police officer, are sitting over drinks. A subsequent scene cuts to the "War Room" in which a "hero NGO," policeman, and social worker are "planning a daring rescue." During the rescue, the "interagency" task force that has convened drives through town bypassing other, more serious incidents, such as a theft, a motorcycle accident, and a violent dispute on the street. The interagency actors arrive at the bar, and what ensues is a comedy of errors as they try to arrest a sex worker as part of their plan to save her. Many of the sex workers on site flee, but the rescue team captures one woman and brings her in for questioning.

Once the group arrives back at the "War Room," the detained worker is asked her age and discloses that she is nineteen years old. Speaking through a well-meaning translator and social workers, the rescue team decides that she is actually sixteen years old and thus can be counted as a victim of trafficking, as Thai law states that those under eighteen cannot consent to participate in sex work. Thus deemed a victim of trafficking, she is sent to the government trafficking-victims shelter, where she is made to work with a sewing machine, a common strategy of rehabilitation for government, secular, and faith-based anti-trafficking organizations alike. In the final scene, the able and empowered worker sews herself a ladder to escape from her captors and the forced "rescue."

FIGURE 18. Promotional poster for the motion picture *Last Rescue in Siam*. Photo by Empower Studio Bad Girls Films.

FIGURE 19. Intertitle in the movie *Last Rescue in Siam*, which features a worker escaping sewing rehab. Video still by Empower Studio Bad Girls Films.

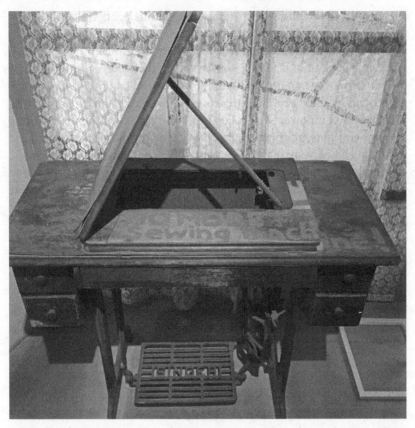

FIGURE 20. "Solidarity Not Sewing Machines" art installation in Empower's This Is Us Museum in Nonthaburi, Thailand. Photo by author.

This satirical Charlie Chaplin–esque film—black-and-white and silent, with subtitles in Thai and English—is based on years of Empower's direct work by and with sex workers whose lives and working conditions have been and are negatively impacted by the global anti-trafficking movement, Thai laws, and law enforcement. Many sex-worker rights organizations around the world have demonstrated that anti-trafficking surveillance, though meant to protect sex workers, has, through police raids and prosecutions, led to a decrease in overall safety and a worsening of other working conditions. In 2012, Empower published the groundbreaking *Hit and Run* report, which documents the collateral harm sex workers experienced at the hands of the anti-trafficking movement in Thailand. Residents of Thai government-run shelters, the report shows, experienced numerous rights violations in the name of their protection as victims of human trafficking.

Empower tells student visitors that there are different types of sex work in Thailand and that precarity within the trade is, as with other types of low-wage work, based on the structured labor relations within each type. In their weekly outreach to sex work establishments across the country, Empower staff focus primarily on educating sex workers about their rights, addressing what they see as the most prevalent issues: nonpayment of wages, maltreatment by entertainment shop owners, random police raids, and forced detention of sex workers in the name of "combating human trafficking." One of the organization's earliest interventions was simple but pathbreaking. In 2006, Empower founded the Can-Do bar, a cooperative, worker-owned establishment that modeled the exemplary labor practices the group felt were missing from the industry. Empower also provides tools for sex workers, such as English-, Thai-, and Japanese-language training and free condoms. It has identified the most vulnerable populations as undocumented sex workers, primarily from Laos, Cambodia, and Myanmar, and stateless hill tribe persons in Thailand. Lacking citizenship, they are more vulnerable to abuse from employers and clients because they have no right to assistance from Thai police and they fear deportation. Street-based sex work, primarily undertaken by non-Thai or transgender sex workers, also occurs under more structurally dangerous conditions because they are more vulnerable to client and police violence.

Empower's work juxtaposes the simplistic, prepackaged scenarios fed to American anti-trafficking tourists with the complex realities of service provision for victims of trafficking in Thailand. Empower's story is much harder to sell. The reality tour offers easily digested narratives of victims and saviors, problems and solutions that require little engagement with structural issues. Unlike those of the human trafficking reality tours sponsored by American organizations, Empower's dissenting narratives of "rights, not rescue" and its calls for "solidarity, not sewing machines" critique the collateral harm that anti-human trafficking efforts have inflicted on sex workers, complicating a landscape of abolitionism in which the act of simply attending a reality tour is understood as a meaningful form of anti-trafficking activism. Yet American consumers continue to readily reach into their pockets and across their networks to raise funds and awareness to save victims of trafficking through these means, selling a version of the issue that generates social capital for tour participants, tour operators, and the expert NGOs that craft the tales of trafficking told on the trip.[28] The prioritization of certain actors, voices, and accounts, and the silencing of others, is an important reminder that transnational social movements are power-laden networks of institutions in which dissenting narratives have little value. Value is created instead by commercial entities that have sought Thailand out as a destination for mass tourism employing packaged narratives about commercial exploits of sex trafficking. The reality tours effectively create echo chambers through which to raise money and political support for anti-trafficking operations led by the same network of international organizations they collaborate with. A cycle of profit creation around dominant forms of anti-trafficking initiatives has thus emerged, whereby anti-trafficking tourists reaffirm narratives and solutions that valorize their own community's efforts.

A TRANSNATIONAL ANTI-TRAFFICKING PARAMILITARY

Fueled by the strong profit motive and political will invigorated by the narratives of anti-trafficking reality tours, a handful of civilian-run military organizations similar to Operation Underground Rescue came to Thailand with the goals of stopping sex trafficking by bolstering local law enforcement. These organizations pursue ends based on the stories anti-trafficking tourists come home with, and they get their means from government and international organization initiatives that have prioritized the capacity building of local anti-trafficking law enforcement. For instance, the Australian-Asia Program to Combat Trafficking in Persons (AAPTIP), which spent 50 million Australian dollars between 2003 and 2016, is funded by the Australian government and Australian AID and managed by Cardno, a private-sector engineering services firm.[29] AAPTIP's work has funded "trainings" of and other support to police officers, prosecutors, and judges to "improve the criminal justice response to trafficking in persons."

Following this alluring model of training law enforcement, a Colorado-based group called Paladin Rescue also claims to dispatch rescue operations to rural Thailand. Daniel Walker, a retired New Zealand police detective and the founder of the New Zealand organization Nvader has also built a nonprofit organization around civilians with law-enforcement backgrounds. Rebranded as LIFT International in 2011, Nvader led a number of renegade rescue operations in Thailand drawing on Walker's experience as a police detective. Due to the nature of their work—ensconced within active law enforcement tactics and ongoing legal cases—nearly all the aforementioned organizations cite confidentiality of their case work to limit transparency around their activities. Like Tim Ballard, the founder of Operation Underground Railroad, Walker is a law enforcement veteran. He served for over twenty years with the New Zealand Police Force and claims to have received training from members of the American FBI and Drug Enforcement Administration undercover programs through the US Law Enforcement Instructors Alliance and US Northeastern Tactical School and from current and former US Special Forces members. He has shared that in his investigations, he would pose as a potential client or a sex tour operator in order to find victims of sex trafficking. He would use cameras to record transactions and speak to victims to gather evidence that could be used to prosecute those guilty of trafficking and trafficking-related offenses. Speaking with a journalist, Walker also noted that during this work, he did not always follow best practices; for instance, he often undertook solo missions without appropriate context and support.[30] Still, Walker applied the knowledge gained during these years to the creation and operation of Nvader.

In 2016, Nvader reported to the Department of Provincial Administration, within the Thai Interior Ministry, that it believed there were three fifteen-year-olds working at Nataree, a Thai-owned massage parlor that had been operating for forty years. Located in central Bangkok, Nataree was just one of around ten "soapy massage" parlors on either side of busy Ratchadaphisek Road. Nataree, one of the oldest, occupied a five-story building with bright neon lights. It employed nearly four hundred workers whose primary service was to bathe clients on a "soapy" table, offer massage, and, allegedly, provide sexual services. Workers reported earning an average of 2,000 USD per month, including both wages and tips.

Much as with OUR, government partners authorized Nvader to conduct its own undercover operation in which it sent clients into the establishment to "interview" workers. After this undercover operation confirmed underage workers, Nvader spent three months planning a raid-and-rescue operation. On June 7, 2017, more than 100 police and officials, accompanied by local media and photographers, initiated a late-night raid during which all workers were apprehended. This included 121 women, including 15 girls ages fifteen to eighteen, who were automatically considered victims of trafficking because they were under eighteen, and 21 foreign nationals who were fined and then designated for deportation. Although the remaining 85 workers were found not to have taken any part in the crime of human trafficking, they were Thai citizens, and were swiftly charged under the Prostitution Act. Some were fined and released, and others were jailed for indeterminate periods of time. Six of the 121 arrested workers were forced to undergo medical exams without their consent. According to *Thaivisa,* the Ratchada Criminal Court issued arrest warrants for Prasert Sukkhee and Sommai Phatsing, the owner and manager of Nataree, on charges of human trafficking and providing underage sex, but, to date, neither owner has been found.[31]

In the days following the Nataree raid, I happened to be teaching afternoon English-language classes at Empower's Can-Do Bar in Chiang Mai, where staff were trying desperately to get information about young people who had been detained. Activists fielded dozens of calls on their personal cell phones from parents and relatives trying to get in touch with their young family members. The sudden disappearance of people who are detained in anti-trafficking rescue operations is common, as detailed in *Hit and Run,* which notes that cell phones are often confiscated in shelters, supposedly out of fear that family members or traffickers might contact workers and retraffic them. This easy slippage between the family member and the trafficker is an intentional blending of the mass-mediated allegation that parents are often responsible for trafficking their own children. This facilitates maternalist interventions by foreign interlocutors who can root out the seeds of bad culture that allegedly underwrite this problem, as seen in chapter 3. This portrait of family irresponsibility and neglect is rarely how migrant rights groups interpreted the situation as they fielded terrified phone calls from family members trying to find their children. The lack of accountability in this forced rescue echoes, once again, Okyere's research into the experiences of nonconsensual rescue and kidnapping of Ghanaian youth living on Lake Volta.[32]

In a 2017 report to the UN Committee on the Elimination of Discrimination Against Women (CEDAW), the Empower Foundation argued that the use of paramilitary organizations was illegal on the basis of entrapment. The report cites several instances when both police and NGOs patronize commercial sex establishments under the guise of being paying clients. Within such operations, these men posing as customers "manipulate the sexual consent of women and girls."[33] The report also noted that entrapment has been publicly decried by the Thai national human rights commissioner as far back as 2003, when CEDAW recognized that police entrapment often leads to serious human rights violations for women in the sex trade. Following the Nataree raid, Thai Human Rights Commissioner Ankaka Neelapaijit spoke out against entrapment once again and asked the government to reconsider its relationship with foreign vigilante anti-trafficking organizations. Given this drastic record of civil rights abuses, publicly denounced by Thailand's human rights commissioner, why do governments cooperate with these groups?

In Operation Underground Railroad's six-part documentary, *Operation Toussaint* (2018)—which raised $1 million for OUR in a single screening—the organization says that it leverages the *TIP Report* to endear itself to government partners.[34] It also offers free technical assistance and infrastructural support. Although OUR is not representing the government in a formal capacity, its government-trained former military and special-ops personnel lend credibility to what otherwise would essentially be a vigilante operation. In a segment of his film titled "The Anatomy of the Rescue," Ballard explains:

> Generally, we find a country that we know, statistically, it's bad. Kids are being hurt; the response has been less than great. And we'll go down, first and foremost, we'll go to the government. We vet the government, usually through our US embassy contacts who—all of us worked with these agencies, and so we have very good relationships with our embassies. And they know who you can trust and who you can't trust. In terms of prosecutors, law enforcement—this guy has been US trained, she has been US trained, polygraphed—the embassy generally has a group of vetted units of people who the government has decided to trust to do joint operations. So we find first and foremost the people we can trust in those countries, and then we sit down with them and say, Look there's a trafficking problem here. And they know that.
>
> The international community, the UN, State Department have done such a great job educating the world and putting that pressure on. There's a problem with human slavery today; it's a real thing. And the other thing the State Department did, in the early 2000s, they created a *TIP Report*. Which is kind of a controversial thing; it's kind of a name-and-shame that they, [the] US government, does every year. They rank every country Tier 1, Tier 2, or Tier 3, based on how good they're doing combating human trafficking. And if you don't get to Tier 1, you lose privileges, you lose grants, you lose support that otherwise you could get. And so the countries, to get to Tier 2, they had to put the laws into place, put the pressure, they felt the pressure, they felt the pressure. So most of these countries we are going to are Tier 2. Tier 2 is: we got the laws in place, but we're not implementing them.
>
> So we sit down and say, "Look, we see you're Tier 2; we can get you to Tier 1. But you have to implement your laws." They say, "Well, we don't even know where to start. How do we find these people and what do we do?" And we lay out all the options, let's say there [are] twelve options . . . everything from teaching them to go on the dark net and find those dirty deals going on and intervene, everything from doing a hard rescue operation, undercover operation, where we have real undercover operators meeting

with bad guys connecting on the beaches and so forth, and everything in between. The government agent will say, "I would like to do number ten, three, two," and we say, Perfect, if you want us to work for you, you have to sign an MOU [memorandum of understanding] with us so that everyone's clear that we work for you. We're not a rogue group; we will not work in your country without your permission.

So then, they just say, "Will you come down and do a training? Teach our guys how to infiltrate the dark net." And so we'll sit with them. Or other times they'll tell us that reports are in, that on this beach or this street corner or this sector of town, we think kids are being hurt, will you bring three of your Western-looking operators, because they like to service Americans, so then we'll go down, and then that's a longer kind of scenario. I'll send three of my operators, and they know what they're doing; they'll sit for a drink at the bar. They'll hang out for a while. Pretty soon they're being introduced to the darkest layers. And the kids are being introduced. We'll have that scenario in ten countries at one time.

We have a hundred contractors, former operators, navy seals, former CIA, and they all have the skill sets—whether its language or technology. We call it the jump team because they have to move that quick. This party is on Saturday. We've got to put together a team. We've vetted all of these guys through an intense training. They'll jump down, go to the party, get the cops, and do the deal. We're in close to fifteen countries and we have lines out right now.[35]

Two decades ago, Janie Chuang presciently warned that the *TIP Report* had created a "global sheriff" epidemic, in which US consular officials were tasked with single-handedly ranking anti-trafficking efforts around the world.[36] Yet the TIP rankings and associated threats of demotion continue to fortify even American civil society actors as they engage with Thai anti-trafficking. Ballard's comments illustrate how the TIP ranking mechanism facilitates new American paramilitary operations in Thailand. Sex workers have long been aware of the impact of the *TIP Report* on their own lives. It is little wonder that, with the promise of a tier upgrade, the Thai Department of Special Investigations and police force would roll out the red carpet for Glenn Beck even though in doing so they trade the safety of their citizens for the vanity project of a anti-trafficking paramilitary force. After these operations succeed (as they determine success), these men return home and raise more funds.

Every year, just before the *TIP Report* is released in June, sex workers prepare for an aggressive series of raids they expect to be staged just after the release. Each year, heads of government protest the rankings while also dealing with the very real economic and trade consequences of a demotion on the three-tier scale. Both the nongovernmental and the state-led initiatives that ostensibly seek to protect the marginalized and vulnerable populations of Thailand fail to take the concerns of those very populations into account. They merely contribute to a feedback loop that serves their own financial and political motives, assisting individuals within their own powerful networks more than the young Thai women they purport to save. A more veiled, subtler exploitation is at play here, but the process is nonetheless the same: wealthy, Western individuals such as Ballard have established an economy in which they are able to profit off the lives, bodies, and stories of these Thai women. While Thai sex workers are getting fined, arrested, and deported, organizations such as Nvader and OUR are getting millions of dollars in funding for their actions.

GLOBAL CALCULUS OF A RACIAL PROJECT

Such new humanitarian operations as OUR and Nvader traffic US imperialist logics throughout the world, neatly repackaged as efforts to combat "modern-day slavery." Invoking the "underground railroad" in its name, OUR exemplifies the abolitionist nostalgia seen elsewhere in the anti-trafficking movement, for instance, William Wilberforce pocket scarves (sold by the anti-trafficking social enterprise Urbane and Gallant) and the Harriet Tubman Award (administered by Truckers Against Trafficking). Operation Underground Railroad suggests that the path to freedom for exploited Thais starts with external paramilitary intervention.[37] Sex and migrant worker activists and the Thai national human rights ambassador have decried this turn to foreign vigilante authority. These contestations emphasize the grave human rights consequences for those who are "rescued" and the irony that the root causes of child sex tourism date back to the US military presence in Thailand during the Vietnam and Indochina wars.

These debates are inaudible amid global North funding priorities and the sentimentality of modern-day abolition. In fact, though, they are amplified by the abundant anti–human trafficking reality tourism programs in Thailand and other countries. The mere act of witnessing poverty, inequality, and difference sits in for an acceptable modern-day abolitionist effort.[38] The overbearing whiteness of these endeavors—encompassing both racial and ethnic forms of American superiority—allows such interventions to be largely uncontested because of the alleged unbiased eyes doing the identification. Finally, such global racial scripts of heroes and victims travel back to the United States to inform new racial vigilante projects that justify the increased surveillance of communities of color in the United States.[39]

The combined market-oriented forces of sexual commerce and mass tourism have made Thailand a site ripe for expansion of the human-trafficking rescue industry.[40] Illustrating the tensions between state ties to global capital and the transnational human trafficking movement, this chapter examines how circulations of sex, global commerce, and tourism align with new transnational consumer, activist, and humanitarian interests in combating human trafficking in Thailand. Alternatively stated, human-trafficking rescue is susceptible to the same market forces that allegedly drive human trafficking and that facilitate mass tourism to Thailand.

Human trafficking reality tours, American university's trafficking-focused study abroad programs, and other instances of global market-based humanitarianism in Thailand demonstrate that the transnational anti-trafficking movement is embedded in race, gender, national forms of power, and capital. Amid the plentiful commerce in anti-trafficking work, the actual sites and symptoms of human trafficking and exploitation are rarely legible to transnational voyeurs, rescuers, and humanitarians. On our reality tour, for instance, we never spoke with organizations that received no funding from, or that operated outside, a brokered institutional arrangement these American interlocutors provided. Everyone left the tour having received exactly what they paid for: a front-row seat to the exploitation of young women in the commercial sex industry and, to ease the resulting feeling of moral discomfort, a solution: helping to save these victims by raising funds and contributing to international anti-trafficking NGOs. These reality tours thus serve to reinforce the dominant narrative of anti-trafficking circles, which depict young, foreign women who need to be saved from vice-ridden cultures and incompetent governments by international actors who have the capacity and moral will to enact change. They drive the moral convictions, financial contributions, and political pressure that enable organizations like OUR and Nvader to exist and profit from their work.

What, then, are the realities that Thai migrants and sex workers wish to share? This book's final chapter explores these realities. One staff member at Empower told me that a true "reality tour" would visit rural farmers who have been victimized by the government's failed and illegal "rice-pledging schemes." The strategy reached its height in 2014, when

Prime Minister Yingluck Shinawatra pledged to buy millions of tons of rice from rural farmers at higher-than-market prices. The government planned to withhold this rice from the market to drive up the global cost of rice. When India unexpectedly lifted bans on rice exports, 10 million tons of rice hit the global market. After Vietnam then lowered its prices, the market price of rice hit rock bottom, devastating Thai farmers who could no longer sell the grain to the free market or to the government. This incident led to a rash of countless suicides in rural areas by farmers in despair because of these slight shifts in global markets. In 2017, Thailand's Supreme Court found Yingluck guilty of failing to stop corruption in the rice-pledging scheme and sentenced her to five years in prison. The sentence will be carried out "in absentia," as the former prime minister is rumored to be living in Dubai.[41]

The Empower staff member who told me the above story from the perspective of how it directly impacted her family reminded me that this issue was vitally connected to human trafficking in that it showed how global markets exacerbate rural and urban inequality. Thailand's rural poor have been systematically left behind by economic development policies that favor the growth of Bangkok's urban core. Such urban-peripheral inequalities drive low-wage migration in a range of service positions, and Thailand's wealth relative to neighboring countries drives undocumented labor migration from countries throughout Southeast Asia. These forms of mobility shed light on the motives for migration and the systemic struggles that may create the preconditions for human trafficking in both China and Thailand; however, the preferred abstractions and refractions of trafficking through red-light districts, commercial sex, and undocumented migration represent the conventional and popular ways the practice in Thailand is understood and consumed. The final chapter takes a look at how these mundane legacies of rural-urban inequality shape a worker's experiences inside and outside of the anti-trafficking industry, and her life after trafficking rescue.

CHAPTER 6

Quitting Rehab

The Promises and Betrayals of Freedom

The struggles that workers in vocational-training rehab programs deal with may lead readers to ask, If rehab is so bad, why do workers stay? On one hand, the answer is complicated. Workers all over the world gripe about work, but they stay because they lack the time or skills to find alternate employment or lack the financial resources to leave. On the other hand, the answer is quite simple. Many do not stay. They quit. In doing so, they engage in one of the most active yet invisible acts of resistance. However, these stories are rarely made public, because they are dispersed, individual efforts that conflict with the melodrama of human trafficking rescue and rehabilitation. To further understand how claims of freedom are a contextual moving target, this chapter looks at life for women once they leave rehabilitation.

I visited Yin in March 2012, just six months after she had left her job at Freedom Unchained and a few days before her twenty-fifth birthday. I boarded a train in Beijing bound for Yiwu, a small port city in China's southeastern Zhejiang province, where China's wholesale manufacturing exports are shipped to hundreds of locations throughout the Middle East and Europe. In describing the city, the *New York Times* observed in 2013, "If it's small, cheap and made of plastic, it can probably be found in Yiwu."

I stepped into a cab with Yin's instructions to find shop E-43 in the jewelry section of the wholesale market outside what is referred to in English as "China Commodity City" (*zhongguo xiao shangpin cheng*).

The taxi meandered through a maze of identical lanes, each with glass storefronts that featured hundreds of beads, stones, pearls, and pendants. It was just 7 a.m., and each storefront had already pulled up its steel security gate and was open for the day's business. As I excitedly stood in the doorway of her shop, I saw Yin crouched behind a glass display case making room within for a new shipment of amethyst that had just arrived from Brazil. Her husband, whom I would meet for the first time, was unpacking the large cardboard carton, sifting through layers of customs documents that detailed the box's journey across several continents.

"Lin Lin," Yin shrieked! Her husband looked up and greeted me in slow, measured, English: "Hello, Lin Lin, How are you?! You can call me Little Cui." The greeting was accompanied by a firm handshake and a salute, which I interpreted as an exaggerated mockery of greetings he had been taught in English class. We quickly reverted back to Mandarin Chinese to exchange pleasantries, during which an older Chinese woman in a hurry walked in, waved her arms, and hollered, "*laobanniang,*" a term of respect and authority meaning "boss's wife," to catch Yin's attention. The customer's left hand was weighed down by bags holding the goods she had gathered from various shops, and her right hand waived the yellow carbon copy of a receipt. Yin glanced up and immediately skipped behind the counter to grab a large bundle bound with brown packing tape. She exchanged the package for the woman's receipt and thanked her for her business. After the customer left, Yin turned to me and explained that this was a typical interaction: the woman was a broker who sourced different jewels to send to her clients around China and, presumably, other parts of the world, and Yin had stayed up until 2 a.m. the evening prior organizing the inventory and preparing the order.

Yin instructed me to leave my bags behind the counter and told her husband she was taking me to breakfast. She nodded goodbye and quickly reminded him which customers were supposed to be stopping in that morning, and which items had yet to be displayed. Yin directed us out of the jewelry section, and we passed through a dizzying maze of near-identical alleys, one selling children's shoes and another selling fake flowers, before reaching a busy intersection that featured several chain restaurants.

Once we turned off the block, her cheeriness dimmed just slightly and she turned to me: "This is the first time I've left the shop to go out to eat since I moved here six months ago."

"What do you mean?" I asked, confused by this seemingly nonchalant admission.

"We have so much work to do at the shop—hundreds of orders some days. We open at 6:30 a.m. and end up staying here very late, sometimes well into the night. The little bit of time we spend at home, I am cleaning up after different relatives who live with us. Because it's a family business, we do all of the work. Cui's parents say we aren't earning enough to hire any additional staff help."

"But I like my job," she quickly interjected, before I could vocalize the concern that was evidently forming between my eyebrows. "As the boss's wife, I have the complete authority to make decisions, and customers treat me with respect," she explained. "But," she added after a pause, "I don't receive a salary. Xiao Cui gives me 20 to 40 kuai (3 to 5 USD) here or there when he tells me to pick up takeout to bring back for us to eat, but I don't collect any money from the business, and I have spent all the savings that I brought here from Beijing."

It was not a coincidence that Yin was now working in another jewelry enterprise. Through her promotion to wholesale buyer for Freedom Unchained, she met Cui and connected the Beijing-based social enterprise to the cheaper wholesale outlet for raw stones and beads in southern China. Their courtship occurred mainly over text messages and WeChat. Seeking to resolve the problem of the long-distance relationship, Cui invited Yin to leave her job at Freedom Unchained and move down to Yiwu to work in his family business. He promised to cover airfare and housing, an offer that felt generous amid a promising romance.

Yin's growing dissatisfaction with work at Freedom Unchained in Beijing made her not just amenable to but enthusiastic about the opportunity to move. Her friends and coworkers in Beijing were hesitant, skeptical, and worried. They pointed out that Yin hardly knew this guy and asked why she would uproot everything to be with him. Yin weighed the decision for several months and eventually decided to take a chance and move to Yiwu. She knew Cui had a thriving family business, and he had promised he would provide her with a stable economic situation. After nearly five years working at Freedom Unchained, she was excited about living on her own, outside a dorm environment. She also told me that she felt stagnant in her employment at Freedom Unchained. Her salary had only increased by a few hundred RMB during her five-year tenure, and she was unsure about the likelihood of further upward mobility in the company. Still, she remained committed to her relationship with Freedom Unchained in Beijing and promised to continue helping the organization as a contact and sourcer on the ground in Yiwu.

We took our time at breakfast as we caught up. Yin ordered nearly everything off the menu, telling me that Cui had given her a 100 RMB bill to make sure that she treated her American friend properly. Midway through devouring the trays of wontons, congee, and crullers, I noticed Yin wasn't eating that much. I remembered that she had once had bad stomachaches back in Beijing and asked if digestion issues were still bothering her. Her faced blushed ever so slightly, and she flashed a bright, excited smile before timidly uttering, "I'm pregnant. Three months."

THE AFTERLIFE OF FREEDOM

Historians of American slavery and abolition have challenged the simplistic binary between slavery and freedom as those concepts are so often narrated in the American retelling of the transatlantic slave trade. A rigorous exploration of the legacies of chattel slavery reveals that freedom and emancipation are not discreet moments of time but have complex lives long after the so-called fractured emancipation and its implementation throughout the United States.[1] Writing about "sexual labor in between slavery and freedom" in antebellum New Orleans, historian Emily Owens reveals how experiences of freedom and enslavement existed on a continuum contingent on gendered and racialized labor. Her fascinating examination of the "brothel clause," an anomalous piece of legislation at the time, reveals how sexual commerce within brothels tied "sexual labor to the behaviors of free people." Owens's attention to the "structural relationship of sexual labor and freedom" marks important reflections for the anti-trafficking movement, particularly for their insights into how the possibilities of freedom changed based on racialized sexual politics.[2]

Freedom—widely touted throughout the anti-trafficking movement—is a Western-grown concept couched in histories of militarized independence following settler colonial conquest. Asian American studies scholar Mimi Thi Nguyen reminds us that the "gift of freedom" is a ruse used to justify US empire and military occupation. Writing about US militarization in Southeast Asia, liberal notions of freedom accrue debt and demand gratitude from refugee and other postcolonial subjects.[3] Such mythologies have in turn been adapted by Western liberalism as tools for justifying "emancipation" in the global South. Culturally and linguistically, "slavery" and "freedom" are simply not used in the same ways in the Chinese and Thai languages, though both Cowboy Rescue and Freedom Unchained flatten such differences when they sell jewelry as a "slave-free good."

While this book pushes back against the metaphor that likens human trafficking to modern-day slavery, a global comparative understanding of freedom is vital to situating the claims that American anti-trafficking organizations rely on. This chapter charts several divergent paths for life after trafficking—and life after anti-trafficking[4]—as just one way to complicate the prevailing assertion that vocational training puts one on a path to freedom. Following Denise Brennan's exploration of life experiences after trafficking in her book about victims of labor trafficking and their disparate journeys in the United States, here I recount four individual stories of life after *anti*-trafficking rescue and rehabilitation. Beneath the glossy appeal of a happy ending for rescued victims of trafficking, Brennan details the mundane character of life afterward—what she refers to as "everyday lifework."[5] Such accounts are rare because it is often difficult for researchers to build relationships with formerly trafficked persons, for an array of reasons ranging from their transience to the manner in which they are protected by the organizations and agencies that assist them.

As the stories in this book have recounted, workers in both China and Thailand had limited opportunities to offer feedback to or seek changes from their employers. As with other low-wage manufacturing jobs throughout the world, in anti-trafficking rehabilitation programs, shop floor discontent has no viable outlet. I observed that concerns voiced against the organization were often summarily dismissed or used against workers to further subject them to regimes of surveillance and control. While dissent was discouraged, sometimes punished, and almost always co-opted by the organization to suit management's interests, a worker always had one absolute option for defiance: she could quit. However, once she did, it was as if her life disappeared from the anti-trafficking discourse or the life-after-trafficking narrative arc. The decision to quit is simply erased from the handpicked narratives of rehabilitative success that organizations peddle and consumers are eager to hear.

During my research with rehabilitation programs, I witnessed more than a dozen workers leave. Some came back and were almost always welcomed by their employers, who firmly believed in the redemptive hope of second—and third, and even fourth—chances. When workers quit, I did my best to stay in touch with them in order to understand the divergent paths they chose after jewelry making. Although this is not a primary source of data for the book, it was important for me to understand quitting as an important part of rehabilitation. Following workers who left has provided access to some of the most telling examples of rehabilitation programs' successes and failures.

From an ethnographic perspective, studying those who "quit" is challenging because it pushes the boundaries of the original social field of the ethnography. Stated differently, when researchers or program evaluators hope to understand a rehabilitation program, they spend time in the rehabilitation center and interview people who work there. It is far more difficult to talk with people who have left. This challenge begins to describe the trap of what social scientists call "sampling on the dependent variable"[6] in warning that qualitative research can be biased by its limited sample frame. For instance, in prior chapters, we learned of neutral observers—journalists, fair-trade authenticators, students, volunteers, and reality tourists—who arrive at both organizations to learn about trafficking survivors' experiences. When NGOs broker the relationship between survivors and visitors, they invariably hope to introduce the public to workers who might affirm the archetypical stories of success that are frequently shared. The jewelry businesses in particular selected only workers who had "good stories" to be interviewed by these short-term guests. This strategy satisfies a business's need for good publicity, but it also allows organizations to suggest that individuals who voice negative experiences may still be "processing trauma" or are "vulnerable to revictimization" if they speak to strangers. When a translator was needed, it was often a staff or volunteer member who represented the organization, further complicating the ability for workers to voice their full range of feedback and not risk employment.

Quitting, then, is a last resort and threatens to make one's story invisible in the organization's archives. When jewelry workers consider leaving rehab, they do what all workers do. They make a calculation based on other work options immediately available, weighed against their previous experiences doing such work, and their present social and economic circumstances. This chapter tells the story of four women who, for various reasons, quit vocational training. Now that they are scattered—some stayed in Beijing or Bangkok, another moved back to her hometown, and another other moved to a different city to start a family—there is no reason why either organization would tell their stories. Yet these accounts reveal the limited range of life options after vocational training. When faced with alternatives to jewelry making, the vast majority end up choosing marriage or jobs in the low-wage manufacturing or service sectors—including sex work.

MARRIAGE AND LOW-WAGE WORK

Like Yin, most workers who left Freedom Unchained in China did so after they entered serious relationships or got married. These relationships offered enough of a social and economic safety net for them to consider life after rehab. Yet, in each case, marriage came with additional low-wage manual labor arrangements outside the home, and forms of unpaid care work for their new families. Jade, now in her late forties, was Freedom Unchained's second worker, recruited in the first days after the organization's founding in 2005. Jade migrated to Beijing from Anhui province when she was eighteen and became a sex worker after becoming dissatisfied with working conditions and pay in restaurant and sales work. After the workday at Freedom Unchained, like other workers, Jade dabbled in different activities to shake off the day. Because of the production facility and dormitory's remote location, most stayed close by. All had cell phones, and as telecommunications improved, many stayed home and could access an entire world from the palm of their hands. They chatted through WeChat, scanned Weibo accounts, and most of all, connected through online dating sites.

In 2009, Jade met Duan in an online chatroom and began seeing him during her time off on the weekends. She said their dates provided a needed respite, an opportunity to experience a world outside the workweek. They would meet in different parts of Beijing, and for a few hours each week, she felt transported away from a workplace that was socially, spiritually, and emotionally all-consuming. About seven months into their budding relationship, Jade began to feel queasy at sporadic points throughout the day and soon discovered that she was pregnant. She disclosed this fact to the small staff and managers, and the reactions were confused, hesitant, and anxious. All were positive when talking of the baby, wanting to ward off any possibility of abortion. The first child "born through Freedom," they exclaimed. But a larger set of anxieties informed the questions they asked behind Jade's back: Who was the person she was dating? Was he a believer? What did we know of him?

Freedom Unchained encouraged Jade to have the child and get married to Duan because of the Christian organization's hardline stance against abortion and extramarital sex. At the same time, the managers expressed reluctance about celebrating her pregnancy, worrying that it might send "the wrong message" to some of the younger women that premarital sex is acceptable. Finally, they expressed concern about the man's character. Manager Fu pulled me aside one day and said, "We don't know if this man is right for Jade. He has not yet accepted Christ into his life. I am not sure if she is ready to live in that environment." Spiritual acceptance and religious conversion were seen as primary goals of rehabilitation, threatened by marriage to a nonbeliever.

Freedom Unchained offered to pay for Jade's wedding, but Jade refused because, as she told me, she suspected she might owe the organization in exchange. Furthermore, she said that paying for her own wedding was a matter of self-respect. It occurred to me that this was Jade's understanding of the "dignity" that so often graced Freedom Unchained's brochures and sales catalogues. Soon after her wedding, Jade and Duan moved to a small apartment that Jade owned on the outskirts of Beijing located two and a half hours from Freedom Unchained's production office. The considerable commute meant that Jade was no longer able to show up to work, Bible study, and small-group sessions. She asked if she could earn her same monthly salary making jewelry at home. The organization frowned upon her absence from the work site because it limited Jade's participation with other workers in the labor of moral discipline and social control. As a compromise, the organization decided to pay her 10 RMB (1.70 USD) for each piece of jewelry that she made off site—pieces that sold for between 15 and 40 USD in the United States—and 100 RMB (17 USD) for each piece that she designed, but it refused to pay for pieces that she designed that were not accepted for production or sale in their catalog.

For a year, Jade was the primary caregiver of her child and designed and made jewelry from home, earning barely more than 1,000 RMB (160 USD) a month. Faced with the diminished economic opportunities and lacking Beijing *hukou* (residency requirements to obtain social welfare) for her daughter in Beijing, she ultimately decided to move back to her home-town near Hefei City, the capital of Anhui province. As the rental market in Beijing began to skyrocket, Jade realized that she would make more money renting out her apartment than working as a freelance jewelry maker. Leaving Beijing and Freedom Unchained demarcated a clear shift in Jade's identities: formerly a sex worker, then labeled a victim of human trafficking by the Freedom Unchained project, and finally, after she decided to leave her rescue program, an anonymous low-wage migrant worker, wife, and mother.

MARRIAGE AS A PATHWAY TO FREEDOM

Jade's and Yin's transitions from wage worker to family worker reveal a universal paradox of marriage. Jewelry workers considered the trade-off attractive, as it offered financial and social independence from the organization. Freedom Unchained also publicly celebrated marriage for its participants and, whenever possible, eagerly shared the good news through social media. One monthly email sent to consumers and prospective donors claimed: "This week at Freedom Unchained, we had a LOT to celebrate! We celebrated Xing Xing's engagement. She will leave Freedom Unchained next fall to start a new life with her husband. We are so happy for Xing Xing that she is emotionally and physically in a place that she can move into this new, joyful, exciting phase of life! We love celebrating these milestones with our women—particularly when that means chocolate cake at the office before 9:00 am!" In both organizations, marriage was often posited as a prime pathway toward successful rehabilitation and redemption. It purported to be the antithesis of prostitution: a consensual and firmly institutionalized relationship sanctioned by the Christian church.

Marriage, in fact, has become a recurrent rehabilitation narrative throughout many US anti-trafficking organizations. In 2013, the Los Angeles–based anti-trafficking organization Freedom and Fashion planned its entire 2013 fashion show around the theme of a wedding ceremony. The organization runs a vocational training program in Los Angeles to teach fashion design to formerly trafficked people. It hosts an annual fashion show where these designs are featured in a marketplace of dozens of other ethically sourced and "slave-free goods." I served as an usher for the 2013 event "Collective X Ceremony" and was asked to be a panelist for the corresponding discussion. Known for its high-end production values, which drew on the donated talent of celebrated designers in the LA area, the fashion show's stage was elegantly draped in white to evoke a traditional Christian wedding. The invitation for the event featured a model cloaked in a white veil, with corresponding text that read, "CEREMONY is about celebrating hope and redemption amidst the grave issue of modern-day slavery. CEREMONY hopes to inspire positive change and mobilize its attendees into action—providing a message of beauty and victory, not just grim statistics or heavy information." A proponent of social enterprises, the fashion show also served as a marketplace: "Attendees will have a chance to shop for these fairtrade and cause-centric products, with purchases that directly support those working to end human trafficking."

This very CEREMONY flier happened to fall out of a folder filled with research paraphernalia one day while I was spending time with sex worker activists in Thailand. After explaining this recurrent theme of marriage as a redemptive exit from sex work, one sex worker named Lee burst out laughing and cut me off mid-sentence in protest: "Well," she insisted, "now they're just giving it away for free!" Referencing an understanding of marriage as an antiquated contractual relationship predicated on patriarchal norms, this criticism was not shared by the American activists drawn to the restoration that marriage promised for heterosexual Christian couples. For Christian social enterprises, marriage was an inevitable exit strategy because it posed the antidote to sex work. The alternatives to paid intimate labor were either paid manual labor or unpaid intimate labor under the contract of marriage. The sanctity of such new bonds was called into question when the romantic partner was not a Christian, but other than that, rarely was it questioned.

Marriage, however, did not always live up to its expectations. I visited Jade in her hometown of Hefei in 2013, three years after she left Freedom Unchained and two years after she left Beijing. She had sold the home in Beijing and lived in a middle-class neighborhood in a two-bedroom apartment in a standard six-floor walkup. The home was fully furnished with items that she had shipped from the Beijing apartment. She and her daughter slept in one of the bedrooms, and her husband, Duan, slept on the couch. The other bedroom had become their daughter's playroom and a storage space for the extra furniture from Beijing that did not fit—vestiges of her former life stacked floor to ceiling like Tetris blocks.

Jade's daughter had just turned three, and Duan had become depressed and indolent because he was having a difficult time finding and keeping a job as a migrant worker in Anhui. During our visit, her husband spent most of his time watching TV. To give us time to talk privately, he took their daughter outside to the park. Because it marked such a rare occasion, Jade's daughter was thrilled to go on an outing with her father. With the apartment to ourselves, Jade showed me around further. She mentioned that her computer was connected to the internet and she knew how to write emails and make online purchases, and could potentially make and sell jewelry from home if I knew of any commercial outlets for her. She also told me that she set a password on the computer so that only she could use it, adding that if she did not, her husband would waste all his time on the computer.

On a walk during my visit, she spent little time making small talk before asking me if I knew a divorce lawyer. She said she recalled that I had worked at a legal aid office in Beijing several years prior. I explained that, unfortunately, the cases of divorce we dealt with at Beijing University's Center for Women's Law Studies and Legal Aid were free only to women who were experiencing domestic violence. She said she had made a cursory inquiry at law firms in Hefei and remarked on how expensive divorce was.

We let the silence linger—a pause pregnant with the weight of impossibility. "It's a shame," she chuckled, if I was still a "victim of trafficking" living at Freedom Unchained, I bet I would be eligible for free legal aid. She was likely correct. Although she may not have been eligible through formal Chinese government social services, Freedom Unchained was connected to such a vast social network of talent and capital that it could likely have crowdsourced either the skills or funding to find and pay a lawyer, as it had previously paid for workers' weddings and violations of the one-child policy. Jade's casual observation revealed a deeply troubling truth about the liberal regime on which human rights, but in particular anti-trafficking work, is based. Rather than call for a widening of social protection resources, anti-trafficking approaches have typically demanded rights on an individual basis, allotting them to deserving subjects based on their victim status. Anthropologist Nick Mai reminds us that this hierarchy of global "sexual humanitarianism" has created an industry in which people must learn to perform appropriate forms of victimhood to be eligible for rights.

During our visit, Jade took me to the factory where she was working for her older sister. It was a small one-room operation that made laces and rope for shoelaces, drawstrings, and lanyards and sold these pieces to large-scale suppliers of shoes, clothing, and bags. She sat behind an industrial loom where brightly colored threads were stitched together at a frenetic pace. Her reflections articulate the major failings not only of heroic efforts to replace sexual labor with manual labor, but also of the limited local economic possibilities for migrant workers across the global South:

> When I first moved back to Anhui, I tried making jewelry to sell everywhere: I walked stall to stall at the market, created a small online shop, and I even tried selling jewelry on the street. I saw how much Americans paid for the pieces I designed and made at Freedom Unchained. I tried for months . . . and no one was interested in buying. Reflecting back, I know why we were able to ask for such high prices: they [Freedom Unchained] told Americans all these tragic stories about our lives, and people felt bad for us. I don't think they needed to say it was horrible as "human trafficking"; they could have just said it the way it is: we have hard lives. We used to work difficult jobs. I've done everything; I used to be a construction salesperson, a waitress, and a sex worker, and jewelry making was just a different kind of work for me, it's all just different kinds of work. . . . Looking back, it was a lost

172 I Quitting Rehab

period of my life. Look at me now, with only enough skills to work for my
sister. I still can't make a stable living, and I just need a job that will allow
me to give my daughter better opportunities in the future.

The realities that Jade and her daughter face are part of a narrative
frequently missing from anti-trafficking freedom festivals and movement advocacy in the United States. Her account complicates the vic-
tim-savior story that pervades the global anti-trafficking movement.
The gap between representation and reality is one of the core failings of
the transnational anti–human trafficking movement. In choosing to
define low-wage workers with transnational tropes of anti-trafficking
victimhood and rescue, rather than as agents who experience global
capitalism, inequality, and state repression in disparate and distinct
ways, the movement overlooks the needs of migrant workers globally.
While marriage offered Jade an opportunity to leave Freedom Unchained,
her relationship also inducted her into a new world of unpaid care work
alongside low-wage manual labor.

INTIMACY, COMMUNITY, AND
MOBILITY IN THAILAND

In Thailand, workers seemed to have a bit more flexibility both in their
romantic relationships and in their engagements with the job market. In
2012, Ploy told her Cowboy Rescue employers that she was leaving her
job to take care of her grandson full-time. Ploy was comfortable at
Cowboy Rescue and certainly considered it a form of retirement from
working in the bars. She left for two main reasons. First, her daughter,
who was living in their family's hometown in Udon Thani province,
wanted to return to full-time work and offered to remit Ploy a portion
of her salary if she could take care of her son. Second, Ploy's long-term
boyfriend, Frances, an American college professor whom she had met
while working as a sex worker, was able to commit to providing financial support to her and their grandson.
    In 2010, Frances helped Ploy put a down payment on a small one-
bedroom apartment located in Samut Prakhan, a province adjacent to
Bangkok. Many Bangkok residents had begun moving out to new housing developments in Samut Prakan due to the rising cost of rent in central Bangkok. The urban sprawl was significant, and her new commute
to the Cowboy Rescue offices took about two hours one way during
rush-hour traffic and included taking a bus, a tuktuk, and Skytrain. On

the times I would travel out to her home, we would splurge on a taxi, and it would only shorten the journey by half an hour at the most because Bangkok's dense traffic was seemingly endless.

When she finally stopped working at Cowboy, Ploy traded her commute and forty-hour workweek to be the full-time caregiver of her grandson, Tao. Around his third birthday, doctors suggested that he might need some testing to assess developmental delays. Her family insisted that he was probably just shy or needed more interaction with kids his age. She insisted that they get a diagnosis and took Tao to dozens of doctors. I accompanied them once and admired her indefatigable spirit. For months, seeking a diagnosis and then therapy, Ploy trotted a toddler on and off multiple forms of public transportation; waited in endless hospital lines; paid bills out of pocket not knowing if, how, or when she would be reimbursed; and was often left with few diagnostic certainties. Eventually, the specialists' consensus was that her grandson had a mild case of autism, and she found a Catholic school that gave him slightly more specialized attention than the local public school.

Once Tao started kindergarten, Ploy's bills began to multiply, and she had to pursue ingenious entrepreneurial endeavors to earn an income from home. Her resourcefulness and creativity were fueled by an unrelenting drive to move forward, and each time I returned to Bangkok, I was excited to hear about her new business ideas. One year, she met me at a shopping mall and immediately led me into a Starbucks. Inside, I watched as she grabbed fistfuls of flat wooden coffee stirrers and handed them to me. She snapped at my dumbfounded gaze and motioned for me to put the stirrers in my bag. She did the same and we walked out with close to fifty—she, of course, made sure as always to leave some for other patrons.

"What are you doing with these coffee stirrers?" I asked. Ploy chuckled, "You'll see when we get home."

Sure enough, when we got there, she unveiled an impressive display of wooden sculptures. She had stacked and interweaved the stirrers together to fashion a large collection of cups, wooden baskets, and vases. Some were covered with paper-mache and a glaze, which she explained provided both waterproof protection and interesting designs. A few years later, she dabbled in making soap and different body salves. The soap business did well for a while, but Ploy always kept busy inventing new ways to hustle. Most recently, she began knitting bags with a kind of thick rope on which she hoped to earn a higher profit margin.

In addition to remitting monthly support that covers the mortgage, Tao's tuition, and living costs, Frances visits once or twice a year and plans to retire in Thailand once he is eligible to receive his pension. He takes care of her. He reminds me to take care of her. We are part of the informal network of people who allow Ploy to piece together a living wage in lieu of adequate state-allocated social welfare provision. Like the anti-trafficking industrial complex, we are not systemic solutions but part of the community that Ploy has built.

These various life choices of love and work after rehabilitation put intimate labor into perspective. Whether formally brokered through the institution of marriage or a feature of intimacy in a long-term partnership or a short-term financial transaction for sex, former sex workers find numerous ways to make a living after quitting rehabilitation. These means often hinged on relationships with men because of limited opportunities in the low-wage work force. Some workers inevitably returned to sex work. Others found ways to do sex work under rehab, even though the organizations considered returning to sex work to be the ultimate failure of rehabilitation and tried hard to prevent it. While some women return to the bars where they used to work, others find it more difficult to go back the longer they have been away. Some have suggested that it's hard to resume after dozens of daily counseling sessions that pathologized sexual exploitation. Others returned sporadically or full-time, driven by the reality that sex work provided far greater economic returns and flexibility than jewelry making.

OTHER SERVICE SECTOR JOBS

Every person who quit rehab faced the challenge of finding another job. Beam, a worker in her late thirties, decided to leave Cowboy Rescue after six years of working there, because she craved a new environment. She considered herself lucky when she found a job at a popular shopping mall in central Bangkok, selling French soaps for a Thai owner. She worked alone managing a small kiosk stocked floor to ceiling with different soaps, lotions, shampoos, and body washes made of olive oil from Marseille, France. Sometimes, she said, she found the work repetitive, selling the same sorts of things from a six-by-six-foot cubicle. But it certainly was never lonely, working in one of the newest, busiest, and most popular malls in Bangkok. Her boss also gave her the ultimate freedom to decide how to display items and engage customers and when to take breaks throughout the day. He rarely stopped in to see her and trusted her completely.

In three years of working there, Beam became supremely well versed in the different types of oils used in making the products she sells, and how to market different products to different clientele. She earned the manager's trust, which gave her tremendous control over her day-to-day schedule. Beam's base salary is slightly lower than her former earnings at Cowboy Rescue, but she has the potential to earn a hefty commission on her sales. Depending on business, Beam can earn between 15,000 and 25,000 baht a month, but as with all commission-based sales jobs, her salary is unpredictable. Her son still lives with her parents, and she is still the only person from her immediate family living in Bangkok. Like millions of other migrant workers, she figured out how to make a living in the service industry.

Then, on March 22, 2020, Thailand announced it would close all malls due to the rise in COVID-19 cases in the country. What began as a temporary, one-month closure ended up lasting over a year, during which time Beam's boss closed the small store. Like millions of retail workers around the world, Beam was left with no way of earning a living. Under the Thai government's COVID-19 economic response plan, because of the mandatory shutdown, Beam was eligible for three months of cash support at 50 percent of her salary. However, because this sum was attached to a formal employer, once the owner shut down the shop, she was no long eligible for state assistance. Between April and June 2020, other informal workers who were labeled temporary workers, freelance, and not registered under the Social Security System were eligible to receive 5,000 baht per month. Further the sex workers' rights group SWING found that some sex workers were denied assistance after disclosing they worked as sex workers. As of this writing, Beam chose to return home to live with her parents, with no permanent work options, because governments around the world have failed to adequately address the long-term economic impact of COVID-19.

THE IMPOSSIBILITY OF JEWELRY MAKING AS A VOCATION

Jade was recruited to join the Freedom Unchained project in 2005 while she was working at a massage parlor near the Lido Hotel in Beijing's Chaoyang District. The hotel, built in 1984 and managed by the American

Holiday Inn franchise, was a popular destination for international tourists in the late 1980s. Catering to Western appetites in particular, businesses in the blocks surrounding the hotel to this day still feature English-language signs selling pirated DVDs, dry-cleaning services, massages, and expat groceries. Also present are a number of small storefronts marked by bright-pink illuminated signs in Chinese advertising massage or adult products, or both. In many of these shops, a customer can pay for sexual services on site, including massages with happy-ending hand jobs, oral sex, or full-service sexual intercourse.

Jade began working at one such shop six years after migrating to Beijing from her hometown in Anhui province in central China. After a failed investment managing her own restaurant and after leaving her husband following several episodes of domestic violence, she faced considerable financial difficulty in paying her mortgage on the two-bedroom home she owned in the southwestern part of the city. She began working at a massage shop in the Chaoyang District at the recommendation of a friend. Armed with a brusque, penetrating, adventurous demeanor, she often told me that sex work was not necessarily difficult for her because it paid the bills. Without fail, clients frequently grabbed her in ways that she didn't like, but she didn't see this as different from the violent episodes that characterized her ex-husband's behavior. Identifying a key distinction of sex work from the domestic violence she endured throughout her marriage, she explained: "At least I never have to see these men again if I don't want to."

Mainstream portrayals of the sex trade typically focus on the supposed horrors of trading sexual services for money—"selling your body," as it is often referred to. But what was most difficult for Jade, she explained, was dealing with management at the massage shop where she worked. Owners typically took a sizable cut of what customers paid, and the middleman fee was often arbitrary; sometimes workers would receive no payment at all. Based on her own calculations, Jade claimed that owners of the massage shop owed her in excess of 10,000 RMB (1,600 USD) in unpaid wages accumulated in the several years she had worked there.

During an ongoing battle with her employer over owed wages, Jade met two American women who began visiting her shop weekly, offering English lessons and stopping in to chat with her and her coworkers while she waited for customers. Jade recalls regarding the friendliness of these two women, the American cofounders of Freedom Unchained, with skeptical curiosity. Why did they want to spend their free time hanging out in a massage parlor, she wondered? But she enjoyed getting to know the Americans as a way to pass idle time in the twelve-to-sixteen-hour days she worked. As Sarah and Yves got to know her and her colleagues, they offered Jade an alternative job making jewelry. Waiting in vain for over a month of owed wages from her owner at the massage business, she and three other women left the shop and became the first recruits at Freedom Unchained in 2006.

As the organization developed over the following decade, Jade became the most senior employee and assumed the role of older sister to others on the shop floor—always offering advice and strategies, both solicited and unsolicited. When I met her in the summer of 2008, she showed me the ropes and taught me how to be a jewelry maker on the shop floor. The lessons included everything from how to insert a centimeter-wide thread into a millimeter-wide eyelet—a task that involves burning the thread as described in chapter 2—to how to cry on cue during group counseling sessions, what Jade called *biaoshi zui,* or "performing sin."

Jade's life story betrayed the tales of despair that filled Freedom Unchained brochures—narratives of women whose desperation to leave sex work was matched only by the gratitude they felt following their rescue by the American social enterprise. Jade's gratitude to Freedom Unchained had many forms: she recognized the job as having many tangible benefits, including medical insurance and weekends off, which most low-wage jobs available to migrant workers in Beijing lacked. As an older worker, she also explained that because some of her younger coworkers lacked the financial stability or the migrant social networks to find jobs outside of sex work, jewelry making was a welcome alternative.

Jade eventually left Freedom Unchained following irreconcilable disagreements with her employers following the birth of her first child. As the primary caretaker for her daughter and a disabled husband whom she married while employed at Freedom Unchained, she asked to work from home in order to care for her family. Managers tried to accommodate Jade's request, but ultimately felt it infringed too much on one of the organization's strictest mandates: that all participants live in the on-site shelter housing. They claimed the shelter requirement protected women from potential traffickers and ensured them a morally safe environment in which to establish their lives after quitting sex work.

Jade maintains that, given a choice, she would have preferred to keep making jewelry for Freedom Unchained; however, in light of the organization's rigid moral guidelines, she quit in 2011. As the organization's most adept jewelry maker—both in speed, skill, and design capability—

and aware of how much Freedom Unchained was able to sell the pieces of jewelry she made in the United States, she hoped to become an independent jewelry producer after her exit. Just weeks into her unemployment, she would soon learn that without the Freedom Unchained marketing team—both their access to US consumers and their unique ability to market the redemptive story of transformation from sexual slavery—jewelry making was not a viable vocation in Beijing. For years after her resignation, each time I visited her, she would be trying her hand at other jobs in different industries, and she would send me home with a few jewelry pieces she had made with a simple request: "When you go back to America, can you sell this jewelry for me, and help me cut out the middleman?"

Jade's simple request, "Can you help me sell this jewelry?" asks us to imagine what is actually for sale when we buy "slave-free goods." Do these programs deliver the promises of rehabilitation from sex trafficking as they claim? Is rehabilitation through vocational training, as it is sold, a sufficient antidote for the challenges migrant workers face in the global South? "Slave-free" jewelry gains marketability only when it is morally embedded with global North values around human trafficking, labor exploitation, and what can be considered "decent work."[7] This marketplace of morality is profitable because it works in concert with the transnational religious and secular social movement to combat trafficking. The impossibility of Jade's earning a living selling jewelry without the help of middlemen brokers like Freedom Unchained, or people like myself, demands increased transparency and accountability from the arbiters of global social movements and the international moral economy market. Jade's question shows that those labeled "rehabilitated victims" of rescue programs are impacted by the moral and economic governance of both anti-trafficking NGOs and the nation-state in which they reside.

GOING BACK TO REHAB

Quitting jewelry making was not always a one-way street. Even after leaving, workers held onto the relationships forged with coworkers and managers, and many saw jewelry making as a backup plan if all else failed. For Yin, after three years of marriage, she grew tired of being an unpaid worker in the family business. She rarely complained about the long hours at the shop, she but could not tolerate the endless stream of work she was expected to do for her husband's family once she returned to the home they shared. She commented that Cui had a "traditional" mother who followed her around demanding that she sweep; scrub the toilets, shower, and bathroom tiles; and generally clean up after all the different relatives who lived together. She felt their family didn't respect her, and Cui deferred to his parents, who fronted the money for their business operations. After enduring years of conflict with Cui and his family, Yin eventually decided to leave Yiwu with her daughter and move back in with her parents and brother. Living with family helped her defray some of the rent, but she still faced pressure to earn an income—particularly because Cui has since disappeared from their daughter's life and offers no financial support.

Once again in a new city, she worked a number of service jobs, including at restaurants around the city, earning at most 2,500 RMB (350 USD) a month if she put in overtime. She described the positions as tiring, typically requiring her to work twelve-hour days marked by routine, disparaging treatment from customers, and absolutely no opportunities for upward mobility. Facing a growing financial burden from her daughter's school and living costs, she contacted Freedom Unchained directors about the possibility of returning to work as a jewelry producer. During her time away from the organization, from 2013 to 2018, salaries at the organization had increased dramatically in line with the cost of living and salaries throughout Beijing. Now at nearly 5,000 RMB (700 USD) a month, the jewelry positions were competitive, which Yin explained was facilitated by the acquisition of a steadier stream of good clients. The director was also amenable to letting Yin take periodic short leaves of absence to visit her daughter. Once her daughter enrolled in full-time kindergarten, Yin decided to ask her parents if they would watch her while she moved back to Beijing to work. They agreed, and Yin has taken one week of unpaid leave every two months to return home to see her daughter.

What changed, I asked? She shrugged her shoulders and explained, "We spent a lot of years talking about vocational training, but I still fundamentally lack an education. The only kinds of jobs I can apply for are service sector jobs that pay very little. I'm already familiar with Freedom Unchained's different requirements, and it's easy work compared to all of these low-wage jobs out here."

The desire of some workers to return to jewelry making brings up two points: while anti-trafficking organizations do not necessarily provide vocational training as an economic pathway, they do fill a vital need for decent jobs that give options to migrants with limited education paths. This last claim is important. However, nothing about it should be restricted to those who have experienced human trafficking. In fact, a broad-based push to create a larger social safety net that prioritizes decent work across the labor market would decrease migrants' vulnerability to trafficking and labor abuse. However, singling out only former sex workers and victims of sex trafficking as those deserving of decent work misses the opportunity to create systemic change. For now, they remain episodic solutions driven by religion, morality, sentimentality, and access to racialized global markets.

Conclusion

Redistribution and Possibilities for
Global Justice

The jewelry collection Perfectly Imperfect, launched in the summer of 2019, features gold and silver earrings, rings, and necklaces in various geometric shapes that are each slightly mismatched—or imperfect, as their branding suggests. Marketed under the hashtag #techforgood, the jewelry line is sold by a new social enterprise that markets jewelry as made by victims of trafficking from India. Free-D—described by its founders as "a portmanteau of 'freed' and '3D'"—trains human-trafficking survivors to use 3-D printers to produce jewelry for sale at global retail outlets. The Umra ring, on sale for $134.44, features a design in which a "perfect square is broken and made imperfect, a celebration of learning and the everyday perfect imperfections that need to be embraced as a part of that journey."[1]

The project was awarded a coveted spot in a 2017 Berlin-based female-empowerment business accelerator program, an opportunity that Free-D's founder likened to "dying and going to feminist heaven." Free-D's pilot project, operating in Mumbai, India, offered "psychological support and 3-D printing training" to ten women whom a local NGO partner labeled victims of human trafficking. The project offered the women internships at an Imaginarium, India's largest 3-D printing factory. In a *Forbes* magazine article detailing its work, Free-D is pitched as equal parts tech startup and social enterprise. The company was founded through the personal investment of one of its founders, and the cofounders promised to raise £500,000 GBP to get the business on its feet. Its online sales portal boasts that a full

"50% of profits from each piece go directly to cover the training or living costs of an at-risk woman beginning her new life with Free-D." Noting that the firm hoped to capitalize on the shift toward 3-D printing in the consumer apparel industry, the *Forbes* journalist asked, "Could CEO [Katherine] Prescott's ambition to become the 'go-to education company' for 3D-printing see her social ambitions flourish? For the sake of the millions in modern-day slavery, we hope so."[2]

Free-D claims to work with girls and women from vulnerable or underprivileged backgrounds recruited from women's shelters or NGOs around Mumbai who are deemed to be at risk and in need of "upskilling." By providing skills training and holistic support through Free-D's vocational training and rehabilitation program, the organization claims, its trainees "gain confidence, find work and move towards financial independence."[3] The latent anxiety around the future of women's employability in a rapidly advancing technological landscape has become a new frontier for the anti-trafficking rescue industry, and a profitable enterprise. Once again, jewelry is the commodity of choice and trafficking is the social issue to be resolved.

Throughout this book, I argue that racialized redemptive labor offers a satisfying antidote to the moral panic regarding global sex work and sex trafficking. Binding ethical consumer activists with former sex workers as virtuous laborers, the "slave-free good" delivers a palatable solution to the economic needs that drive sex work and satisfies the moral imperatives of rehabilitation for sex workers. Jewelry is just one of the numerous commodities sold as part of the anti–human trafficking movement in a concerted effort to leverage the marketplace to raise funds and awareness about sex trafficking. Vocational training—here in the skills of making jewelry—is marketed as a technical solution that brings global development goals around human trafficking into sharp focus while obscuring the equally powerful faith-based objectives of missionary work and the abolition of prostitution. Profit and religious proselytization become invisible as motives when shrouded in the sentimentality of entrepreneurship and rehabilitation as pathways to "freedom." These forms of power are equally invisibilized when the state relies on global North NGOs and vigilante and paramilitary entities to pursue anti-trafficking rescue efforts. By transforming sexual labor into low-wage manual labor, such organizations have created racialized redemptive and virtuous labor arrangements. For consumers, the promises of rehabilitation meld Christian morality and salvific evangelism with secular development goals promising decent work.

This book aims to open a conversation about transparency and the integration of local perspectives in global development frameworks. I seek to initiate a dialogue that considers American anti-trafficking interventions alongside the realities of migration, sex, and commerce in China and Thailand. To that end, this book also focuses on how anti-trafficking rehabilitation programs are reciprocally shaped by the state and market forces in the countries where they operate. In Thailand, vocational training work embodies the neoliberal free market, while in China, labor relations reflect the authoritarian character of the state. The distinct character of vocational training in each place is attributed to the divergent political economic contexts of low-wage labor relations in China and Thailand, yet these important distinctions are invisible across movement organizing in the United States, and they reveal how victims experience anti-trafficking rehabilitation projects in different national contexts.

These disparate cases should temper the ongoing excitement over vocational training, given its perilous past. NGOs, social enterprises, and governments alike have responded to global gendered poverty by introducing a host of interventions, from ethnic handicraft industries responding to rural poverty beginning in the 1980s, to the advent of "slave-free goods" in response to human trafficking in the 2000s, to developing possibilities in technology-specific vocational training to keep up with the "future of work." However, continual technocratic innovations in vocational training often fail to deliver on their promises under the racist and discriminatory work structures of global capitalism. The racial wages of rescue place power in the hands of those inventing and administering the trainings and of the consumers whose spending supports these projects. They uphold the virtuous industries of manual labor rather than amplify resources to help working-class migrants navigate the varied terrains in which they already live and work. Power for workers—from exercising greater social autonomy to remediating workplace discontent—is intentionally removed from the equation, as all of these solutions involve labor organizing and resistance at their core.

REFLECTING ON TWO DECADES SINCE THE PALERMO PROTOCOL

In the two decades since the passing of the United Nations Palermo Protocol and the United States Trafficking Victims Protection Act, human trafficking has rapidly risen to the top of global human rights agendas and has drawn unparalleled interest from global governance institutions, transnational civil society, nation-states, and civilian activists alike. A social concern that engages faith-based and secular groups in both democratic and authoritarian nation-state contexts, the global movement to combat human trafficking has become a pivotal transnational social movement. Since the year 2000, the cause has transformed civilian-consumer activist engagement and coupled it with state and market power both in the United States and abroad.

Stemming from UN protocols and global governance compliance pressures, and codified through national law, the global movement to combat trafficking has embedded and instituted new forms of state and market power across China and Thailand. The carceral state, in particular, now works with nonstate actors in novel ways, ways that have led to the further subordination of women globally. The way the state wields power over global social movements differs in authoritarian China versus democratic Thailand. The movement is beholden to authoritarian state interests in China, which trades access to organizational survival for government partnerships and oversight. This exchange has largely stifled the creation of a transnational human-trafficking rescue industry in China, relative to other parts of the world. Multinational corporations seeking cheap manufacturing labor and the Chinese government, which profits from foreign manufacturing contracts, purport to prioritize anti-trafficking responses, all the while lacking any provisions for worker safety or security, and certainly having no provisions to secure worker organizing. In more democratic Thailand, the movement is less beholden to political power than to global market power, in which a vigilante and free-market humanitarianism parallels the political economic priorities of tourism and foreign investment as engines of Thai economic growth. The large market for global human trafficking rescue parallels state investment in tourism and sexual commerce, revealing how economic development and humanitarian rescue are co-constituted.

Human trafficking rescue and rehabilitation have become accessible to everyone from law enforcement officers to citizen consumers, thereby creating new spaces of civilian vigilantism outside the state. The proliferation of renegade civic engagement parallels the increasing abundance of market-based movement responses, illustrating the convergence of public and private, state and nonstate, and secular and faith-based efforts.[4] As the Chinese and Thai cases—and their transnational connections through the United Nations and sites of activist organizing and consumption in the United States—demonstrate, this convergence has occurred despite differences across political economies, though the movement has taken on the characteristics of authoritarianism in China and the free market in Thailand.

The book argues that differences in nation-state particularities are important, but these distinctions are often glossed over through global North activist scripts. I home in on China and Thailand to show that, despite nearly identical forms of rehabilitation via vocational training for jewelry, rehabilitation programs absorb the labor regimes of low-wage migrant work peculiar to each place. In China they embody the character of authoritarianism in a moral appeal to capitalism that masks religious affiliations in this atheist, one-party state. In Thailand, working conditions resemble those of free-market firms. The Chinese organization Freedom Unchained transposes state authoritarianism onto its workplace because of fear of government censorship, and employs labor control strategies that resemble the collective working arrangements of the postsocialist *danwei*, or work unit. By contrast, Thai workers at the Cowboy Rescue see jewelry making as equivalent to many other low-wage jobs and experience greater independence in terms of housing and taking other part-time jobs after the workday has ended. In both cities, labor control strategies such as mandatory weekly Bible study, Christian life counseling, and per-minute wage deductions for arriving late for Christian worship and for infringement on nightly curfews represent new ways such organizations blend tactics of labor management with moral reform. China's restrictions on Christian missionaries and commercial sex work impose an authoritarian regime on Freedom Unchained movement activists, which they transfer onto their workers. Meanwhile, Cowboy Rescue activists working in Thailand can receive missionary visas and work alongside numerous state and civil society partners that engage the commercial sex industry. The primary differences between these anti-trafficking movement interventions in China and in Thailand boil down to legislative postures toward Christianity and the commercial sex industry, and political economic orientations toward foreigners, tourism, humanitarianism, and global markets.

COUNTERHEGEMONIC GLOBALIZATION AND SOCIAL MOVEMENTS

Motivated by a fundamental concern with how and why counterhegemonic movements may reproduce the same hegemonic power structures that they aim to combat, this book shows how transnational social movements can obscure a highly stratified organizing base that claims counterhegemonic intentions while simultaneously reinforcing and reproducing existing hegemonic structures.[5] Shedding light on how power is embedded in social movements through different institutional resources—those of the state or the market, or both—answers sociologist Peter Evans's call to explain how, when, and why counterhegemonic globalization is possible and when its opportunities are foreclosed. As evidenced in its inherent contradictions, the transnational anti-trafficking movement supports Michael Burawoy's critique of the "false optimism" embedded in social movement scholarship.[6] Burawoy and many labor movements scholars have demanded that social movement scholarship be more attuned to state and market power.[7] In this book, I illustrate ways the Thai and Chinese states and global markets facilitate or absorb the goals of the anti-trafficking movement. At the same time, I also pay attention to the race, class, nationality, and gender identities of global North rescuers, as these identities inscribe additional forms of power, motivation, and interest across the movement. Taken together, they strengthen new forms of US empire and foreclose alternatives that center organizing for workplace rights and economic justice.

In the case of faith-based activism through the market—including the commodity chain of "slave-free" jewelry and human-trafficking reality tourism—ethical consumption appears to be impossible when the labor relations of production and tourism are still bound by the features of neoliberal global capitalism. In both faith-based and secular activism, through the state in China and the market in Thailand, social justice grounded in the demands of local activists and migrant workers appears to be incompatible with interagency efforts to build transnational solidarity, because these efforts consistently fail to center worker-driven forms of resistance, organizing, or expertise.

Most social movements struggle with inherent contradictions and inconsistencies because they must appeal to a range of audiences and include a great number of constituents; in social movement language, they must develop a set of common grievances embedded in networks of solidarity and must frame these grievances in a culturally resonant way. This need for a coherent frame may make divisions and dissent within these social movements illegible. In other words, what may be considered problematically hegemonic varies significantly within a global movement. While many social movements have targeted the state to demand change, others find that any sort of state engagement cannot be detached from the penal and carceral dimensions of nation-state power. Alternatively, growing numbers of social entrepreneurs, microcredit lenders, and consumer activists find the market an appealing resource and target, given the dominance of global capital. Yet the stated beneficiaries of such social programs—who are also often the producers of commodities that fuel entrepreneurship—report subordination through labor practices and unequal labor relations. Such inequality appears distinct from traditional labor arrangements of global capital in the varying moral and social requirements that exist alongside labor requirements, but ultimately not in how capital is distributed.

Many stakeholders in the global North who have contributed to its design, funding, and propagation consider the global movement to combat trafficking a success. In the United States, most college campuses have at least one human-trafficking awareness club, more than four thousand faith communities have joined together for an annual "Freedom Sunday" of worship each April, and in 2010, President Barak Obama designated January "National Human Trafficking Awareness Month."[8] On January 11, 2021, commemorative activities included a 5K "Freedom Walk" in stiletto heels to raise awareness about gender inequality, a human trafficking film festival, and numerous fundraisers for American anti-trafficking organizations working domestically and abroad. Such advocacy campaigns and efforts to heighten awareness have inspired a decade of social engagement spanning the consumption of slave-free goods, international human trafficking reality tours, and vigilante rescue operations in working-class immigrant and racial minority neighborhoods in the United States.[9]

Many others have found the global movement to combat human trafficking to be marked by failure, especially in its impact on the "trafficked" women the movement purportedly helps.[10] These failures, most often attributed to ambiguous goals and unclear definitions and organizing tenets, have consistently led to the surveillance and patrolling of low-wage women workers around the globe. As a market-based strategy that turns to American consumers to raise funds against and awareness of human trafficking, this form of humanitarian assistance sells the version of human trafficking that generates the most social capital for tour participants, tour operators, and the expert NGOs that craft the trafficking narratives recited on the trips—and receive donations from tour revenues.[11] Opportunities to hear alternative perspectives that explicitly critique human-trafficking rescue, such as the "Bad Rehab" and "Last Rescue in Siam" videos, created by the Asia Pacific Network of Sex Workers and Empower Foundation, challenge the simplistic narratives that facilitate consumer activism. Scholars of transnational advocacy networks have long recognized that a coherent frame that focuses on "practices that result in bodily harm to vulnerable individuals" is the surest route to transforming a particular human rights concern into a broadly appealing justice movement.[12] By invoking simple narratives of slavery and freedom, the anti-trafficking movement has mobilized against universally recognized rights violations and, by so doing, has managed to bypass most critiques that the movement is Western-biased and imperialist.

Complicated narratives from allegedly trafficked women that reveal the slavery framing to be flawed or false threaten the entire premise of the movement, and they are a dangerous challenge to the activists who have propelled the issue of human trafficking to international prominence. These competing narratives have the potential to impose material, reputational, and ideational costs on these movements—endangering their funding, legitimacy, and accumulated social capital, as well as their own understandings of themselves as moral actors. These high stakes, and equally high profits, underlie the strategic silencing of these voices, despite their bold claims for solidarity and global sisterhood.

This book is particularly invested in how social movement subjects—"victims" of human trafficking, as they are ubiquitously labeled by anti-trafficking activists and the movement at large—regard the movement. In addition to victims—formally or informally identified by anti-trafficking laws or marked as such by large anti-trafficking NGOs—I argue that another cohort of social movement subjects exists among migrants and sex workers who have become the targets of human-trafficking interventions, ranging from state surveillance and detention to NGO reeducation through labor. However, their lives are made visible only if they are recognized as trafficking victims, and the legibility of their struggle represents complicity in some narratives that largely remove their agency.

The subjects of governmental and nongovernmental anti-trafficking efforts include many individuals who do not identify as "victims of trafficking." Nonetheless this label provides anti-trafficking activists with enormous political and social capital. Under an anti-trafficking global governance regime that prioritizes and rewards quantifiable measures of "prevention, protection, and prosecution," nation-states are evaluated by the quantity of cases identified and numbers of victims assisted. The Tier 3 TIP ranking that US State Department recently assigned to China and Thailand has been attributed to low numbers of prosecutions and protection. Detaining greater numbers of "victims of trafficking" within government shelters in Thailand and "repatriating"—a euphemism for deporting—undocumented Burmese marriage migrants from China are two strategies that appear to result in quantifiable improvements in the Thai and Chinese governments' metrics with respect to human trafficking.

In addition to political capital, tremendous social capital is accumulated by global North anti-trafficking activists and rescuers as they claim to represent human-trafficking victims and connect with larger transnational advocacy networks and funding streams. In practice, this social capital is converted into economic capital as anti-trafficking activists trade fabricated stories of victimized women and fantastical tales of rescue and freedom to raise funds and as justification for product markup. I document this phenomenon empirically in this book by examining the rise of a cottage industry of "victim repair" through vocational training.

Social movement organizations like Freedom Unchained and Cowboy Rescue purport to provide "freedom" to victims of trafficking, yet they perpetuate the same forms of injustice that they aim to challenge by interweaving racism and classism with labor discipline and new-abolitionist morality. Despite the differences in political regimes in China versus Thailand, the interventions staged by both organizations reproduce inequality by reinscribing low-wage workers onto the global orbit of capitalist production. These workers' victim identities are inseparable from their alleged freedom—and their past labor as sex workers—in part because of the presumption that their freedom can be bought through clients' consumption of the workers' now-virtuous wage labor.

If they reject the label "victims of trafficking," what identities do the alleged subjects of this movement choose instead? Consistent with a growing body of research, I found that they have self-identified as migrant laborers, sex workers, immigrants, parents, lovers, activists, and organizers.[13] Their unique individual experiences as the subjects of the global movement to combat human trafficking constitute a bevy of stories of increased surveillance with few tangible efforts to change their lived realities as people existing at the margins of political power, wealth, and appropriate heteronormativity. This marginalization is exacerbated by the fact that policy makers, NGOs, and activists consistently exclude subjects from anti-trafficking movement-building conversations. Subjects of the movement have shared that when they are asked for their perspectives, it is either through—often uncompensated—interviews with journalists or researchers, or with authors of books and articles that rarely yield any tangible benefits for migrant workers' rights. The ongoing struggles confronting workers mentioned in chapter 6—Jade, Yin, Beam, and Ploy—are conveniently erased from global concern now that they are no longer employed by anti-trafficking NGOs.

GLOBAL RESISTANCE: "SOLIDARITY, NOT SEWING MACHINES"

Rather than rescue, sex workers across the globe have long asked for enforcement of policies concerning employer accountability, health and safety, and protection from police abuse.[14] Sex workers and working-class immigrants have become the unwitting victims of the anti-trafficking movement, and nowhere did I find such efforts more audible than in Thailand, where sex worker and migrant worker rights organizations have launched aggressive campaigns against rescue and rehabilitation efforts by both government shelters and nongovernmental organizations. These interventions—including research about sex workers *by* sex workers, transmission of legal knowledge into the hands of the sex workers, and arts-based responses to injustice—represent formidable models of counterhegemonic movements in that they use the strategies of the carceral state to demonstrate means of survival within it. Two examples of such activism include the creation of a legal manual that explains anti-trafficking laws to sex workers (along with ways to articulate that one is not a victim of trafficking) and the formation of the political activist entity called SWASEAN, Sex Workers of ASEAN, which builds on the ASEAN political economic process and convenes sex workers throughout Southeast Asia for annual advocacy and strategy development.

Organizations like the Empower Foundation struggle with sustainability, organizational autonomy, and survival. The hard line of withdrawal of USAID funding from organizations that support sex work as an occupation represents just the tip of the iceberg in a long-standing global funding regime that prioritizes prostitution's abolition over the health, safety, and rights of sex workers. To understand the enduring effects of sex work's stigmatization in the contemporary era, one need not look much further than the Freedom and Fashion conference, a *New York Times* article, or the latest sensationalist Hollywood exposé that points to sex trafficking as the issue requiring the most advocacy, attention, and financial support in the fight against modern-day slavery. The sensational and moral focus on sex—and the emphasis that sex work is not dignified work—silences important discussions of pervasive global labor exploitation.

The realities of limited low-wage opportunities in the global work-force have been highlighted through numerous forms of international sex worker activism against sex-trafficking abolition. Faced with the onslaught of vocational training programs designed as "exit" strategies from sex work, the Asia Pacific Network of Sex Workers and Thailand's Empower Foundation have designed banners, T-shirts, art installations, and social media campaigns around the themes "Rights Not Rescue" and "No More Sewing Machines," efforts I describe in chapter 3. In China and Thailand, it is primarily gendered forms of low-wage work that are available as alternatives to jewelry making and sex work, including waitressing, garment factory work, and domestic work. In fact, many sex workers have told me that they chose sex work specifi-cally because of the higher wages and abysmal working conditions in garment factories and domestic work.

ORGANIZING FOR MIGRANT WORKER RIGHTS

The labor rights of global migrants continue to be a missing piece of the global movement to combat human trafficking, despite the fact that transnational UN protocols include labor and sexual forms of labor in their definitions. Discussions of (1) vocational training as rehabilitative labor for sex workers; (2) the recruitment of a labor rights NGO to write songs about trafficking; and (3) the disparate global activist poli-tics around sex versus labor trafficking in Thailand all aim to bring critical analysis of labor rights into understandings of the global move-ment to combat human trafficking. In sum, the preceding chapters illustrate how different forms of transnational action through the state and market lead to the global subordination of low-wage women workers. Ultimately, such transnational action is shaped by political economic opportunity structures and constraints in China and Thai-land, and are governed by the motives of nation-states, global govern-ance institutions, NGOs, and activists, yet rarely by the needs of the low-wage migrant workers whom anti-trafficking interventions aim to assist.

If the Empower Foundation's sex worker activism in Thailand chal-lenges the hegemonic social movement agendas described throughout much of this book, what is the response in China? Searching for this answer, I often came up empty-handed during my research in China, where the government has actively suppressed sex worker and labor rights organizing. In June 2014, Chinese sex worker rights activist Ye

Haiyan was barred from leaving the country to attend the International AIDS Conference in Melbourne, Australia, because of her reputation for sex work and HIV advocacy on Twitter.[15] Because Chinese sex worker activists see government corruption and abuse as their primary target, the Chinese sex worker rights movement has maintained little connection to the global anti-trafficking movement.[16] Similarly, China's labor movement has not looked to the global anti-trafficking crusade as a potential source of solidarity or competition. This incompatibility between local and global movements is best highlighted by the collaboration, described in chapter 4, among the New Workers' Artist Troupe, global governance institutions, and the Chinese state. Despite the successful launch of five anti-trafficking rock concerts and a commercial CD, the primary facets of the NGO's actions to raise awareness about labor safety and migrant worker rights are still seen as deeply problematic and destabilizing to government authority.

Amid the pervasive state repression, the global movement to combat trafficking occupies a precious position, as the coveted terrain in which China can build political capital through selective compliance with transnational human rights. The benign position that human trafficking has attained within China's Ministry of Public Security, and the narrow definition of trafficking in Chinese law, has limited the development of an international anti-trafficking rescue industry in China. Although the authoritarian state has precluded vibrant opportunities for counter-hegemonic organizing, it has *not* foreclosed opportunities for sex workers to become inculcated into American rehabilitation programs in Beijing—suggesting the potency of social entrepreneurship even under authoritarianism.[17] This asymmetry between sex worker rights and labor rights organizing in China and Thailand reveals the sharp distinctions that political economies effect in global social movements. Overall, I have argued that the global anti-trafficking movement in China has taken on the characteristics of the state, while the movement in Thailand takes on those of the free market.

FETISHIZING TRANSPARENCY AND THE GLOBAL SUPPLY CHAIN

Long before the term *global supply chain* entered our everyday vocabulary to account for the commodity scarcities caused by COVID-19, its use had begun to pick up speed within the antitrafficking movement. In

2010, the California Supply Chain Transparency Act (SB 657) was the first US law passed of its kind. It requires corporations with global profits in excess of $100 million to provide formal action plans that "disclose their efforts to eradicate slavery and human trafficking from their direct supply chains for goods offered for sale." To date, Walmart, KFC, Lululemon, Amazon, Walgreens, Facebook, Adidas, Hasbro, Pepsi Co, and Apple are among the hundreds of corporations that have issued public statements that outline measures to ensure that "human trafficking and slavery" do not exist in their supply chains—typically statements drafted by a firm's corporate social responsibility departments.[18] Similarly popular legal interventions like the European Union's 2015 Modern Slavery Act and the United Kingdom's 2015 Supply Transparency Act promise that increased supply chain transparency will foster accountability to improve labor conditions. These calls for transparency placed enormous power in the hands of multinational brands and corporations. In this manner, they are similar to jewelry projects in that they call on market-based interventions to remediate workplace abuses.

However, such interventions are underpinned by the exigencies of economic efficiency, which do not consistently align with workers' needs and therefore cannot be depended upon to protect workers' interests. In fact, the United Kingdom Home Office's 2021 independent review of its Modern Slavery Act found that the legislation lacked necessary "teeth" for "businesses [to] take seriously their responsibilities to check their supply chains."[19] Others have similarly argued that the millions of dollars corporations have poured into writing modern-day slavery statements and creating responsible sourcing divisions has really produced scant results, since there are limited measures for implementing these laws.[20] Workers in these supply chains are still grappling with tremendous workplace abuse, conditions that worsened during the pandemic and its aftermath.

Transnational labor activists have demanded private-sector corporate accountability following several disastrous labor rights tragedies during the past decade. The 2013 Rana Plaza building collapse, where 1,129 workers were trapped and killed inside a building that housed more than 5,000 garment workers, primarily suppliers for global retail brands including Walmart, Benetton, and The Children's Place, is an excellent example. Victim advocates and labor rights groups sought compensation for death and injury, as well as improved worker safety and protection. Two global unions, UNI and IndustriALL, came together to negotiate the Bangladesh Accord, which requires workplace safety inspections, reports, and legally binding measures for compliance.[21] When a handful of corporations refused to sign the accord, advocacy groups launched naming-and-shaming campaigns; for instance, several viral internet videos pressured companies such as H&M and the Gap into compliance with the Bangladesh Accord.[22] In a manner parallel to the way jewelry consumers are posed as proponents of change, global North consumers also called on brands to sign the accord. Writing a decade later, however, activists have found scant improvements in occupational health and safety and have argued that the accord's "compliance efforts are a charade" and have done little to achieve justice in the Bangladeshi garment industry.[23]

This book shows that sex workers often turn to sex work after, or concurrently with, working in a host of other low-wage types of work. Fundamentally, I argue, this means that anti-trafficking efforts must account for the garment industry and manufacturing, service, and care work sectors alongside sex work and sex trafficking. In other words, we must care as much about restaurant workers and massage workers as we seemingly do about sex workers. By emphasizing care, I don't mean to suggest that we employ the same types of maternalist rescue and white savior tropes to save women workers in those other industries, but that we devote equal energy and resources to improving working conditions and access to decent work throughout the region. In other words, heeding the call that a rising tide lifts all boats, how can we broaden media attention to demand social protections regardless of type of work or gender?

Fetishizing private sector accountability also strengthens state power: for instance, Chinese and Thai economic desires to promote an environment welcoming to foreign manufacturing has stifled worker protest. These state contexts are important for understanding the precarious legal positioning of labor unions in authoritarian China, where they are run by the government, and in Thailand, where only a small and select group of industries have a union.[24] The pandemic threw into sharp relief the limits of relying on the norms and interests of consumptive habits and transnational policies of the global North. Worker-led efforts, rather than corporation- or consumer-led ones, change the focus to the ideas and needs of workers themselves. Rarely have efforts toward supply chain transparency brought attention to worker organizing; in fact, most have overshadowed it.

APPROACHES TO WORKER ORGANIZING

What, then, is a worker-organizing approach, and how is it different from prevailing anti-trafficking approaches? Stories and examples of worker organizing efforts have been folded into the preceding chapters in many ways. In China, the New Worker Artist Troupe fought to incorporate accounts of everyday workplace abuses, and in particular students intern abuses, in songs that the United Nations had commissioned them to write about human trafficking. The Asia Pacific Network of Sex Workers' "Bad Rehab" music video depicts the violence that Cambodian sex workers have experienced in anti-trafficking programs run by the government and NGOs alike. Asia Wage Floor Alliance and Global Labor Justice have launched numerous campaigns that call for an end to gender-based violence and discrimination in garment factories throughout Southeast Asia. In addition to the numerous forms of organizing and advocacy already outlined in these chapters, during the pandemic, Empower ran a mutual aid effort that redistributed rice, tampons, and other essentials to workers who were excluded from Thai government assistance. The notable exclusions included sex workers and those who lacked a Thai identity card. Commenting about Empower's mutual aid work, a Burmese migrant worker told a Reuters journalist, "If it wasn't for Empower, I would have committed suicide."[25] Empower's Can-Do Bar has, since 2006, modeled the sex worker–owned cooperative business. Worker-owned cooperatives present one way to shift the relationships of power inherently built into businesses and offer a new horizon of powerful forms of organization for formerly incarcerated workers, sex workers, and migrants.[26] The above are all forms of organizing that prioritize building worker power, as opposed to raids, rescue, and rehabilitation.

Elsewhere in the region, worker organization led by women is reaching formidable and unprecedented heights. In 2019, the Federation of Garment Workers Myanmar (FGWM) formed the first women-led industrial union in Yangon. Despite limited financial and popular support for building worker capacity to organize, and limited media reporting of worker strikes, Myanmar garment workers have mobilized diverse forms of collective action in recent years. Reports estimate that thousands of workers have participated in myriad forms of protest, calling for reforms including an improvement in working conditions, arbitration mechanisms for internal disputes, and more severe consequences for employers who violate labor laws. At one factory in 2019, management agreed to all forty-five demands initiated by the striking garment workers, including addressing concerns over health and safety, wages and benefits, and excessive working hours. Strikers have even joined in solidarity to call on officials to enact and enforce their policies, demanding resignations for lack of action. The strikes led by garment factory workers in Myanmar demonstrate direct organizing's broader importance and potential as a means through which laborers can alter decidedly unjust working conditions; however, workers also participate in less visible modes of resistance. Facing various threats if they staged a strike, workers have also turned to internal factory actions, including workplace sit-ins, singing songs, and wearing red bandanas as ways of mounting unified protest during their workdays. Surviving both a pandemic and a coup, the worker organizing capacities of FGWM translated into political organizing savvy that placed them on the front lines of the civil disobedience movement following the 2021 military coup in Myanmar.[27]

Women workers in South Asia have also demonstrated the power of worker organizing across intersecting identities. In April 2022 a Dalit-led and majority women trade union of textile workers helped bring forward the *Dindigul Agreement*, an enforceable agreement which promotes the elimination of gender-based violence and harassment and raises standards in the global garment industry. The collaboration between worker organizers in the Tamil Nadu Textile and Common Labour Union alongside the Asia Floor Wage Alliance and Global Labor Justice-International Labor Rights Forum, demonstrates the power of organizing at the intersection of gender, labor, and caste-based justice.

Worker organizing is not always possible in situations of employer or state repression or under the criminalization of migration and sex work, but worker resistance is always present. Organizing amplifies the ability of individual acts of resistance to gain voice and traction, as seen throughout this book. Organizing offers a path out of employer co-optation of resistance—likely a reason that so many workers have turned to organizing in the Asia-Pacific region. Worker-organizing strategies reframe relationships of power and authority and weaken the propensity of worker exploitation. Their successes indicate that the existing problems in a supply chain, especially regarding exploitation and accountability, would be best addressed by turning more power directly over to workers, in contrast to efforts at alleviating abuses via allocating additional power to governments, corporations, and consumers. Organizing workers is brutally mundane, grinding work, however. It is not sexy. The wins are rare. The gains are often invisible and thus remain drastically underfunded. Worker-organizing strategies need political support, and they need funding.

REDISTRIBUTION AND DEFUNDING ANTI-TRAFFICKING

In 2021 alone, a select number of US anti-trafficking organizations described within this book cumulatively reported revenues of just under 200 million USD. According to GuideStar, an independent American nonprofit organization database, Cowboy Rescue and Freedom Unchained have combined total gross receipts over 3.3 million USD. Paramilitary group NVADER/Lift International's 2021 annual budget was 1.89 million USD, while Operation Underground Railroad's annual income reached 44 million USD. The Nomi Network, which runs vocational training programs for victims of trafficking in Cambodia and India, reported an annual budget of 3.6 million USD, while the Polaris Project, which runs the US anti-trafficking hotline, had a 2021 annual revenue of 22.9 million USD. The evangelical Christian organization International Justice Mission tops all of these with an astounding 140 million–USD annual budget to support its anti-trafficking work in Thailand, Myanmar, Cambodia, Ghana, and other places around the world.[28] These annual revenue figures suggest that there is no shortage of funding available for anti-trafficking work.

Racialized anti-trafficking rescue and rehabilitation narratives are indisputably popular. As such, they cast an enormous shadow on alternative mobilizations already undertaken by groups working toward systemic forms of racial and economic justice. What would a world look like if the 2021 revenues of these anti-trafficking efforts were redistributed to workers themselves? There are already many possible ongoing policy proposals that map out how this might be possible: by organizing universal basic income programs, supporting worker-organizing capacity training, offering reparations for legacies of militarized sexual commerce throughout Thailand, and by supporting efforts to decriminalize sex work and end the racialized policing of poverty. Can we, for instance, envision anti-trafficking vocational training programs that do not mandate exit from sex work, or that offer possibilities through industries that don't teach gendered, niche crafts like making jewelry, tote bags, or pajamas? Can we pair vocational training with a dramatic shift in labor relations so that employer-employee relations are more just? One example of shifting labor relations is worker-owned cooperative businesses, which drastically shift power relations in the workplace. How can we critically conceive of a process of redistribution, as the evidence urges us to do?

Because anti-trafficking organizations have not embraced redistributive ethics yet, groups organizing at the intersections of sex worker, migrant, and racial justice have already strategized ways of funding their work outside the anti-trafficking industrial complex. In 2019, Red Canary Song, a grassroots collective of migrant workers, sex workers, and their allies in New York hosted its first annual fundraiser, "Red Canary Screams." Envisioned by queer BDSM educator and professional dominatrix Yin Q, the event was produced by Kink Out, a BDSM art and culture collective. The event raised nearly 23,000 USD, garnered through paid flogging and boot-licking stations around the periphery of the dance floor, a silent auction of BDSM gifts and services, merchandise sales, and sold-out ticket sales. Red Canary Song used the no-strings-attached cash to support monthly mutual aid to massage workers in Flushing throughout the COVID-19 pandemic—at the same time that anti-trafficking organizations were raising funds to police Asian massage work as a site of human trafficking. Sex worker groups have long demonstrated the promises of mutual aid and community care as just some possible pathways to liberation. Rather than seek funding in the fraught anti-trafficking landscape, they have generated funding from within Asian diasporic sex worker communities.[29]

Defunding anti-trafficking is about not merely massively redistributing the donations and profits accumulated by anti-trafficking interventions, but also shifting sources of expertise to focus on impacted communities. The call to decenter expertise requires journalists, mass media, and funders to shift their attention away from reporting from the perspectives of global North NGOs and their founders. It also calls upon university researchers like me to move out of the way so as not only to bring underrepresented voices to the table but also to allow them to create the agenda and be amply compensated for doing so. This involves moving beyond tokenizing models of community-engaged research toward the roadmap that Linda Tuhiwai Smith has sketched for Indigenous research, which disperses power from institutions that have historically subjugated Indigenous knowledge while grossly profiting from it.[30] While Smith and many other Indigenous scholars write particularly of settler colonial sources of institutional power and knowledge consolidation, I believe these are powerful lessons and roadmaps to apply to cases of militarism, imperialism, and racist legacies of research design and implementation. For instance, of Smith's powerfully articulated twenty-five Indigenous research projects, Empower's Hit and Run research and embroidery work strikes a resonant chord. These works and numerous other research projects are conceived, funded, directed, acted, threaded, and researched entirely by sex workers from the global South.

Connecting the threads of this project, from vocational training programs to state-sponsored awareness campaigns, to government shelters and global activism, and across spirituality, morality, and politics, one central question connects most actors: What constitutes good work?[31] Posing this simple query across different levels of the movement reveals the contrasting institutional and moral commitments that different actors hold. Evangelical Christian activists suggest the frame of dignified work, which to them means work that aligns with morally acceptable Western notions of family, gender, and sexuality. Global governance institutions like the United Nations align with nation-states and stand behind legal parameters of work and decent working conditions, as delineated in national laws and law enforcement. Low-wage women workers and migrant laborers (including men) appear to be consistently caught between limited opportunities, oppressive morality, and unsatisfactory laws. Equally important, they seek racial, gender, caste-based justice and the decriminalization of sex work, migration, and poverty. As long as projects to help workers are founded chiefly to satisfy the emotional needs of the racialized global North—or, as Teju Cole has tweeted, "the emotional needs of white people and Oprah"[32]—we will continue to miss these vital pieces.

The global, ubiquitously sentimental use of the phrase "modern-day slavery," synonymous now with "human trafficking," subordinates considerations of the nuanced political economies of sexual commerce and nonsexual labor, which are subsumed by the promise of transnational movements and fair-trade markets to replace and correct abusive state power and employer relationships. These human trafficking interventions reproduce the subordination of women across racial and national borders at the discursive and labor process levels. The resulting and reinforced assumptions about Asian women's labor in China and Thailand—and American women's consumption and activism on their behalf—have created new racial-national hierarchies across the global governance of human trafficking and the grassroots lives it intends to impact.

Acknowledgments

The best part of closing an ethnography about rehabilitation, redemption, and salvation is thanking all the people who have saved me along the way. This alternate framing of rescue was first offered to me by the sex workers and activists of the Empower Foundation in Chiang Mai, Thailand. Chatchalawan Muangjan, Maleerat Van Driesdan, Mai Cando, and Liz Hilton buoyed me with their wit, insight, and irreverence and inspired me with their research, advocacy, and dedication to accessibility. Their patience in the face of a four-decade-long struggle for sex worker and migrant worker rights is matched only by their boundless creativity while leading a global movement that demands accountability from the government and everyone who walks through the doors of the Can-Do Bar. In Bangkok, the Global Alliance Against Traffic in Women (GAATW) offered me desk space in which to think, write, and collaborate. Thank you to Bandana Pattanaik, Alfie Gordo, Apivart (Nong) Chaison, Bobby Garasimov, Kate Scheill, and Rebecca Napier-Moore for sheltering me in the Sivalai compound. Also in Bangkok, the Asia Pacific Network of Sex Workers (APNSW) community offered immense inspiration through art, photography, and other musings. Thanks to Dale Kongmot, Tracey Tully, and the late Andrew Hunter for sharing books and stories, along with good art and beer.

In 2005, Fu Guosheng rescued me from my first United Nations conference in Ruili, a small border town on the China-Myanmar border. 果果 and I shared mutual restlessness over the excess of global experts and conference banquets, and we left the conference early to bring fancy restaurant leftovers to youth living in a nearby town. Her politics of redistribution and care have grounded this work for two decades. That same year, David Feingold and the late Heather Peters were kind enough to meet me at the Blue Bird café in Kunming, China. I had just graduated from college and was thrilled to be researching human trafficking in China. They graciously advised me to dial the enthusiasm down several notches in order to understand the nuance and interrogate the space between global and local understandings of trafficking. Lin Lixia and Guo Jianmei, at the Beijing University Center for Women's Law Studies and Legal Aid, were outstanding teachers and hosts, for years after my yearlong internship in 2005. At the United Nations Inter-Agency Program on Human Trafficking, I thank Wu Yiping, Wang Yi, He Yunxiao, Ms. Wang, and Lisa Rende-Taylor.

This project is indebted to numerous organizations, both at the grassroots and global governance levels. I thank the anonymous evangelical Christian social enterprises for allowing me to participate as a volunteer with their work in Bangkok, Beijing, and Los Angeles. This book is forever inspired by the women workers I am lucky to know and write about; thank you for your trust, friendship, and wisdom.

I returned to graduate school in the sociology doctoral program at UCLA in 2007. Bill Roy's love of music and social movements inspired me to want to study them. Ruben Hernandez-Leon, Roger Waldinger, and Adrian Favell helped me find my space within the international migration canon and continued to support me when I strayed from it. Vilma Ortiz, Min Zhou, and Ed Walker rounded out my grad school education in the areas of race, ethnicity, and political sociology and, most pivotally, inspired me with how they mentor grad students. Gail Kligman was the chair of my MA committee, member of my dissertation committee, and created a thriving intellectual community at UCLA in which to study human trafficking. Gabriel Rossman, the second reader on that MA committee, gave me crucial foundations for how to think at the intersection of anti-trafficking markets and their cultural inflections. Chris Tilly helped me make connections between microscale labor politics in vocational training and broader histories of labor organizing in the United States and across the global South.

My dissertation advisor, Ching Kwan Lee, met me at every stage of this project, providing profound insights, inspiration, encouragement, and motivation to make it better. I would return from months in China and Thailand, and CK would help me digest my fieldwork and then immediately challenge me to find and explore bigger and more fascinating empirical and theoretical puzzles. CK's work has unveiled so much about power in every realm of my personal and professional life. I value her investment in ethnography as an important tool for understanding the relationship between power, subjugation, and resistance. Her research has answered so many questions, and inspired so many more.

I have had the privilege to travel, research, plan conferences, and write with Elizabeth Bernstein. Thank you for planting the seeds of so many ideas and giving me space and encouragement to develop them. Thanks also for rearranging them when needed, providing venues for me to share my work, and introducing me to a vibrant community of sex worker scholars and activists in North America and Thailand.

In Los Angeles, I found a wonderful community for developing my sociological imagination. I met Hyeyoung Oh Nelson, Rennie Lee, Caitlin Patler, and David Trouille on the first day of graduate school and relished the communities we built outside Haines Hall. Forrest Stuart's passion for the perfect vignette has filled our lives with magical ethnographic storytelling, now perfectly repurposed for toddler story hour. Laura Orrico has gifted me friendship filled with never-ending talks about gender, power, and ethnography. Anthony Ocampo made our computer labs livable with grocery store rotisserie chicken and a West Hollywood escape plan. AJ Kim and I have been in each others lives since college and have shared nearly two decades of all-nighters and collaborative hustling. Jennifer Musto and Diya Bose have been wonderful interlocutors and friends who have shared stories on the front lines of anti-trafficking research. A fellowship from the Social Science Research Council International Dissertation Research Fellowship brought me into a lifetime intellectual community and friendship with Mimi Kim, Janice Gallagher, and Marie Berry. Thanks to Montae Langston and Luis Medina for listening to me talk about this work for years and offering your insights and criticisms. Tony Ochoa, Raymond Contreras, JR Sambrano, and Marcos Santiago: your love is a massive safety net that has drowned out recurring doubt; thanks for always catching me when my flip-flops slip out from under me.

I am indebted to a lineage of critical anti-trafficking scholars. I read Kamala Kempadoo's work with awe as an undergraduate and never thought I'd be so lucky as to work with Kamala as a feminist anti-racist collaborator. Janie Chuang and JJ Rosenbaum are badass lawyer scholar activists whose brilliance has paved the way for this work and inspires me endlessly. Samuel Okyere is always ready to tell me a story that causes me to lose sleep, and I'm so grateful to have him as a comrade working across the world. Gabriella Sanchez, Cameron Thibos, and Julia O'Connell Davidson round out a formidable OpenDemocracy *Beyond Trafficking and Slavery* editorial team, and I am lucky to learn from ongoing collaborations with them. Kimberly Kay Hoang, Maria Cecilia Hwang, and Rhacel Parreñas have offered brilliant and generous comradery as Asian / American feminist ethnographers working on sexual politics in Asia: I have learned so much from your work and am grateful for every word of mine you have read and made better—I am deeply influenced by your insights. Nicola Mai and Sine Plambech's visual ethnographies and films have been incredible teaching and learning tools. Rebecca Surtees has been a cherished mentor, welcoming me with a cold beer and unparalleled research advice and ethical guidance. Finally, Lyndsey Beutin's "no shortcuts will suffice" attitude toward unearthing and squashing every last node of white supremacy makes her the best cheerleader, wordsmith, and late-night texting and accountability partner; thank you for getting me to the finish line.

Sex worker rights activists at BAYSWAN, Butterfly Migrant Sex Workers Project, and Ocean State A$$ have been energizing collaborators. Carol Leigh, Elene Lam, Julianna Brown, prabh singh kahal, and Claire Macon have been a constant source of inspiration. Yin Q, Charlotte, Yeonhoo Cho, Eunbi Lee, Esther Kao, Yves Tong Nguyen, Wu, Edward Ye, Lisa, Lyn, and Chong Gu of Red Canary Song, lead the way in anti-carceral and sex worker–led models of organizing that talk back to paternalistic anti-trafficking interventions and have made RCS an empowering site of retreat and growth the past four years as I finished the book.

A wonderful community of scholars, mentors, collaborators, and friends was vital to this book. We met as budding researchers in Beijing twenty years ago, and legal scholars Alex Wang and Aaron Halegua continue to teach me today. Eli Friedman's ethnographic work and labor organizing around China are an inspiration to me. Julia Chang is my sounding board around feminist academic motherhood and models how to navigate our challenging occupational hazards. Hae Yeon Choo, Leisy Abrego, Nishant Upadhyay, Mimi Thi Nguyen, Jennifer Jihye Chun, Pei-Chia Lan, and Joya Misra have been formidable feminist mentors and friends. Catherine Scheer and the team at ARI Project on Religion provided incredible feedback on the techno-politics of vocational training alongside religious development initiatives in Southeast Asia. Ye Yint Khang Maung, Ma Moe Sandar Myint, Thet Hnin Aye, Ben Harkins, and Jenna Holliday gave me their patience and inspiration in discussing parallels between these cases and those of powerful women workers and rehabilitation programs in Yangon.

Many people read portions of this work and offered deep editorial insights. Chanelle Adams, Katherine Chin, and Ricardo Jaramillo taught me so much about the craft of writing through their own lyrical prose. Anitra Grisales offered vital developmental edits that helped me move from dissertation to book and encouraged me to find my own voice. My wonderful UC Press editor, Naomi Schneider, shepherded me through the intimidating process with encouragement and offered a wonderful home for this book. Rene Almeling and Sharmila Rudrappa offered generous comments and criticisms of multiple drafts of this manuscript throughout the pandemic. Steven Baker's copyediting and Emily Park's production expertise have been last-stage gifts of skill and care to make my manuscript legible to the world. Sanya Hyland composed the index for this book, an aside to her masterful artistic inspirations and friendship. Glynnis Koike illustrated the book's cover, visualizing this work beyond my wildest dreams.

This research would not have been possible without generous funding from UCLA's Graduate Division, Department of Sociology, Center for the Study of Women, Institute for Research on Labor and Employment, Asia Institute, Center for Chinese Studies, and Center for Southeast Asian Studies. I received invaluable fellowships that supported fieldwork, writing, and offered mentorship through the Social Science Research Council, Ford Foundation Dissertation Fellowship, Institute for Citizens and Scholars, and the American Sociological Association Minority Fellowship Program. Sidney Tarrow and Doug McAdam were intrepid leaders of the Contentious Politics Gang through the SSRC Dissertation Proposal Development Fellowship, and their support and feedback have been vital to this project. A faculty fellowship in Human Trafficking and Modern Day Slavery, at Yale University's Gilder Lehrman Center for the Study of Slavery Resistance and Abolition, allowed me time to write and brought me into wonderful community with David Blight, Michelle Zacks, Wendy Hesford, Jessica Pliley, Genevieve LeBaron, and Christienna Fryar.

In 2014, I moved to Providence, Rhode Island. Brown University's Watson Institute was a special landing spot for a postdoc where I enjoyed late-night conversations over Clément with Janice Gallagher and Deepak Lamba-Nieves. Rick Locke, a preeminent expert on labor and global supply chains, embraced this work and offered detailed comments that helped a sociologist speak to larger global conversations about supply chains. Coteaching a course with Michael Rodriguez Muniz fostered a friendship anchored in my deep admiration of Michael's approach to community-based work, his humility, and will-ingness to drop everything and join me in a probing internet search. The Watson Institute hosted a book manuscript workshop and invited Rene Almeling, Janie Chuang, and Andre Willis as wonderfully generous and brilliant commentators. Rene happened also to be my assigned mentor as a first-year graduate student at UCLA and, since 2007, has been a wonderful and generous sounding board against doubt, tears, and fears, and simply, the best role model.

As a junior faculty member in the Department of American Studies and Eth-nic Studies, I have the most loving and supportive community. Adrienne Keene is an unrivaled partner in the forensic obsession with truth and deception, and a body of water to plunge into. Her selfless approach to public engagement inspires me endlessly. Letitia Alvarado has shared so much wisdom with me, and her texts about cool Latinx sex worker art activations from her own research have illustrated the beauty of interdisciplinary friendship. Susan Smulyan saw and understood this work as an American studies and ethnic stud-ies project from day one and encouraged me to push the boundaries of interdis-ciplinarity. Susan has also kept my family fed and well read. Matt Guterl has been a sounding board for everything from weird idioms to urgent crises to random citation recommendations and everything in between. Evelyn Hu De-Hart, Bob Lee, and Debbie Weinstein have paved the way with equal parts inspiration, levity, and love. Kiri Miller, Aliyyah Abdur-Rahman, and Ralph Rodriguez supported me through the years with detailed work pouring through annual reviews, accompanied with wonderful feedback and mentorship. I am lucky to call our department administrator extraordinaire, Carrie Cardoso, a dear friend. Across the quad, Nitsan Chorev, Jose Itzigsohn, Michael Kennedy, and Patrick Heller have made the Department of Sociology a welcome second home and have been so generous with their time and mentorship.

My incredible colleagues at the Center for the Study of Slavery and Justice have supported the successive incarnations of this work through our Human Trafficking Research Cluster. Thanks so much to Tony Bogues, Shana Wein-berg, and Maiyah Gamble Rivers. The Center for the Study of Race and Ethnic-ity in the Americas has also been a vital home where I could cultivate ideas, revise them, and share them with a brilliant community of scholars. Thanks to Tricia Rose and Stéphanie Larrieux for fostering a community that grounds joy and justice. Colleagues across the university offered so much inspiration: Emily Owens has been an intellectual inspiration, and it's been fun discussing the stun-ning parallels in our work while our kids play together. Daniel Rodriguez and Susan Rohwer immediately made Brown feel like home when they threw the Spread sex worker book event my first year there. Francoise Hamlin and Nancy Khalek have built and nurtured a Faculty of Color network at Brown and have been cherished mentors and friends. Thanks to research assistance from Penel-ope Kyritsis, Aarish Rojiani, Beka Yang, Agnes Chang, and Angie Baecker.

Sarath Suong and Kohei Ishihara welcomed and inspired me into a beautiful movement family in Rhode Island and have nourished my flesh and soul with food from the farm and secret-recipe ingredients to keep things spicy. Yvette Koch, Wes Parker, and Gina Rodriguez–Drix have been birth and life doulas, offering vital support, a shoulder to cry on, and reminders to celebrate. Frances

Smith, thank you for years of Thai interpretation, linguistic and everything else. Sometimes we can go years without having a three-way Skype call, yet the rush of tears and laughter each time remind me of the deep and loving respect I have for the life you and Ploy have built together. Sam Shweisky taught me that it's important to find a routine, so you can chart a path off of it. My cousins Jenny Yang, Isabella Wang, Debbie Chang, and Rebecca Kaye have shown me a lifetime of sisterhood. My lifelong friends Michelle Lo, Morna Ha, and Sarah Kalhorn continue to celebrate every landmark along the way and never stopped asking about my book.

I remain ever grateful for my undergrad advisors at Pomona College, Samuel Yamashita, Kyoko Kurita, David Elliott, Laura Kuo, Nana Osei-Kofei, and the late Katherine Hagedorn, for teaching me how to read and write, giving me the confidence to pursue doctoral work, and challenging me to see the interdisciplinary possibilities in Asian studies and women's studies.

I owe a great debt to my family. My uncle Dali asked me to read this book to him while he was dying, and he moved the oxygen mask aside to tell me, "The sentences are too long," a loving jab to the academy that he knew so well, and bravely left. He and his wife, June Ritchie, always brought humor and a healthy dose of reality to the graduate school process. My brother Kevin has been my partner in crime in so many life pursuits—as a beach volleyball partner, as a fellow undergrad at the Claremont Colleges, through graduate school, and as junior faculty. It's such a delight to watch you, Ellen Wang, Caden, and Rio grow together. Joyce and Donald Larson sheltered our family in so many places; thank you for your newspaper clippings, recipes, and endless love and care.

My dad taught us that everything he ever needed to learn he learned on the volleyball court, and that is where I learned how to be an ethnographer. My mom taught me to question everything relentlessly and always offered a healing refuge when I had burned the candle at both ends. She is how and why motherhood and care work were main pillars of my orientation even before I had kids. This book is dedicated to my amazing parents, Ruby and Davi.

Eric Larson fills our house with library books, Tupperware, scavenged posters, tracked changes, and more love, wit, music, and single socks than anyone could possibly pair. Thank you for cultivating the deep love language of labor organizing into our life and work together across three continents. Whether in Ruili or Pawtucket, on Calle Citlaltepetl or Lilac Lane, I am so lucky to build a home with you wherever we go. Rui Rui and River, thank you for a life full of bedtime stories and bedtime protests: here is one more.

The Embodied Currencies and Debts of Global Feminist Fieldwork

My fieldwork was marked by equal parts joy, fear, guilt, and rage. It began in an ethnographic methods course during my first semester of graduate school at UCLA with discrete assignments and a certain and necessary bounded space. Fifteen years later, it has unraveled into a sprawling mess that is bounded neither by geography nor by time but rather by beautiful friendships, inventive ways of communicating transnationally, and shared rites of passage encompassing birth, death, breakups, and all that exists in between. I was elated to form relationships with workers that allowed me to understand the everyday processes of resistance and survival. I was enraged by the power asymmetries that permitted certain narratives to travel well while largely silencing others. I embodied those very asymmetries with the global mobility of a US passport that enabled me to travel freely in between the sites of production and consumption of a global ethical commodity chain. And I was crippled with guilt that I would not tell these stories in a way that the world needed to hear them, or fear that I would tell them in a way that would bring on only more surveillance, scrutiny, or silence over workers lives. Workers taught me to become comfortable with those silences. And to live at peace that certain "data points" would not make it into these pages because they would jeopardize the small interstitial ways that workers have carved out paths of daily survival.

My Institutional Review Board (IRB) at UCLA required me to use pseudonyms for the organizations and people with whom I conducted ethnography. While I have strived to remove identifiable features from their descriptions, I have struggled with who and what such anonymity protects. Liz Hilton at the Empower Foundation once told me that my choice to not name organizations made my academic written work a "soft cock." I remain troubled by how the ethical responsibility to the IRB often betrays responsibilities to people who are living under repressive state regimes and oppressive labor systems. Even in attempts to write about power, powerful institutions remain protected. My own fears of litigation were realized when one of the peer-reviewed journal editorial boards I sit on was threatened with a libel lawsuit by a prominent anti-trafficking organization—whose name appears in these pages—that disagreed with a researcher's article about them. When trying to explain the concept of libel to Chinese and Thai workers, we quickly arrived at a shared understanding that the threat of a libel suit is often used to uphold status quo relations of power.

Heeding the call to explore power in varying dimensions, I followed "slave-free jewelry" from its sites of consumption in Los Angeles to its sites of production in Beijing and Bangkok. As a participant-observer volunteer in different organizations, I gained access to different actors in the movement—government officials, the United Nations, consumers, NGO workers, activists, trafficking survivors, and sex workers. My mobility through these different sites has required critical assessments of my positionality, and I have drawn from the foundational premises of reflexive feminist ethnography, which demands that researchers address and acknowledge fundamental power inequalities between researchers and research subjects, in search of an "ethical field relationship."[1] Feminist ethnographers have the responsibility to take an active role in creating a more egalitarian research relationship: "Discussions of feminist methodology generally assault the hierarchical, exploitative relationship of conventional research, urging feminist researchers to seek instead an egalitarian research process characterized by authenticity, reciprocity, and inter-subjectivity between the researcher and her 'subjects.'"[2] Early scholarship in feminist ethnography critiqued the fact that most research was conducted by women of privilege about research subjects with considerably less race and class privilege.[3]

Women of color and Third World researchers contributed to these debates by discussing methodological issues of "insider" versus "outsider" status. Pat Zavella's Chicana identity, and thus her position as a coethnic insider, allowed her unique access to and firsthand knowledge of her research subjects: "Insiders are more likely to be cognizant and accepting of complexity and internal variation, are better able to understand the nuances of language use, will avoid being duped by informants who create cultural performances for their own purposes, and are less apt to be distrusted by those they study."[4] At the same time, the insider deals with another set of political exigencies, which do not necessarily indicate that this work is biased or lacking rigor, as will sometimes be accused: "With one's insider status comes the responsibility to construct analyses that are sympathetic to ethnic interests."[5]

Feminist reflections on researcher positionality are useful for explaining how global ethnographic approaches are appropriate to studying transnational social movements. Maria Mies argued that a researcher's ethnic or class identity is not as significant for good research as is one's outlook, and advocates a "view from below."[6] Seeking to resolve power inequalities between researchers and their subjects, feminist ethnographers have advocated "studying up" rather than "studying down." In shifting the research agenda in this direction, they seek to examine how power is created and maintained.[7] Studying those in positions of power can reveal the underlying structures that create and sustain ideologies of dominance. While "studying up" resolves some ethical dilemmas regarding power dynamics between researchers and subjects, Tsing points out, doing so in isolation does not necessarily "de-colonize" the center, as some have hoped, but rather more deeply ensconces power as a static and unfixed object.[8] Rather than study up or down, my global ethnography studies the transnational anti-trafficking movement across particular positions in order to examine how power is relational and mutually constructed and contested.

As a middle-class Chinese American graduate student in sociology, I was at once an insider and an outsider across the different sites in this research and, accordingly, have framed my methodological approach to ethnography as one who transcends "studying up" and "studying down" by aiming to "study across" the intersubjective layers of the anti-trafficking movement. This approach is motivated by a belief that the practice of global and multisited ethnography offers many possibilities for studies of transnational social movements.

ACCESS AND ETHICS

This global ethnography began in Southern California in the fall of 2007 when, almost weekly, one could find a human trafficking event happening somewhere around town. As part of an ethnographic methods course during my first year of graduate school at UCLA, I sought out these venues as "sites" for the field practicum component of the class. I spent about eight hours a week attending anti-trafficking meet-up groups, church seminars, academic talks and conferences, art shows, public lectures, movie screenings, music concerts, and numerous anti-trafficking fairs.

It was through the large anti-trafficking fairs that I first learned of Cowboy Rescue's and Freedom Unchained's work in Thailand and China. I was excited to discover the global connections of this work, having just moved back to the United States after spending three years in China. Just prior to beginning graduate school, I spent two years building a community art program on the China-Myanmar border, which provided no-cost arts education to ethnic-minority youth dealing with drug trafficking, the HIV/AIDS epidemic, and parental incarceration. I stumbled upon these jewelry projects at a moment when I was vitally interested in researching and writing a PhD dissertation that explored forms of cultural activism, and my excitement was piqued because of the creative and transformative possibilities of making jewelry as a part of trafficking rehabilitation.

I inquired about volunteer opportunities at Cowboy Rescue and Freedom Unchained offices in Los Angeles, and shared that I was a graduate student at UCLA developing a Master's thesis on human-trafficking activism. Cowboy Rescue's US director welcomed volunteers and mentioned that many other full-time students were participating in summer-long or semester-long internships. Volunteers were in high demand to staff the large, twice-monthly jewelry sales events held at various venues. Each quarter, the LA office would also perform a large inventory analysis to assess which pieces were needed from the Bangkok office. Many volunteers also met weekly for Bible study that focused on human trafficking, did a human trafficking street-walk outreach to identify trafficked persons, and attended worship services together at a social justice–oriented nondenominational evangelical Christian church in Los Angeles.

Freedom Unchained also had a small base of operation in Los Angeles, run primarily by a graduate student in public health at UCLA who was also one of the organization's cofounders. By spring 2008, I was embedded as a weekly volunteer at both Freedom Unchained and Cowboy Rescue. For a total of twenty nonconsecutive months of fieldwork in Southern California over four years, I assisted in the office once a week, participated in outreach, attended church services and meetings, and sold jewelry in various venues. Cowboy's Los Angeles office was a base for shipment, sales, and marketing, and it also ran several anti-trafficking awareness and outreach programs in the area. I assisted with all matters relating to the business side of operations, including collecting inventory; packing and shipping jewelry orders; liaising with customers and the Bangkok office; organizing and hosting jewelry sales; and participating in local outreach activities. Freedom Unchained did not have a formal office in Los Angeles; however, its main operations director was based in the city and organized home jewelry sales, advocacy, and awareness events. As a volunteer for both organizations and participant observer of the anti-trafficking movement at large, I have attended more than forty different formal sales events, primarily at local churches, large anti-trafficking conferences, and fair trade craft fairs. I have worked as a host selling jewelry in more than a dozen in-home jewelry parties.

I took my first trip to the sites of jewelry production in Bangkok and Beijing in June 2008. I was jittery with excitement as I imagined finally meeting the women who made the jewelry I had become so intimately familiar with. Well versed in the marketing scripts for the jewelry, I also felt nervous. It seemed I had been speaking on behalf of these women for nearly half a year before meeting them in person, and my feminist sensibilities were unsettled by the audacity of such a relationship. As a full-time volunteer at Cowboy Rescue and Freedom Unchained's offices in Bangkok and Beijing, I was in the company of several other short- and long-term volunteers on church-organized mission trips. Unlike those volunteers who were guided by their faith relationship with the organizations, I accessed both organizations via three intersecting identities and interests: (1) my prior volunteer work for the organizations' Los Angeles offices, (2) my experience establishing an arts program for ethnic minority youth and migrant street youth on the China-Myanmar border, and (3) my curiosity as a graduate student conducting research on various pathways to human trafficking assistance.

In Beijing and Bangkok, I spent about four hours every day making jewelry, cooking, and participating in worship alongside the workers, and an additional four hours assisting activists with administration, programming, and outreach. I continued this daily routine for three summers, in 2008, 2009, and 2010. During the workweek at Freedom Unchained in Beijing, I helped translate for visiting English-speaking groups and organized leisure activities for workers after the workday, including craft activities and different workshops in the dormitory. More informally, I developed friendships with workers as we prepared meals, shopped, went to internet cafés, and sometimes took extended weekend trips to visit their hometowns.

In Bangkok, my volunteer duties were more regimented because of Cowboy's institutionalized international volunteer and missionary program, which hosts four to five short-term missionaries per year. Having previously volunteered over two hundred hours at Cowboy Rescue's inventory and sales distribution sites in Los Angeles, I was able to process online sales orders, take inventory, and occasionally assist with English-language classes in Bangkok. When the workday ended, I left with the workers and participated in their lives outside work. In Beijing this was restricted to short walks about the compound or, on rare occasions, taking a twenty-minute bus ride to the nearest commercial center to buy cosmetics or hair supplies. In Bangkok, the after-work activities were more diverse, usually taking the form of walks in the park, followed by dinner at a local food stall. Sometimes I would accompany workers to their second jobs, at local restaurants or at the train station, to get a sense of how work at Cowboy Rescue contrasted with other work in Bangkok.

By my third summer of research, in 2010, I reached the point that ethnographers refer to as saturation: I was continuing to see the same "data points" emerge day in and day out. However, my decision to leave the jewelry shop floor was not informed by a calculus of methodological rigor. From a research design perspective, my advisor, Ching Kwan Lee, encouraged me to understand this as a political sociology project and shift to a secular-versus-faith-based case comparison. Around this time, I personally sought a shift in ethnographic research sites because I felt my presence was becoming intrusive: workers entrusted me with both the joys and frustrations of work, but activists were unwilling to respond to different criticisms that had been launched. Although I started my fieldwork optimistic about jewelry making as a form of cultural activism, as I immersed myself in the participant observation on the shop floor, workers seemed to interrogate the confusing duality between manual labor and spiritual reform. During my first two years of research, I rarely spoke back to activists, whom I considered to be my generous hosts. However, by my third summer of research, I often raised questions with activists, but found them to be quickly shot down or, as evidenced in chapter 3, co-opted sometimes to enact more rigid forms of surveillance on workers. I began to feel as if we had reached a stalemate, an impasse that motivates many of the questions in this book: workers often shared that expectations of religious observance and virtuous behavior posed intrusions into personal rights and autonomy in the workplace; by contrast, activists believed that the lack of spirituality was one of the root causes of human trafficking.

Since I left the jewelry production sites in 2010, I have stayed in contact with a handful of workers from both programs; some have retired, others have moved to other jobs and cities, and still other women remain in the vocational training programs. I remain friends with some—relationships that live completely outside the confines of the organization, though I know without those organizations these friendships would not exist. Those tend to be the voices that resonate most strongly with me because, as dissenting voices, I worry that there is no place for them in the living archive of these organizations' work, or in the global anti-trafficking movement.

RACE, FAITH, AND GLOBAL MOBILITY

My identity as an agnostic Chinese American woman set me apart from other volunteers and activists, who were primarily white, North American or Western European Christian women with extensive prior missionary experience. This difference created a bond between me and many of the workers, who on numerous occasions expressed feelings of solidarity based on our shared identities as Asian women, despite differences in class and nationality. I openly disclosed the fact that I am not Christian, and though I would attend daily church worship with workers, I chose not to engage in proselytizing or prayer circles. Although I am not Christian, I sought to understand the religious convictions and commitments of activists. In Los Angeles, I regularly attended church worship at several of the Los Angeles–based churches that these projects were affiliated with, and in February 2011, I participated in a twelve-week social justice training course with one such church to understand the sources of social justice in theology and religious practice.

Qualitative researchers have discussed the dynamics involved in a non-Christian researcher studying conservative Christian practices. For instance, Tanya Erzen's ethnography of sexual and Christian conversions in the American evangelical church details the fraught negotiations around research access when the researcher does not share the same Christian beliefs of the organizations she is studying. At New Hope Church, Erzen's genuine curiosity, continued presence as a volunteer, and technical skills as a web designer earned her access to a religious community of which she was very much an outsider, and I similarly traded different forms of labor to maintain my research access at Freedom Unchained and Cowboy Rescue. I offered translation skills, as well as hundreds of hours of work related to marketing, inventory, and jewelry sales and distribution. Like Erzen, I also experienced episodes when I became the subject of religious conversion techniques, though, unlike Erzen, who also became the target of gay conversion techniques, my volunteer status, middle-class background, and American passport shielded me from the behavioral expectations and social control that is exerted on former sex workers.[9]

Due to my long-standing presence as a volunteer and researcher, there were moments when I met new activists, volunteers, and workers who assumed that I was Christian because faith had drawn most of the activists together. If there was no clear-cut occasion to address the fact that I am not Christian, I made no effort to change their perceptions and interpreted their assumptions as part of the religious social field in which I participated. I think it was clear to most that I had no fluency in Christian religiosity; for instance, nothing was more awkward than the one time when I was asked to say grace before lunch in Bangkok. As I became emboldened to ask more questions of activists, the fact that I am not Christian did create some problems with the activists with whom I interacted more closely. These individuals consistently asserted that my faith, or lack thereof, posed a barrier to my interpretation and understanding of their beliefs, actions, words, and spirituality, as well as their role in the anti-trafficking movement.

As I was one of the only nonwhite outreach participants, and one who can speak Chinese and some Thai, outreach participants always hoped that my language skills would come in handy during outreach to immigrant communities in the United States. It was these particular forms of racial and ethnic social capital, along with my stated interest in and research on anti–human trafficking programs in China, Thailand, and the United States, that made me an acceptable member of the anti-trafficking groups, though I do not share their faith. This trade-off between personal skills and experience in exchange for access occurred frequently throughout my research. Accompanying that trade-off was always the tension-inducing realization that in order to be immersed, I often engaged in practices with which I disagreed—illustrating for me how ethnographic immersion was facilitated by my mobility, class standing, and privilege. In the name of research and immersion, and to uncover the subjective motivations and tactics of the actors involved, I occupied public spaces in the same manner that I critique in my research subjects, and have even enacted specific moments of my own surveillance through outreach as ethnographic encounter—for instance, when I participated in street outreach in Beijing, Bangkok, and Los Angeles. At the same time, I voiced my concerns about problematic activities as they arose in context, as is also mentioned in the book, in the hope of sharing research findings with both organizations.

Conversely, I have also become a subject of hopeful reform and proselytization. In one instance, I was surprised to find a group of hands slowly hovering above me during lunch in Thailand. The pastor was leading the group in a prayer for me as a nonbeliever. Moments like these remind me that research was often isolating; I slept in the volunteer house and would come home every night and write fieldnotes. There was no Wi-Fi in the volunteer house, and I had a cheap data plan because of my grad student budget. Sometimes to escape the solitude of rehashing what had happened that day through writing fieldnotes, I rebelled by sneaking out onto the balcony to smoke a lone cigarette. I wasn't a smoker, yet this act seemed defiant and reminded me of a larger world outside this Christian missionary project.

Researchers have discussed the moral dilemma that arises for some ethnographers whose research activity is, at least on the surface, "morally or ideologically reprehensible."[10] The more immersed I became in the shop floor realities of jewelry production, the more I began to find these projects mired in a moral and political objective that was antithetical to my personal understandings of migrant, racial, and sex worker justice. I looked to other scholars to help understand the undertones of white supremacy and ethnography and was guided by Katherine Blee's research on women's participation in anti-Semitic and racist groups such as the Ku Klux Klan. Her reflections reveal methodological insights about how to manage emotions when you fundamentally disagree with the group you are studying. Blee maintained professional and fruitful relationships with her respondents by taking a stance that was "distant but not neutral."[11] Furthermore, a critical researcher of Korean American proselytizing missions, Ju Hui Judy Han writes that researchers are "neither friends nor foes" and can achieve objective observations through "empathetic proximity" and "critical distance."[12] These terms reflect fundamental tensions in conservative religious spaces, and Han argues that "it is precisely the tension in-between that has the potential to generate the most revealing insights about the complex social worlds that we all inhabit."[13]

UNDERSTANDING THE POSTSECULAR

During my three years of fieldwork in evangelical Christian anti-trafficking social entrepreneurship, the global anti-trafficking movement in China and Thailand grew, and it became clear to me that these two American evangelical Christian rescue projects represented just one facet of a larger terrain of social engagement. There were several distinct moments of convergence, or lack thereof, that struck me. In Thailand, Cowboy Rescue had collaborated with the United Nations and the International Labor Organization to conduct raids and fund repatriations of trafficked people, whereas the China-based organization isolated itself from any other foreign or Chinese NGOs, primarily as a way of staying below the government's radar. Interested in how the secular dimensions of anti-trafficking activity connected with the faith-based groups, I moved on to conduct an additional twelve months of ethnographic fieldwork at secular anti-trafficking organizations in both cities.

Hoping to understand the connections between faith-based organizations and secular and state anti-trafficking actors, I conducted additional fieldwork with secular and state-run anti-trafficking projects between 2011 and 2014. Between September 2012 and February 2013, I spent six months as a full-time research assistant at the China office of the United Nations Inter-Agency Project on Human Trafficking (UNIAP) in Beijing, where I participated in several UN-led research and advocacy projects administered in collaboration with various Chinese government bodies and local and international NGOs. During my research tenure, I assisted with a program that trained the New Workers' Artist Troupe, the band affiliated with a well-known Chinese labor rights NGO, to compose and perform songs about human trafficking. I was also a lead researcher for a five-country study on experiences of reintegration for victims of trafficking led by Rebecca Surtees and coordinated through UNIAP's regional management office in Bangkok.

For the purpose of consistent research design, I had intended to complete a parallel six months as a researcher at the UNIAP office in Bangkok. However, because of extensive structural changes within UNIAP during that time, my research on the secular anti-trafficking response became more dynamic and multisited. Having operated as an independent and temporary project for five years, UNIAP underwent a large-scale program evaluation, which determined that the organization needed to be folded into the United Nations Development Programme (UNDP), its name changed to UNACT, and its entire management team overhauled.

I spent the latter half of 2013 in Thailand, where I was generously provided with office space at the Bangkok office of the Global Alliance Against Traffic in Women (GAATW). I shared space with a group of intelligent, thought-provoking feminist activists who were working with anti-trafficking, migrant labor, and women's rights organizations in the region and throughout the world. As a hub for anti-trafficking, migration, and labor rights mobilization for the Southeast Asian region, Bangkok was an ideal geographic location for frequent meetings with staff from international organizations such as the Asia Pacific

Network of Sex Workers, the Asia Foundation, Save the Children, and various UN agencies.

My time at GAATW placed me near the heart of the anti-trafficking world in Bangkok, and I traveled out of the city often to conduct participant observation as a volunteer at the Empower Foundation, in its office and its sex worker–owned bar in Chiang Mai. During the six nonconsecutive months I spent at the Empower Foundation, the staff was patient as I occupied numerous roles: researcher, English teacher, sometime Chinese-language teacher, outreach worker, failing graphic designer,[14] and customer at the Can-Do Bar during its hours of operation between Wednesday and Saturday nights. In 2017, I brought a group of twelve Brown University students to Empower as a pedagogical exercise to re-envision and redo the "reality tour" that appears in chapter 5. Empower suggested drastic and innovative revisions to the reality tour itinerary that would ground it in migrant and sex worker justice. For the seven days of our travel, the Empower gang's patience, humor, food, games, interpretation, and love sustained our class, and it is this combination of forces that make Empower feel like one of the most important places of retreat and clarity throughout my research. The community they have created through sex worker organizing has been a salve through the isolating and seemingly impossible moments of fieldwork. It is important to me that I never pursued a "collaborative" research project with Empower. Through the power of what the foundation calls "experitainment," they have shown that sex workers must be central to the research conception, design, analysis, and dissemination of work about their lives. Since I am not a sex worker and have never worked in Thailand, I should not occupy this space.

In August 2012, with Elizabeth Bernstein, I participated in a weeklong human trafficking reality tour to Bangkok, Chiang Mai, and Chiang Rai.[15] Elizabeth and I traveled as researchers; at the time, she was finishing a book on the global manifestations of sex and capital, and I was finishing my dissertation research, for which she was one of my advisors. Our research agendas shaped what we hoped to understand through this trip—for Elizabeth, a case of how American sites of redemptive capitalism traveled throughout the world and, for me, an interest in how reality tourism differed from other kinds of American anti-trafficking interventions in Thailand and China. This global purview of the anti-trafficking movement has allowed me access to the different ways the anti-trafficking endeavor is commodified within transnational efforts to combat human trafficking. These disparate secular sites constitute my "secular" case for the Chinese and Thai contexts that animate chapters 4 and 5 of this book, and allowed me to explore state, market, and social movement relationships in each case, broadening the political economic contexts of the initial fieldwork on evangelical projects.

In closing, my ethnographic research was characterized by an embodied negotiation of trade-offs and tensions. I often traded my personal skills and labor to gain research access to organizations. In addition to the exchange of my labor for access to social movement organizations, I also accumulated a serious debt to the numerous low-wage women workers who generously confided their experiences with me. These ethnographic possibilities and responsibilities have been facilitated by my mobility, class standing, and other privileges. The fluidity of my access to such different people, perspectives, sites, and stories across this movement is a constant reminder of my responsibility to shed light on structural power and inequality that privilege certain voices and prevent others from being heard. In this book, I have attempted to do justice to these accounts.

Notes

PREFACE

1. See Beutin 2023 and the websites of The New Abolitionists (https://www
.thenewabolitionists.com) and Operation Underground Railroad (https://
ourrescue.org/).

2. Carol Leigh, "Anti-trafficking Industrial Complex Awareness Month (2nd
Edition)," Gilder Lehrman Center for the Study of Slavery, Resistance, and Abolition, Yale University, accessed September 1, 2022, https://glc.yale.edu/sites
/default/files/pdf/anti-trafficking_industrial_complex_awareness_month_2nd_
edition_with_images_carolleigh_stori.pdf.

INTRODUCTION

1. Throughout this manuscript I use pseudonyms to refer to organizations
and individuals that I encountered through ethnographic participant observation, except in instances where they explicitly requested they be named a particular way. In cases where I draw on publicly available data about an organization or individual, I make fair use of the actual name as presented to the public.

2. Here I am answering ethnographer George Marcus's invitation to "follow
the thing"—a provocation to accompany the trail of objects to trace their social
and political meanings (Marcus 1995).

3. Kempadoo 2001, 2005; Kempadoo, Sanghera, Pattanaik 2005; Agustín
2007; Doezema 2010; Bernstein 2008a; Chapkis 2003; Weitzer 2010.

4. Bernstein 2007b.

5. Anderson 2007; Raymond, Hughes, and Gomez 2001.

6. Agustín 2003; Srikantiah 2007.

7. Chacòn 2006; J.A. Chuang 1998, 2006b; Gallagher 2010; Kotiswaran
2011; Haynes 2006.

8. Anderson and Andrijasevic 2008; Sharma 2006, 2017; O'Connell Davidson 1998.

9. J. A. Chuang 2010; Doezema 2001; Hoang and Parreñas 2014; Parreñas 2011.

10. Agustín 2007.

11. Mai 2013.

12. J. A. Chuang 2014.

13. Tier 1 represents the highest ranking, followed by Tiers 2, 2 Watch List, and 3.

14. See also J. A. Chuang 2006a, 2010; Gallagher 2006; M. Goodman 2005; and Harvey 2003. While this book observes the year 2000 as a critical juncture for American anti-trafficking activism, international engagements with human trafficking predate the 2000 UN and US laws. During international women's conferences in the 1980s, feminists convened to discuss trafficking under the broader rubric of violence against women. The Coalition Against Trafficking in Women (CATW) was founded in 1989, following the Trafficking in Women conference in Manila. CATW claimed to be the first international anti-trafficking NGO and was granted consultative status by the United Nations Economic and Social Council (ECOSOC) in 1989. The coalition's founders included several American feminist groups, such as Women against Pornography and Women Hurt in Systems of Prostitution Engaged in Revolt (WHISPER). Many CATW opponents charge that these leaders brought their existing anti-prostitution agenda to the anti-trafficking movement (CATW 2022).

Disagreeing with what they felt was the prioritization of the sex-trafficking agenda, a separate group of feminists in 1994 founded the Global Alliance Against the Traffic in Women (GAATW). GAATW claims to take a "human rights approach"; this acknowledgment of and attention to sex worker and migrant-worker rights distinguishes the organization from others, it claims (GAATW 2008). GAATW founders were keen to point out differences in power between CATW activists and their subjects, claiming that the former's position as First World feminists led them to devalue lived experiences of Third World women: "We acknowledged that the vision of global sisterhood is fraught with numerous tensions—including those of class, race, sexuality and nationality—and began to understand that they need to listen before speaking on behalf of other women" (GAATW 2005).

15. Dummermuth 2019; Hughart 2020.

16. See, e.g., Bernstein 2010; Musto 2016; and Shih 2016.

17. Kempadoo 2007.

18. Beutin 2017, 2023. See also O'Connell Davidson 2015.

19. For the purposes of political economic comparison, I have simplified the Chinese and Thai states into more democratic and authoritarian classifications here but elaborate on these distinctions in the following sections. A notable elaboration on this simplification is that Thai military repression and state control have taken on authoritarian strains in recent political history. Thailand became a Western-style constitutional democratic monarchy in 1932. Characterized by free elections for its prime minister, the nation has also been governed by periods of military rule stemming from its contentious history of political

coups. Since 2006, Thailand has been plagued by a series of political coups that have overthrown two prime ministers: Thaksin Shinawatra in 2006, and Yingluck Shinawatra in 2014. This contentious political environment reveals a deep-seated divide between Thailand's rural and urban populations, as discussed at length in chapter 5. While these uprisings were met with authoritarian military repression, in the context of this book's focus on state-society relationships, I interpret such uprisings as evidence of a relatively open political environment. Furthermore, as discussed in chapter 5, such civil unrest has had limited impact on the range of anti-trafficking activities undertaken in Thailand, which further underscores that, even in the face of political upheaval, commerce, tourism, humanitarian interventions, and the rescue industry remain relatively untouched.

20. Whyte 1985; Huang 2008.

21. The People's Republic of China (PRC), founded in 1949, is a one-party state ruled by the Chinese Communist Party (CCP), led by President Xi Jinping. China's transition away from socialist rule began in 1978 when Deng Xiao Ping led the nation through a decade of economic reforms.

22. The contemporary rural-urban divide may be attributed to two foundational state policies. In 1950, in order to properly distribute land following land reforms initiated in 1949, the CCP instituted two forms of residency categorization: permanent urban and permanent rural residents. The *hukou* system of family registration institutionalized these categories by assigning persons either agricultural or nonagricultural residency status. This dramatically impacted citizens' land rights; for example, only those with nonagricultural household status can obtain housing or residence in towns and cities.

23. Gaetano and Jacka 2013; K. Chan 2009.

24. Friedman 2022; Walder 2002.

25. China National Plan of Action on Combating Trafficking in Persons 2008, 2013, 2021. For further analysis of the legislative influence of the National Plans of Action on human trafficking in China, see, e.g., B. Ling 2018 and M. Dong 2019.

26. The comprehensive body of scholarship on sex work in China includes Pan 1999; Zheng 2009a, 2009b; Hershatter 1997; Jeffreys 2004, 2006, 2010; Jeffreys and Huang 2009; and Boittin 2013.

27. Ren 1999.

28. For an important discussion of sex work and its relationship to the governance of HIV/AIDS, see, e.g., Hyde 2010; Uretsky 2016; and Peters 2013.

29. Amnesty International 2013; *Global Times* 2014; Human Rights Watch 2013; Jeffreys 2004.

30. Lee and Shen 2009; Friedman 2009.

31. Lee and Zhang 2013; J. Chuang 2014; Minzner 2013.

32. Thailand is a former constitutional monarchy and the only Southeast Asian nation not to have been formally colonized. The lack of colonial rule has often been cited as one reason why Thailand holds one of the strongest religious traditions in Southeast Asia. In Thailand, the king is the head of state and the prime minister is the head of government. With Buddhism as Thailand's official religion, the government observes national Buddhist holidays, and many customs such as weddings and burials follow Buddhist spiritual tradition.

33. Pollock and Aung 2010; Feingold 2013; Huguet and Punpuing 2005.

34. According to a 2018 report by the Thai Office of the National Economic and Social Development Council (NESDC), Bangkok's GDP represented 47.5 percent of Thailand's total GDP (Office of the NESDC 2018).

35. Lim 1998; Empower Foundation 2016; Wilson 2004; Jeffrey 2002; Molland 2012.

36. Wilson 2004; Skrobanek, Boonpakdi, and Čhanthathīrō 1997; Chamratrithirong 2007; Phongpaichit and Baker 1998, 2002; Baker and Phongpaichit 2014.

37. This is a morally and ideologically based argument that has been refuted by numerous studies on the ground. See, e.g., Agustín 2007; Empower Foundation 2011a, 2011b, 2012.

38. Empower Foundation 2012.

39. Enloe 1989; Cohen 1996; Wilson 2004; Parreñas, Thai, and Silvey 2016.

40. Shih 2017.

41. Thailand Anti-Trafficking in Persons Act, B.E. 2551, 2008. According to the act, "'Exploitation' means seeking benefits from prostitution, production or distribution of pornographic materials, other forms of sexual exploitation, slavery, causing another person to be a beggar, forced labour or service, coerced removal of organs for the purpose of trade, or any other similar practices resulting in forced extortion, regardless of such person's consent." The expansion to include male victims is significant, as this act explicitly replaced and repealed the 1997 Measures in Prevention and Suppression of Trafficking in Women and Children Act, B.E. 2540: "'Forced labour or service' means compelling the other person to work or provide service by putting such person in fear of injury to life, body, liberty, reputation or property, of such person or another person, by means of intimidation, use of force, or any other means causing such person to be in a state of being unable to resist."

In recent years, global human-trafficking activism has called for increased attention to cases of nonsexual labor trafficking involving undocumented Burmese and Cambodian fishers in the deep-sea fishing industry. Hodal and Kelly 2014.

42. Bernstein 2007b, 2010, 2015; Zimmerman 2013. See also projects such as the Freedom Business Alliance, an industry facilitator of businesses that works to address human trafficking (https://www.freedombusinessalliance.com/)

43. See, e.g., "Our Values," Expression 58, accessed October 28, 2022, http://expression58.org/values/.

44. Bernstein 2007b; Zimmerman 2013.

45. King and Pearce 2010.

46. Jenkins and Perrow 1977; Ganz 2000; E. Walker, Martin, and McCarthy 2008; Chasin 2001.

47. Chasin 2001.

48. Polanyi 2001 (1944).

49. Zelizer 1979, 1985 1994, 2005.

50. Almeling 2011; Rudrappa 2015.

51. Wherry 2008.

52. Jaffee 2007: 26.

53. For a compelling discussion of "fair trade feminism," see Heiliger 2013.

54. Fassin 2011; see also Ticktin 2014.

55. Aijazi 2014: 14; Kapoor 2006

56. Chomsky 2008; Nguyen 2011.

57. These humanitarian projects and sentiments extend to global "voluntourism" in Latin America and Africa; postwar "reconstruction" in the Middle East, Southeast Asia, and Afghanistan; and civilian-led sex trafficking raid and rescue in East and Southeast Asia. Voluntourism collides with anti-trafficking in novel ways; the forms of activism are detailed throughout this book. In particular, in 2010, Cowboy Rescue introduced Los Angeles–based efforts to identify victims of trafficking through street outreach in that city. This is part of a larger cohort of not-in-our-backyard initiatives within the United States that train volunteer civilians how to identify and report victims of trafficking in the United States. Shih 2016.

58. Mostafanezhad 2013; Jaffee 2007; Wherry 2008; Heiliger 2008; Einstein 2013; Vrasti 2012; Clarke 2008.

59. T. Cole 2012; Kempadoo 2015.

60. Beutin 2023; Mensah and Okyere 2019.

61. Brooks 2005.

62. Mies 1998.

63. hooks 1992. See also Wilson 2011 and Lekakis 2022.

64. Agustín 2007; Leigh 2015; Bernstein 2014; J. A. Chuang 2015. See also Carol Leigh, "Anti-trafficking Industrial Complex Awareness Month (2nd Edition)," Gilder Lehrman Center for the Study of Slavery, Resistance, and Abolition, Yale University, accessed September 1, 2022, https://glc.yale.edu/sites/default/files/pdf/anti-trafficking_industrial_complex_awareness_month_2nd_edition_with_images_carolleigh_stori.pdf.

65. See, e.g., Molland 2012.

66. Bernstein 2007b; 2019.

67. See, e.g., Hung 2002; Tucker, Ren, and Sapio 2010; Davis 2001, 2011; Weiss 2001; Haney 2010.

CHAPTER 1. THE BUSINESS OF REHAB

Some material in this chapter is adapted from Elena Shih, "Globalising Rehabilitation Regimes: The Moral Economy of Vocational Training in After-Trafficking Work," in *Forcing Issues: Rethinking and Rescaling Human Trafficking in the Asia-Pacific Region,* edited by Sallie Yea, © 2013 by Routledge, reproduced by permission of Routledge; and from Elena Shih, "Free Market Evangelism: The Technopolitics of Vocational Training for Modern Day Abolition," in *The Mission of Development: Religion and Techno-politics in Asia,* edited by Catherine Scheer, Philip Fountain, and Michael Feener, © 2018 by Brill Press, reproduced by permission of Brill Press.

1. Vance 2012: 207.

2. See, e.g., Karim 2011; Radhakrishnan 2021; Siddiqi 2009; Nawaz 2019.

3. Altan-Olcay 2014.

4. See, e.g., figure 1; Bernstein 2007b, 2008b, 2015; and "Shop for Good," Not For Sale, accessed October 22, 2022, https://store.notforsalecampaign .org/.

5. Email message from Nomi Network, May 11, 2017: "Nomi Network's Gala was a Huge Success! Thank you for joining us." When I attended the Nomi Gala in 2017, I was surprised to find many seats around me vacant despite the fact that the event was sold out. I learned that Nomi had sold tables to corporate sponsors for $10,000 apiece and up, though in many instances, those companies did not find enough guests to fill the seats.

6. Nomi Network 2021: 48–49.

7. Zimmerman 2013.

8. For a fascinating exploration of the often-hidden evangelical Christian foundations of the Kony 2012 movement (a viral campaign launched by the American NGO Invisible Children to have Joseph Kony arrested), see Kron 2012.

9. The International Labor Organization (ILO) initiated the category "decent work" in 2015 as part of the 2030 Agenda for Sustainable Development. The four pillars of decent work are employment creation, social protection, rights at work, and social dialogue.

10. Melucci 1989; Somers and Gibson 1994; Tilly 1978; McAdam, Tarrow, and Tilly 1996; Guidry, Kennedy, and Zald 2000.

11. Conca 2005.

12. Sassen 2006; Soysal 2012.

13. Evans 2005.

14. Adams 2013; Einstein 2007; O'Neill 2015; Kron 2012.

15. Benshoff 2019; Adams 2013; Scheer, Fountain, and Feener 2018.

16. Bornstein 2004; Hirono 2008.

17. Hirono 2008.

18. Pascoe 1990.

19. Keck and Sikkink 1998.

20. "Our Vision and Values," World Vision, accessed September 5, 2022, http://www.wvi.org/vision-and-values-o.

21. Zimmermann 2013.

22. Quoted in Zimmerman 2013: 5.

23. Zimmerman 2013: 91.

24. Australian Catholic Religious Against Trafficking in Humans 2015. See also Pope Francis's keynote address at the 2019 Conference on Pastoral Orientations on Human Trafficking. "Address of His Holiness Pope Francis to Participants at the International Conference on Human Trafficking," La Santa Sede Francesco, April 11, https://www.vatican.va/content/francesco/en/speeches/2019 /april/documents/papa-francesco_20190411_conferenza-trattadipersone.html

25. Bernstein 2007b, 2019; Zimmermann 2013.

26. Masenior and Beyrer 2006; Kinney 2006.

27. National Institute of Justice 2013. Sex worker rights activists and advocates across the globe challenge the explicit focus on labor trafficking because commercial sex is still not recognized as a form of legal work, with needs including wage regulations, benefits, and occupational safety.

28. US GAO 2006, 2007; Chacòn 2006; Parreñas 2011.

29. Bernstein 2008a: 2; Cheng 2008; Soderlund 2005.

30. Gasaway 2014; Hondagneu-Sotelo 2006.

31. Soerens and Yang 2009.

32. Myers and Colwell 2012.

33. Religious organizations have become so adept at seeking funds through the market that several secular anti-trafficking NGOs have now partnered with evangelical social enterprises for funding. For instance, in 2013, the Coalition to Abolish Slavery and Trafficking (CAST) partnered with a small Christian company called Gallant Suits that sells business suits "ethically made" by seamstresses rescued from trafficking in Cambodia. The suit company held a fundraiser in which it sold handmade men's suits for about $1,000 apiece, a clothing line that promised to "usher in a new era of masculinity" not predicated on "sexual exploitation." Male models wearing the suits posed alongside CAST's Survivor Advocacy Caucus, as CAST eagerly accepted donations from the proceeds of the event.

34. Kitiarsa 2008.

35. Reeb and Wellons 2006; Silvoso 2010.

36. Johnson 2011; Rundle 2012; Rundle and Steffen 2011; Bronkema and Brown 2009; Lai 2006.

37. Miller and Yamamori 2007: 48.

38. Radosh 2008.

39. Hildebrandt 2011. In China, many small NGOs choose to register as private enterprises or use existing organizations as fiscal conduits for their operations.

40. Pangsapa 2015; Chaitanat and Leeds Co., Ltd. 2013.

41. Vincent 2003.

42. Doezema 1998: 46.

43. Kempadoo and Doezema 1998: 127.

44. See, e.g., Spivak 1988, 1999; Trinh 1989, 1999; Mohanty, Russo, and Torres 1991; and Tarrow 2005.

45. UN Palermo Protocol 2000.

46. McDaniel 2010.

47. Betsy Anderson, "How Jewelry Is Saving Women from Human Trafficking," CNN, updated March 25, 2016, https://www.cnn.com/2016/03/25/world/iyw-saving-women-from-human-trafficking-with-ingenuity-education/index.html.; Lori Basheda, "Former Sex Slaves Make Jewelry with OC Women," *Orange County Register,* January 5, 2009, https://www.ocregister.com/2009/01/05/former-sex-slaves-make-jewelry-with-oc-women/; See also, Kassidy McIntosh, "Jewelry Gives Hope to Human Trafficking Survivors," *New York Minute Mag,* April 21, 2017, https://www.newyorkminutemag.com/jewelry-gives-hope-to-trafficking-survivors/

48. Nguyen 2022.

49. Chavisa 2014.

50. Adam Jacot de Boinod, "Travel in Numbers and Colours: Wear Pink for Luck on Tuesdays in Thailand," *Independent,* June 2, 2015, https://www.independent.co.uk/travel/news-and-advice/travel-in-numbers-and-colours-wear-pink-for-luck-on-tuesdays-in-thailand-10290964.html.

51. Human Rights Watch 2018.
52. Haney 2010; McKim 2017.
53. US TVPA 2000.
54. Ghimire 2012.
55. Weeks 2011.
56. See, e.g., Chan, Ngai, and Selden 2015; Su 2010; Friedman 2022; Chan and Ngai 2010; Chan 2014.
57. Jacobs 2019.
58. Across all three countries a growing body of literature investigates the limits of different vocational training approaches. The ways that China's turn towards vocational training has enabled workplace exploitation of student interns is detailed in Chapter 4. Thailand's vocational training law, the Skill Development Promotion Act (B.E. 2545), was introduced in 2002 and has provided limited access for migrant workers. Empower has advocated that training should expand to include legal literacy and human rights awareness.

CHAPTER 2. MANUFACTURING FREEDOM

1. Beales et al. 2016.
2. This is a claim similarly rehearsed by popular books on the subject, as described in chapter 5.
3. This was the salary range between 2008 and 2012, when I conducted ethnographic fieldwork. In subsequent years, salaries have increased in keeping with the local minimum wage in each city.
4. E.P. Thompson (1971) and James Scott (1977) have used the "moral economy" concept to describe the norms and ethics that characterize social and economic exchange among peasants and working-class people in agrarian societies. More recently, Paul Gilroy's (2010) revitalization of the concept in relation to Du Bois's seminal works has integrated an analysis of race and globalization into the moral economy framework. I build upon these prior theorizations to extend the moral economy lens in order to understand the circuits of affect and sentiment that circulate among transnational movement activists as they construct both labor and consumption as righteous, dignified, and just.
5. Hoang 2015.
6. See, e.g., Shimizu 2007; Le Espiritu 2001; Okazaki 2002; and Pascoe 1990. For a corollary discussion of Black and Latina women's hypersexualization, see, e.g., Miller-Young 2010; and S. Brooks 2010.
7. Wesley 2004; Spengler 2007.
8. Yang and Guo 1996; Jacka and Gaetano 2007.
9. Kuruvilla, Lee, and Gallagher 2011; Friedman 2014; C.K. Chan and Peng 2011.
10. Burawoy 1982.
11. Global Labor Justice and Asia Floor Wage Alliance 2019; Halegua 2021.
12. For rich analyses of gendered service sector work in China and Thailand, see, e.g., Hanser 2005, 2008; Otis 2011; Paitoonpong and Akkarakul 2009; and Phananiramai 2002.
13. Musto 2011.

14. The pure linguistic and semantic inconsistencies between definitions in Thailand, China, and other countries that have adopted transnational law reveal further confusion between transnational and local legal and colloquial understandings of *human trafficking, freedom, exploitation,* and *slavery*—terms frequently used in the public discourse around human trafficking. These complications over pure definition and linguistic translation are discussed at length in chapters 5 and 6, which examine how the movement combines with global governance objectives to enforce state and market goals. This is particularly illuminating when discussing the contexts of labor exploitation and sexual commerce in each place.

15. The similarities between garment work and work under rehabilitation are vividly detailed in the graphic novel *Threadbare: Clothes, Sex, and Trafficking,* by Anne Elizabeth Moore. Though pervasive, this is not a new phenomenon. Historically, Jessica Pliley's feminist work on the carceral roots of the modern FBI point to similar histories of work and reform: "A majority of the thirty-four Jewish sex workers who violated probation in 1905 had first worked as garment workers in New York City." Pliley 2014: 47.

16. See, e.g., Hoang 2015; Agustín 2007; Bernstein 2007a; Brents, Jackson, and Hausbeck 2010; Shah 2014.

17. These are the prevalent reasons sex workers offered in both programs. Employee respondents at both locations also described the reasons for deciding to leave sex work: violence, social stigma, unhappiness, loneliness, or general curiosity about work opportunities available under foreign bosses. In the text, I highlight the less frequently heard narratives and illustrate the stark contrast between lived reality and activists' framing of reality.

18. Chin 2012.

19. Hunt 1988: 401.

20. Pascoe 1990; Lui 2009; Pliley 2014.

CHAPTER 3. BAD REHAB

Some material in this chapter appears, in a form since revised, in "Duplicitous Freedom: Moral and Material Care Work of Sex and Migration," *Critical Sociology,* 44(7–8), 1077–1086. © 2018. Reproduced by permission of Sage Publications.

1. APNSW, "Somaly Uh Uh: Bad Rehab extended remix," YouTube, December 15, 2010, https://www.youtube.com/watch?v=GMor7N1rIMI.

2. Empower Foundation has used the term *sentences* to push back against a criminal justice regime that suggests that arrest is synonymous with "rescue." See Arnott and Crago 2009.

3. Marks 2014.

4. Arnott and Crago 2009.

5. This maternalist language, though recurrent for women and girl victims of trafficking, is also used with young boys. Using the slogan "Boys cannot be baht," Urban Light, another American NGO, working in northern Thailand, refers to young men over age eighteen as "boys" because sex work presumably robs them of their innocence. Referring to them as boys confers a certain victim

identity that could be called into question if they were referred to as adult male workers.

6. Goffman 1961.

7. Surtees 2008, 2013.

8. Brunovskis and Surtees 2007; Empower Foundation 2012.

9. Empower Foundation 2012.

10. Ramachandran and Walters 2018; Walters 2016.

11. Bose 2016.

12. Surtees 2013.

13. Chab Dai Coalition 2012.

14. In the decade since its drafting, the Chab Dai Charter has expanded to include organizations throughout Southeast Asia, and in 2017, the Chab Dai Coalition began sponsoring an international conference for all types of anti-trafficking organizations, not just the faith-based ones.

15. Urry 2002 (1991).

16. Mahdavi 2022.

17. Chuang 2014.

18. In a corollary discussion of maternalist power structures of humanitarianism and adoption, geographer Mary Mostafanezhad (2013) has discussed celebrity humanitarianism as a site of First World "gendered" generosity whereby the celebrity of public figures like Angelina Jolie and Madonna serves to bolster and extol their adoption of Third World children—uncontested subjects of maternal humanitarian action.

CHAPTER 4. TRAFFICKING BENEVOLENT AUTHORITARIANISM IN CHINA

1. Biao 2007; Chang, Dong, and MacPhail 2011.

2. For a discussion of the educational struggles of migrant families in China, see, e.g., Dong and Goodburn 2020; Goodburn 2009; M. Ling 2019; K. W. Chan and Yuan 2022; Chang, Dong, and MacPhail 2011; and Friedman 2022.

3. Su 2012; D. Chan 2011; J. 2013; J. Chan and Ngai 2010.

4. Lee and Shen 2011: 174.

5. Ong 2016.

6. Harney 2015.

7. Cain Nunns, "China's Foreigner Crackdown: Much Ado about Nothing?" *The World* (Public Radio International), June 13, 2012, https://www.pri.org/stories/2012-06-13/china-s-foreigner-crackdown-much-ado-about-nothing.

8. Harney 2015.

9. Ngai and Austin 2018; Friedman 2009.

10. See, e.g., Shih, Rosenbaum, and Kyritsis 2021.

11. China National Plan of Action on Combating Trafficking in Persons 2008–2012.

12. Huang 2008: 1.

13. B. Ling 2018.

14. J. Chang 2014.

15. Lee and Zhang 2014; Lee 1998, 2007; Friedman and Lee 2010; Ngai 2005.

16. China National Plan of Action on Combating Trafficking in Persons 2021–30.

17. Shih 2013b. The spurious conflation of deportations as "humanitarian repatriations" is not unique to the Chinese context and has been demonstrated in Sine Plambech's (2014) work on the deportation of Nigerian migrants from Western Europe, and throughout global contexts in the work of Nandita Sharma (2005).

18. For an in-depth discussion of how arrested Chinese sex workers are subject to the Chinese government's "custody education" program for rehabilitation and reform, see, e.g., Amnesty International 2013; *Global Times* 2014; Human Rights Watch 2013.

19. Andrew Hunter, interview with author, 2012; Human Rights Watch 2013.

20. Lee and Zhang 2013.

21. J. Yang 2010; Walder 1984.

22. Taking Peters and Feingold's insights to heart, I deeply admire the longstanding cultural interventions to mitigate trafficking that they have undertaken throughout Yunnan and Southeast Asia since the late 1990s.

23. Zaloznaya and Hagan 2012: 346.

24. On the New Workers' Art Troupe, see Qiu and Wang 2012; Liu 2018; and Connery 2019.

25. Hildebrandt 2013.

26. This assessment was based on observations and data collection over the course of my six-month research tenure at the UNIAP China office. In this small office of only three full-time staff members, everyone was called upon to assist with regional conference planning, travel logistics, and communications.

27. Gold, Guthrie, and Wank 2002; Xin and Pearce 1996.

28. "Our Mission Statement," World Vision, accessed October 23, 2022, https://www.wvi.org/our-mission-statement.

29. World Vision Staff, "Prayer for an End to Human Trafficking," World Vision, updated May 27, 2021, https://www.worldvision.org/child-protection-news-stories/pray-end-human-trafficking.

30. For discussions of the All China Women's Federation and its relationship to women's rights in China, and NGO and GONGO politics, see Saich 2000; N. Zhang 2020; Kaufman 2012; and Jie 2006.

31. For a discussion of the Chinese government's oversight of NGOs, see Hildebrandt 2011; Deng 2010; G. Yang 2005; Shieh and Deng 2011; Ma 2002; Saich 2000.

32. Chan and Ngai 2010; Chan 2014.

33. Su 2012.

34. The IMOAT installed an insidious, seemingly mundane system of surveillance in the UNIAP China office. One part-time staff member was hired purely to translate all English-language reports into Chinese to send over for ministerial approval. Such documents often went back and forth through

several rounds of review, delaying completion of the office's regional work plan. In one instance, I created a human trafficking referral sheet for potential victims and was required to submit it to the Ministry of Public Security (MPS). I was asked to reformat the document that displayed a checklist of services offered by referral agencies (for instance, legal aid, psychological counseling, and housing). Government officials asked that the check marks be removed because they provided a visual—and somehow more quantitative—assessment of the amount of trafficking services available. Instead, I was asked to describe the services in prose paragraphs rather than in checklist form.

35. Criticism of the "newness" of anti-trafficking activism is a sentiment shared by sex worker activists who have argued that the sudden rise of human trafficking as the current cause cèlébre takes attention away from longer-standing human rights abuses.

36. Goldman 2005.

37. "The New Workers Art Troupe," Institute for Public Art, accessed October 23, 2022, https://www.instituteforpublicart.org/case-studies/the-new-workers-art-troupe/.

38. Despite the US State Department's downgrade of China to Tier 3, in the same year, the United Nations awarded IMOAT director Chen an international "Social Media Engagement" prize for his anti-trafficking Weibo site, a microblog platform (similar to Twitter) that allows users to report cases of trafficking directly on the page. This site promises that local public security bureau resources will be allocated to address all posted cases. IMOAT enthusiastically reports that many cases have been pursued and solved through this platform, cases predominantly of school-aged children being kidnapped on their way to school—a crime not typically treated as a trafficking offense in other countries. The Ministry of Public Security conveniently labels child kidnapping a crime of human trafficking, allowing it to cite solved cases of child kidnapping as a demonstration of its anti-trafficking efforts.

39. In my earliest trip to rural Yunnan in 2005, accompanying a research team from Minzu University of China, I could already see the influence of global anti-trafficking protocols. A local women's federation representative in the Lancang Lahu Autonomous County (located near the China-Laos border) guided us to a rural elementary school labeled a "special pilot school" for anti-trafficking prevention, where a chalkboard displayed the Chinese translation of the UN Palermo Protocol in bright-colored chalk.

40. Desai 2007; Bob 2001; Maney 2000.

41. Bandy and Smith 2005: 11.

42. Brooks 2007: 136. For a corollary discussion of child rights and child trafficking, see Okyere 2013.

43. Okyere 2013, 2017, 2022.

44. US Department of State 2022. The 2003 Trafficking Victims Protection Reauthorization Act (TVPRA) specified that a Tier 3 ranking would be accompanied with economic sanctions; however, this has not proven to be a significant deterrent for China, given its relatively low reliance on aid. China's manufacturing and export economy was not affected following its Tier 3 ranking (Ponnudurai 2013).

45. Chinese citizens have criticized the *Trafficking in Persons Report* for its neoimperialist gaze. Reading through the comments on a news article that discussed the demotion to Tier 3, I found three that referenced the US history of chattel slavery during the transatlantic slave trade. One commenter wrote: "A certain Western country, whose history is already heavily tainted with a record of human trafficking, and where the problems of slavery, forced labour, the smuggling of people etc. still exist, has no right to take the moral high ground/ be the moral authority on the issue of human trafficking." Echoing this point, 國色 wrote: "America was built on the trafficking of persons, and their numbers of missing children are extremely high as well. If we factor in the relative populations of the two countries, the issue of trafficking in America is worse than in China." The third commenter tried to keep the rankings in comparative perspective. 仰韶 wrote: "How many ancestors of Asians in America today were kidnapped and trafficked to America for labor? If the ultimate representative of trafficking in persons calls itself number two on the list, who dares to call itself number one?" "The US Government Announced That It Would Place China on the List of Countries with the Worst Levels of Human Trafficking," China Gate, June 27, 2017, http://www.wenxuecity.com/news/2017/06 /27/6348907.html.

46. Trump 2018.

47. According to news reports (e.g., Associated Press 2017), other brands identified by China Labor Watch as customers of the Ganzhou factory include Nine West, Naturalizer, BCBG Max Azria, Jessica Simpson, and Tory Burch.

48. Kinetz 2017.

49. As Plambech (2014) has demonstrated in the European context, the Chinese government has used the framework of "repatriation" to measure its anti-trafficking activism. Large anti-trafficking actions in 2013 included the rescue and repatriation of youth from Myanmar. Alternatively read, such repatriation is arguably just the deportation of undocumented migrants; however, the government did not grant access for me to conduct interviews with such victims so as to make an independent assessment of this possibility.

CHAPTER 5. VIGILANTE HUMANITARIANISM IN THAILAND

Some material in this chapter appears, in a form since revised, in "Freedom Markets: Consumption and Commerce across Human Trafficking Rescue in Thailand," *positions: Asia Critique*, 25(4), 769–94 © 2017, reproduced by permission of Oxford University Press; "The Travels of Trafficking," pages 98–127 in *Brokered Subjects: Sex Trafficking and the Politics of Freedom,* edited by Elizabeth Bernstein, © 2018 by The University of Chicago, reproduced by permission of The University of Chicago Press; and "The Erotics of Authenticity: Sex Trafficking and 'Reality Tourism' in Thailand," *Social Politics: International Studies in Gender, State, and Society*, 21(3), 430–46, © 2014, reproduced by permission of Oxford University Press.

1. US Congress Committee on Foreign Affairs 2015.

2. Vice News journalists Anna Merlan and Tim Marchman published a meticulously researched and reported, multipart investigative report on how

OUR's work was often exaggerated or outright fabricated the facts. The report reveals that Tim Ballard faced criticisms from law enforcement officials around the world who claimed he had falsified tales of their partnerships. Merlan and Marchman 2020, 2021a, 2021b.

3. "Operation Underground Railroad," Candid: Guidestar, accessed September 25, 2022, https://www.guidestar.org/profile/46-3614979.

4. Petrova 2017.

5. Elizabeth Bernstein and I previously explored the merging of humanitarian sentiment and commerce in this reality tour—what we described as an "erotics of authenticity." Bernstein and Shih 2014.

6. Fittipaldo 2018.

7. Varley 2018.

8. Bales 2004 (1999): 78.

9. Phongpaichit 2004.

10. Office of the NESDC 2018; Wilson 2004; Skrobanek, Boonpakdi, and Chanthathīrō 1997.

11. Kedmey 2013.

12. Manning 2006.

13. Phongpaichit and Baker 2004.

14. US military presence in Thailand during the Vietnam War and other Indochina wars, including the stationing of American troops in Thailand and the flow of other foreign troops for R and R, bred one of the earliest infrastructures for tourist exchange and commercial sex tourism in the world (Ditmore 2011: 454). Referring to US militarism in South Korea, Sealing Cheng (2011) and Hae Yeon Choo (2016) have also demonstrated the presence of sexual humanitarianism in former and current US military bases throughout the country, revealing the force of geopolitical power in contemporary migrant worker lives and the humanitarian campaigns that seek to discipline them.

15. Wilson 2004.

16. Walk Free Foundation, "Resources," accessed December 4, 2014, https://www.walkfree.org/resources.

17. Chuang 2006a ("global sheriff"). The influence of Western economies is merely an extension of the same phenomenon that Chuang outlines in problematizing the US *Trafficking in Persons Report*'s connections to binding economic sanctions from the World Bank and International Monetary Fund. For critiques of the Global Slavery Index, see Gallagher 2014.

18. Lawrence and Hodal 2014. The Thai government has also begun issuing its own country report in response to the US TIP Report. See Royal Thai Government 2021.

19. The Rohingya are an Islamic ethnic group that lives predominantly in Burma. The United Nations has named them one of the most persecuted ethnic groups in the world. An estimated 100,000 Rohingya live in refugee camps on the Thai-Burma border. Tan 2014.

20. Empower Foundation 2012.

21. "Anti-Slavery Directory: Thailand," End Slavery Now, accessed October 23, 2022, https://www.endslaverynow.org/connect?country=3398&state=&city=.

22. Andrew Drummond, "The Greyman and the Akha," YouTube, January 5, https://www.youtube.com/watch?v=aqO4xKDdiZ8.

23. To maintain their anonymity, I use pseudonyms to refer to the reality tour provider. These pseudonyms are consistent with those used in the article on which this chapter draws, Bernstein and Shih 2014.

24. Although the website promised three-star hotels, the group was placed in backpacker hostels that cost 5 USD per person per night. When I confronted the guide about the inaccurate description on the organization's website, he explained, once again, "Don't forget that this is Thailand, still a poor Third World country, and these accommodations are the equivalent of three-star hotels in Thailand." Other tourists seemed pleased with this explanation, eagerly nodding in agreement, seemingly pleased with their own ability to "rough it" and to experience local realities firsthand. Kimberly Hoang (2015) describes this phenomenon as a fascination with "Third World poverty" in her ethnographic accounts of Western men's "benevolent remittances" to Vietnamese sex workers, whom sex tourists assume to be "virtuous" Third World subjects.

25. For examples of the aforementioned instances of tourism, see, e.g., Parreñas 2011; Bloul 2012; Vrasti 2012; Steinbrink 2012; Linke 2012.

26. Fathers were not a beneficiary population of such "anti-trafficking" services. In fact, several of the organizations' comments about fathers suggested that Burmese men were part of the problem, subjecting their wives and children to the cruel fate of poverty and the temptations of drugs and crime. The organization's many references to creating "home" and "family" for mothers and children encouraged escape from the deficient families they were born into.

27. Cultural forms of activism in Thailand have a rich history dating back to the democracy struggles in the 1970s, and this film is just one of many artistic interventions that sex workers rights organizations have made in anti-trafficking work. In 2013, Empower Foundation launched an art show at the Bangkok Art and Culture Center featuring works by sex workers from Malaysia, the Philippines, Laos, Cambodia, Vietnam, Thailand, Indonesia, Myanmar, Timor Leste, and Singapore. During the COVID-19 pandemic in 2021, Empower workers mailed their high-heeled shoes to the government as a group performance to show some of the impacts of being prohibited from working.

28. Bernstein and Shih 2014.

29. Australian Government 2016.

30. Nealon 2014; Enting 2014; "Daniel Walker," Intervarsity Press, accessed October 30, 2022, https://www.ivpress.com/daniel-walker.

31. *Bangkok News* 2019.

32. Okyere 2017.

33. Empower Foundation 2017: 4.

34. DNA Films, "Operation Toussaint: Operation Underground Railroad and the Fight to End Modern Day Slavery." YouTube, posted July 28, 2020, https://www.youtube.com/watch?v=7q8dYM9oPJA.

35. "Video #4: The Anatomy of the Rescue." Operation Underground Railroad, accessed September 25, 2022, https://ourfilm.org/anatomy-of-the-rescue, 16:45 ("How do you find these children?")

36. Chuang 2006a.

37. Beutin (2017, 2023) argues that such abolitionist nostalgia profits from a pervasive anti-Blackness in the invention and invocation of the term "modern-day slavery," which explains its global success.

38. For a discussion of "bearing witness" in trafficking cases, see, e.g., Fukushima 2019.

39. For a detailed discussion of civilian vigilante rescue efforts in the United States, see Shih 2016.

40. Agustín 2007.

41. Ono 2017.

CHAPTER 6. QUITTING REHAB

1. Kelly 2003; Hartman 2008.

2. Owens 2017: 184.

3. Nguyen 2012.

4. This distinction reflects an important intervention made by Denise Brennan and Sine Plambech (2018), guest editors of issue 10 of the *Anti-Trafficking Review,* titled "Life after Trafficking." https://www.gaatw.org/resources/anti-trafficking-review/975-no-10-special-issue-life-after-trafficking.

5. Brennan 2014: 4.

6. Winship and Mare 1992; Berk 1983. For a related argument regarding research on refugee resilience, see Cole 2021.

7. The International Labor Organization (ILO) created the category "decent work" in 2015 as part of the 2030 Agenda for Sustainable Development. The four pillars of decent work are employment creation, social protection, rights at work, and social dialogue. See "Decent Work," International Labor Organization, accessed October 1, 2022, https://www.ilo.org/global/topics/decent-work/lang--en/index.htm.

CONCLUSION

1. Free-D, accessed January 18, 2019, www.free-d.org.uk.

2. Knowles 2018.

3. Free-D, accessed January 18, 2019, www.free-d.org.uk.

4. Shih 2016; Bernstein 2010, 2019.

5. Evans 2005.

6. Burawoy 2010: 7.

7. Lee 2007; Seidman 2007; Silver 2003.

8. White House 2010.

9. Shih 2016.

10. Kempadoo, Sanghera, and Pattanaik 2005; Kempadoo and Shih 2022; Okyere 2017; Beutin 2023; Agustín 2007; Bernstein 2019; Chuang 2014; Doezema 2010; Empower Foundation 2012; Gallagher 2014; GAATW 2007; Parreñas 2011.

11. Bernstein and Shih 2014.

12. Keck and Sikkink 1998: 195.

13. Hoang 2015; Hwang 2017, 2018; Bernstein 2007a; Shah 2014; Cheng 2011; Agustín 2007.

14. "Solidarity Not Sewing Machines," and "Rights Not Rescue" are two prominent slogans used by the Asia Pacific Network of Sex Workers, and Empower Foundation. See APNSW, "Don't Talk to Us about Sewing Machines—Talk to Us about Workers' Rights, Part 1," YouTube, April 30, 2012. https://www.youtube.com/watch?v=-CfYvmGIzRE.

15. Yu 2014. See the Global Network of Sex Worker Projects (2013) letter of support for Ye Haiyan.

16. For instance, sex worker activists in China campaigned against the Chinese Ministry of Public Security's public-shaming tactics whereby arrested sex workers were paraded barefoot through city streets after their apprehension. In July 2010, the MPS officially banned the use of such tactics, asking that police act in a "rational, calm and civilized manner." (http://www.ipsnews.net/2010/08/china-a-parade-less-a-step-forward).

17. In an interview with an Asian American Christian social entrepreneur in Southern California, I learned that Christian businesses-as-missions have long pursued business as a strategy for evangelism in authoritarian contexts that are closed to missionary presence. Tutti Frutti, a popular frozen yogurt chain based in Orange County, California, that is also a Christian business-as-mission enterprise boasts that most of its global satellite franchises are in authoritarian or non-Christian locations, in countries such as Bahrain, China, United Arab Emirates, Myanmar, Iraq, and Saudi Arabia. http://tfyogurt.com/home/locations_other/.

18. See ASDA, "Modern Slavery Statement 2022," 2022, https://corporate.walmart.com/media-library/document/modern-slavery-statement-2018/_proxyDocument?id=00000163-b28c-dd8b-adef-bfed2c110000; KFC 2020. "KFC Modern Slavery Statement," https://modernslaveryregister.gov.au/statements/489/; Lululemon, "Modern Slavery Statement," 2020, https://info.lululemon.com/about/modern-slavery-statement; Amazon 2020. "Modern Slavery Statement," https://sustainability.aboutamazon.com/2020-modern-slavery-statement.pdf; Walgreens Boots Alliance, "Modern Slavery and Human Trafficking Statement," 2021, https://www.walgreensbootsalliance.com/news-media/position-statements/modern-slavery-and-human-trafficking-statement; Facebook, "Anti-Slavery and Human Trafficking Statement," 2021, https://s21.q4cdn.com/399680738/files/doc_downloads/2021/06/2021-Facebook's-Anti-Slavery-and-Human-Trafficking-Statement.pdf; Adidas, "Modern Slavery Act Transparency Statement," 2018, https://www.adidas-group.com/media/filer_public/02/e5/02e51e8a-220e-4dbb-9291-bdc33921f4cd/modern_slavery_act_transparency_statement_2018.pdf; Hasbro, "Hasbro Global Modern Slavery Statement," 2021, https://csr.hasbro.com/en-us/news/policy?id=csr_global_modern_slavery_statement#:~:text=Hasbro%20is%20committed%20to%20regularly,regulations%20and%20Hasbro%20core%20values; PepsiCo, "Modern Slavery and Human Trafficking Statement," 2021, https://www.pepsico.com/docs/default-source/sustainability-and-esg-topics/2021-pepsico-modern-slavery-

and-human-trafficking-statement.pdf?sfvrsn=e21d9563_3; Apple, "2021 Statement on Efforts to Combat Modern Slavery in Our Business and Supply Chains," 2021, https://www.apple.com/supplier-responsibility/pdf/Apple-Combat-Human-Trafficking-and-Slavery-in-Supply-Chain-2021.pdf.

19. "Independent Review of the Modern Slavery Act," United Kingdom Home Office, 2021, https://www.gov.uk/government/publications/independent-review-of-the-modern-slavery-act-final-report/independent-review-of-the-modern-slavery-act-final-report-accessible-version.

20. See, e.g., Shih, Rosenbaum, and Kyritsis 2021; LeBaron et al. 2022.

21. IndustriALL Global Union, "Bangladesh Accord on Fire and Building Safety Released," May 14, 2013, https://www.industriall-union.org/bangladesh-accord-on-fire-and-building-safety-released; see also Taylor and Shih 2018.

22. Anner, Bair, and Biasi 2013.

23. Rahman and Yadlapalli 2021.

24. China's only labor union is the government-sanctioned All-China Federation of Trade Unions (ACFTU), whose leadership consists of Communist Party officials and whose primary goals have been to promote an increase in the number of formal labor contracts. At both the central and provincial levels, union federations maintain close relationships with management, and union organization within workplaces is weak (Friedman 2014). By contrast, the Thai Constitution protects the right to form unions and to bargain collectively, but only 1.5 percent of 40 million workers in Thailand belong to unions (Napathorn and Chanprateep 2011).

25. Wongsamuth 2020.

26. See, e.g., Johnson et al. 2022; Sobering, Thomas, and Williams 2014.

27. Zin 2019; Business and Human Rights Resource Centre 2019.

28. New Zealand Government 2022; GuideStar 2022a, 2022b; Operation Underground Railroad 2021; Nomi Network 2021; International Justice Mission 2022.

29. Red Canary Song pursues this approach as diametrically opposed to hegemonic forms of policing Asian massage work *as* anti-trafficking rescue. Examples of approaches that endorse policing as a means of combating trafficking include, the Polaris Project's Illicit Massage Business project, along with The Network (formerly Heyrick Research), which employs large datasets to surveil Asian massage workers in the name of protecting them (Lam 2018a, 2018b; Shih 2021; Polaris Project 2019; Heyrick Research 2022).

30. Smith 2012. See also Tuck 2013.

31. See also Kathi Weeks's (2011) thought-provoking treatise on the fundamental problems of the good-work paradigm. Weeks's insights prompt us to ask instead, Why are we obsessed with good work as the only possible solution for economic justice for women? Grappling with a similar question, the ILO has made "decent work" a globally sustainable goal to be achieved for labor. In its "Indicators to Measure Decent Work" it outlines a set of general norms that accommodate differences across political economic contexts and industries. International Labor Organization, http://www.ilo.org/integration/resources/mtgdocs/WCMS_115402/lang—en/index.htm.

32. Cole, Teju [@tejucole], "4- This world exists simple to satisfy the needs—including, importantly, the sentimental needs—of white people and Oprah," *Twitter*, March 8, 2012, https://twitter.com/tejucole/status/177810073740001281.

METHODOLOGICAL APPENDIX

1. Berik 1996.
2. Stacey 1988: 22.
3. Wolf 1996.
4. Zavella 1993.
5. Wolf 1996: 139.
6. Mies 1999: 28.
7. Nader 1972; Yanagisako and Delaney, 1995.
8. Tsing 2005.
9. Erzen 2006: 7.
10. Kraska 1998: 89.
11. Blee 1993: 385.
12. Han 2010.
13. Han 2010: 14.
14. At the time, Empower was reprinting its English-language textbook, based on an original that lacked a digital copy.
15. See Bernstein and Shih 2014.

Bibliography

Adams, Vincanne. 2013. *Markets of Sorrow, Labors of Faith: New Orleans in the Wake of Katrina*. Durham, NC: Duke University Press.

Agustín, Laura. 2003. "Sex, Gender, and Migration: Facing Up to Ambiguous Realities." *Soundings*, 23, 84–98.

———. 2007. *Sex at the Margins: Migration, Labour Markets, and the Rescue Industry*. London: Zed Books.

———. 2014. "'Sex Work Is Not Sex Trafficking': An Idea Whose Time Has Not Come." Naked Anthropologist, September 19, 2014. http://www .lauraagustin.com/sex-work-is-not-sex-trafficking-an-idea-whose-time-has-not-come#comments.

Aijazi, Omer. 2014. "The Imaginations of Humanitarian Assistance: A Machete to Counter the Crazy Forest of Varying Trajectories." *UnderCurrents: Journal of Critical Environmental Studies, 18*, 46–51.

Almeling, Rene. 2011. *Sex Cells: The Medical Market for Eggs and Sperm*. Berkeley: University of California Press.

Altan-Olcay, Özlem. 2014. "Entrepreneurial Subjectivities and Gendered Complexities: Neoliberal Citizenship in Turkey." *Feminist Economics, 20*(4), 235–59.

Amnesty International 2013. "China's 'Re-education through Labour' Camps: Replacing One System of Repression with Another?" December 2013. https://www.amnesty.org/en/latest/news/2013/12/china-s-re-education-through-labour-campsreplacing-one-system-repression-another/.

Anderson, Bridget. 2007. *Troubling Trafficking: Why I Am Worried about Motherhood and Apple Pie but Don't Endorse Slavery*. Copenhagen: Danish Institute for International Studies.

Anderson, Bridget, and Rutvica Andrijasevic. 2008. "Sex, Slaves, and Citizens: The Politics of Anti-trafficking." *Soundings, 40*, 135–45.

Andrijasevic, Rutvica, and Bridget Anderson. 2009. "Anti-trafficking Campaigns: Decent? Honest? Truthful?" *Feminist Review,* 151–55.

Anner Marc, Jennifer Bair, and Jeremy Blasi. 2013. "Toward Joint Liability in Global Supply Chains." *Comparative Labor Law and Policy Journal, 35,* 1–44.

Anzaldua, Gloria. 1990. *Making Face, Making Soul/Haciendo Caras: Creative and Critical Perspectives by Feminists of Color.* San Francisco: Aunt Lute Books.

Arnott, Jayne, and Anna-Louise Crago. 2009. *Rights Not Rescue: A Report on Female, Male, and Trans Sex Workers' Human Rights in Botswana, Namibia, and South Africa.* Open Society Institute, June. Retrieved from NSWP, Global Network of Sex Work Projects, https://www.nswp.org/sites/nswp.org/files/rightsnotrescue_20090706.pdf.

Asia Foundation. 2013. "Thailand Adopts Nationwide Minimum Wage Policy amid Controversy," January 30. http://asiafoundation.org/in-asia/2013/01/30/thailand-a dopts-nationwide-minimum-wage-policy-amid-controversy/.

Associated Press. 2017. "Workers from Factory Making Ivanka Trump Shoes Tell of Long Hours, Low Pay, Abuse." *Voice of America.* June 28. https://www.voanews.com/a/workers-from-factory-making-ivanka-trump-shoes-long-hours-low-pay-abuse/3920047.html.

Australian Catholic Religious Against Trafficking in Humans. 2015. "Prayer and Action against Human Trafficking." Justice and Peace Office, Catholic Archdiocese of Sydney. https://www.dfat.gov.au/sites/default/files/aaptip-fastfacts.pdf.

Australian Government, Department of Foreign Affairs and Trade. 2016. "Australia-Asia Program to Combat Trafficking in Persons (AAPTIP) Program Fact Sheet." January.

Baker, Chris, and Pasuk Phongpaichit. 2005. *A History of Thailand.* Cambridge: Cambridge University Press.

Bales, Kevin. 2004 [1999]. *Disposable People: New Slavery in the Global Economy.* Revised ed. Berkeley: University of California Press.

Bangkok News. 2019. "Controversial Bangkok Soapy Massage Ordered Shut Down Again—Before It's Even Opened." ASEAN Now, June 27. https://aseannow.com/topic/1108586-controversial-bangkok-soapy-massage-ordered-shut-down-again-before-its-even-opened/.

Bandy, Joe, and Jackie Smith, eds. 2005. *Coalitions across Borders: Transnational Protest and the Neoliberal Order.* Lanham, MD: Rowman and Littlefield.

Banet-Weiser, Sarah. 2012. *Authentic™: The Politics of Ambivalence in a Brand Culture.* New York: New York University Press.

Barry, Kathleen. 1995. *The Prostitution of Sexuality: The Global Exploitation of Women.* New York: New York University Press.

Batsone, David B. 2010. *Not for Sale: The Return of the Global Slave Trade—And How We Can Fight It.* Revised ed. New York: HarperOne.

Benshoff, Laura. 2019. "Fugitives from ICE: A Family Finds Sanctuary in a Pennsylvania Church." *All Things Considered,* March 7. National Public

Radio. https://www.npr.org/2019/03/07/700215924/fugitives-from-ice-a-family-finds-sanctuary-in-a-pennsylvania-church.

Berik, Gunseli. 1996. "Understanding the Gender System in Rural Turkey: Fieldwork Dilemmas of Conforming and Intervention." Pp. 56–71 in D. L. Wolf, ed., *Feminist Dilemmas in Fieldwork*. Boulder, CO: Westview Press.

Berk, Richard A. 1983. "An Introduction to Sample Selection Bias in Sociological Data." *American Sociological Review*, 48(3), 386–98.

Bernstein, Elizabeth. 2007a. *Temporarily Yours: Intimacy, Authenticity, and the Commerce of Sex*. Chicago: University of Chicago Press.

———. 2007b. "The Sexual Politics of the 'New Abolitionism.'" *Differences*, 18(3), 128–51.

———. 2008a. "Introduction: Sexual Commerce and the Global Flow of Bodies, Desires, and Social Policies." Special issue, *Sexuality Research and Social Policy*, 5(4), 1–5.

———. 2008b. "The Sexual Politics of the 'New Abolitionism': Imagery and Activism in Contemporary Anti-trafficking Campaigns." Paper presented at Center for the Study of Women, University of California, Los Angeles, February.

———. 2009. "To Plead Our Own Cause: Personal Stories by Today's Slaves." *Contemporary Sociology: A Journal of Reviews*, 38(5), 437–39.

———. 2010. "Militarized Humanitarianism Meets Carceral Feminism: The Politics of Sex, Rights, and Freedom in Contemporary Antitrafficking Campaigns." *Signs*, 36(1), 45–71.

———. 2012. "Carceral Politics as Gender Justice? The 'Traffic in Women' and Neoliberal Circuits of Crime, Sex, and Rights." *Theory and Society*, 41(3), 233–59.

———. 2014. "Introduction: Sexual Economies and New Regimes of Governance." *Social Politics: International Studies in Gender, State, and Society*, 21(3), 345–54.

———. 2019. *Brokered Subjects: Sex, Trafficking, and the Politics of Freedom*. Chicago: University of Chicago Press.

Bernstein, Elizabeth, and Elena Shih. 2014. "The Erotics of Authenticity: Sex Trafficking and 'Reality Tourism' in Thailand." *Social Politics: International Studies in Gender, State, and Society* 21(3), 430–60.

Beutin, Lyndsey P. 2017. "Black Suffering for/from Anti-trafficking Advocacy." *Anti-trafficking Review*, 9(2), 14–30.

———. 2022. "The Anti-trafficking Apparatus Has a Racial Justice Problem." Pp. 47–63 in Kempadoo and Shih 2022. New York: Routledge.

———. 2023. *Trafficking in Antiblackness: Modern-Day Slavery, White Indemnity, and Racial Justice*. Durham, NC: Duke University Press.

Biao, Xiang. 2007. "How Far Are the Left-Behind Left Behind? A Preliminary Study in Rural China." *Population, Space, and Place* 13(3), 179–91.

Blee, Katherine. 1993. "Evidence, Empathy, and Ethics: Lessons from Oral Histories of the Klan." *Journal of American History*, 80(2), 596–606.

Bloul, Rachel. 2012. "Ain't I a Woman? Female Landmine Survivors' Beauty Pageants and the Ethics of Staring." *Social Identities*, 18(1), 3–18.

Bob, Clifford. 2001. "Marketing Rebellion: Insurgent Groups, International Media, and NGO Support." *International Politics,* 38(3), 311–34.

Boittin, Margaret Leith. 2013. "New Perspectives from the Oldest Profession: Abuse and the Legal Consciousness of Sex Workers in China." *Law and Society Review,* 47(2), 245–78.

Bornstein, Erica. 2004. *The Spirit of Development: Protestant NGOs, Morality, and Economics in Zimbabwe.* London: Routledge.

Bose, Diya. 2016. "Dhaka's 'Victims of Trafficking': Locked Up for Their 'Own Good.'" *openDemocracy,* February 19. https://www.opendemocracy.net /en/beyond-trafficking-and-slavery/victims-of-trafficking-in-bangladesh-locked-up-for-their-own-good/.

Bravo, Karen E. 2007. "Exploring the Analogy between Modern Trafficking in Humans and the Trans-Atlantic Slave Trade." *Boston University International Law Journal,* 25, 207.

Brennan, Denise. 2014. *Life Interrupted: Trafficking into Forced Labor in the United States.* Durham, NC: Duke University Press.

Brennan, Denise, and Sine Plambech, eds. 2018. "Life after Trafficking." Special issue, *Anti-trafficking Review* (10).

Brents, Barbara G., Crystal A. Jackson, and Kathryn Hausbeck. 2010. *The State of Sex: Tourism, Sex, and Sin in the New American Heartland.* New York: Routledge.

Bronkema, David, and Christopher M. Brown. 2009. "Business as Mission through the Lens of Development." *Transformation,* 26(2), 82–88.

Brooks, Ethel C. 2007. *Unraveling the Garment Industry: Transnational Organizing and Women's Work.* Minneapolis: University of Minnesota Press.

Brooks, Siobhan. 2010. "Hypersexualization and the Dark Body: Race and Inequality among Black and Latina Women in the Exotic Dance Industry." *Sexuality Research and Social Policy,* 7(2), 70–80.

Brunovskis, Anette, and Rebecca Surtees. 2007. *Leaving the Past Behind: Why Some Trafficking Victims Decline Assistance.* Oslo: Fafo Institute and NEXUS Institute to Combat Human Trafficking.

———. 2013. "Coming Home: Challenges in Family Reintegration for Trafficked Women." *Qualitative Social Work,* 12(4), 454–72.

Burawoy, Michael. 1982. *Manufacturing Consent: Changes in the Labor Process under Monopoly Capitalism.* Chicago: University of Chicago Press.

———. 1998. "The Extended Case Method." *Sociological Theory,* 16(1), 4–33.

———. 2000. *Global Ethnography: Forces, Connections, and Imaginations in a Postmodern World.* Berkeley: University of California Press.

———. 2010. "From Polanyi to Pollyanna: The False Optimism of Global Labor Studies." *Global Labour Journal,* 1(2), 301–13.

Burningham, Kate. 2000. "Using the Language of NIMBY: A Topic for Research, Not an Activity for Researchers." *Local Environment,* 5(1), 55–67.

Business and Human Rights Resource Centre. 2019. "Myanmar: Labour Activists Charged for Role in Garment Factory Strike Over Working Conditions."

CATW (Coalition to Abolish Traffic in Women). 2022. "Our Work." Accessed October 27, 2021. http://www.catwinternational.org/.

Chab Dai Coalition. 2012. "Chab Dai Charter Assessment Tool: Commitment to Excellence in Protection, Collaboration, Participation, and Transparency." Third Annual Interdisciplinary Conference on Human Trafficking, 2011. Digital Commons at University of Nebraska, Lincoln. https://digitalcommons.unl.edu/cgi/viewcontent.cgi?article=1002&context=humtraffconf3.

Chacón, Jennifer M. 2006. "Misery and Myopia: Understanding the Failures of US Efforts to Stop Human Trafficking." *Fordham Law Review,* 74, 2977.

———. 2010. "Tensions and Trade-Offs: Protecting Trafficking Victims in the Era of Immigration Enforcement." *University of Pennsylvania Law Review,* 1609–53.

Chaitanat and Leeds Co., Ltd. 2013. "How to Register an NGO in Thailand." Retrieved October 10, 2014. https://www.youtube.com/watch?v=cB72Qy44IL8.

Chamratrithirong, Aphichat. 2007. "Research on Internal Migration in Thailand: The State of Knowledge." *Journal of Population and Social Studies,* 16(1), 1–20.

Chan, Chak Kwan, and Zhaiwen Peng. 2011. "From Iron Rice Bowl to the World's Biggest Sweatshop: Globalization, Institutional Constraints, and the Rights of Chinese Workers." *Social Service Review,* 85(3), 421–45.

Chan, Debby. 2011. "Activist Perspective: The Social Cost Hidden in the Apple Products." *Journal of Workplace Rights,* 15(3–4).

Chan, Jenny. 2013. "A Suicide Survivor: The Life of a Chinese Migrant Worker at Foxconn." *Asia-Pacific Journal,* 11(31), 1–22.

———. 2014. "The Labor Politics of Global Production: Foxconn, the State, and China's New Working Class." PhD dissertation, Royal Holloway, University of London.

Chan, Jenny, and Pun Ngai. 2010. "Suicide as Protest for the New Generation of Chinese Migrant Workers: Foxconn, Global Capital, and the State." *The Asia-Pacific Journal,* 37(2), 1–50.

Chan, Jenny, Ngai Pun, and Mark Selden. 2015. "Interns or Workers? China's Student Labor Regime." *Asian Studies,* 1(1), 69–98.

Chan, Kam Wing. 2009. "The Chinese Hukou System at 50." *Eurasian Geography and Economics,* 50(2), 197–221.

Chan, Kam Wing, and Yuan Ren, eds. 2022. *Children of Migrants in China.* New York: Routledge.

Chang, June, 2014. "China Needs an Amber Alert System to Fight Child Abductions." *China Daily.* October 14.

Chang, Grace, and Kathleen Kim. 2007. "Reconceptualizing Approaches to Human Trafficking: New Directions and Perspectives from the Field(s)." *Stanford Journal of Contemporary Research,* 317–44.

Chang, Hongqin, Xiao-yuan Dong, and Fiona MacPhail. 2011. "Labor Migration and Time Use Patterns of the Left-Behind Children and Elderly in Rural China." *World Development,* 39(12), 2199–2210.

Chapkis, Wendy. 2003. "Trafficking, Migration, and the Law: Protecting Inno-
cents, Punishing Immigrants." *Gender and Society* 17(6), 923–37.

———. 2005. "Soft Glove, Punishing Fist: The Trafficking Victims Protection
Act of 2000." Pp. 51–65 in Elizabeth Bernstein and Laurie Schaffner, eds.,
Regulating Sex: The Politics of Intimacy and Identity. New York: Routledge.

Chasin, Alexandra. 2001. *Selling Out: The Gay and Lesbian Movement Goes
to the Market.* New York: Palgrave Macmillan.

Chavisa, Pear. 2014. "The Meaning of Color in Thailand: Pear Chavisa Graphic
Design." Chavisa Pear Design. March 23. https://pppear.wordpress
.com/2014/03/23/the-meaning-of-color-in-thailand/

Cheng, Sealing. 2008. "Muckraking and Stories Untold: Ethnography Meets
Journalism on Trafficked Women and the US Military." *Sexuality Research
and Social Policy,* 5(4), 6–18.

———. 2011. *On the Move for Love: Migrant Entertainers and the
US Military in South Korea.* Philadelphia: University of Pennsylvania
Press.

Chin, Angelina. 2012. *Bound to Emancipate: Working Women and Urban Citizenship in Early Twentieth-Century China and Hong Kong.* Lanham, MD:
Rowman and Littlefield.

China National Plan of Action on Combating Trafficking in Women and Children. 2008–12. https://www.notip.org.cn/UserImages/00000570.pdf

China National Plan of Action on Combating Trafficking in Persons. 2013–20.
https://www.nwccw.gov.cn/2017-05/26/content_158795.htm.

———. 2021–30. https://www.chinalawtranslate.com/en/countertrafficking-
plan2021thr2030/.

Chomsky, Noam. 2008. "Humanitarian Imperialism." *Monthly Review,* 60(4),
22–50.

Choo, Hae Yeon. 2013. "The Cost of Rights: Migrant Women, Feminist Advocacy, and Gendered Morality in South Korea." *Gender and Society,* 27(4),
445–46.

———. 2016. "Selling Fantasies of Rescue: Intimate Labor, Filipina Migrant
Hostesses, and US GIs in a Shifting Global Order." *Positions: East Asia Cultures Critique,* 24(1), 179–203.

Chow, Rey. 1991. *Women and Chinese Modernity: The Politics of Reading
Between West and East.* Minneapolis: University of Minnesota Press.

Chuang, Janie A. 1998. "Redirecting the Debate over Trafficking in Women:
Definitions, Paradigms, and Contexts." *Harvard Human Rights Journal,* 11,
65.

———. 2006a. "United States as Global Sheriff: Using Unilateral Sanctions to
Combat Human Trafficking." *Michigan Journal of International Law,* 27,
437.

———. 2006b. "Beyond a Snapshot: Preventing Human Trafficking in the
Global Economy." *Indiana Journal of Global Legal Studies,* 13(1),
137–163.

———. 2010. "Rescuing Trafficking from Ideological Capture: Prostitution
Reform and Anti-trafficking Law and Policy." *University of Pennsylvania
Law Review,* 1655–1728.

———. 2014. "Exploitation Creep and the Unmaking of Human Trafficking Law." *American Journal of International Law*, 108(4), 609–49.

———. 2015. "Giving as Governance? Philanthrocapitalism and Modern-Day Slavery Abolitionism." *UCLA Law Review*, 62, 1516.

Chuang, Julia. 2014. "China's Rural Land Politics: Bureaucratic Absorption and the Muting of Rightful Resistance." *China Quarterly*, 219, 649–69.

Clarke, Gerard. 1998. Non-governmental Organizations (NGOs) and Politics in the Developing World." *Political Studies*, 46(1), 36–52.

Cohen, Erik. 1988. "Authenticity and Commoditization in Tourism." *Annals of Tourism Research*, 15(3), 371–86.

———. 1996. *Thai Tourism: Hill Tribes, Islands, and Open-ended Prostitution*. Collected Papers 4. Bangkok: White Lotus.

Cole, Georgia. 2021. "Sampling on the Dependent Variable: An Achille's Heel of Research on Displacement?" *Journal of Refugee Studies*, 34(4), 4479–4502.

Cole, Teju. 2012. "The White Savior Industrial Complex." *The Atlantic*, March 21.

Conaway, Jessica. 2004. "Reversion Back to a State of Nature in the United States Southern Borderlands: A Look at Potential Causes of Action to Curb Vigilante Activity on the United States/Mexico Border." *Mercer Law Review*, 56, 1419.

Conca, Ken. 2005. *Governing Water: Contentious Transnational Politics and Global Institution Building*. Cambridge, MA: MIT Press.

Connery, Christopher. 2019. "New Workers' Culture: An Interview with Xu Duo." *Boundary 2: An International Journal of Literature and Culture*, 46(2), 255–62.

Crawford, Adam. 1997. *The Local Governance of Crime: Appeals to Community and Partnerships*. Oxford: Clarendon Press.

Cunningham, Hilary. 2000. "The Ethnography of Transnational Social Activism: Understanding the Global as Local." *American Ethnologist*, 26(3), 583–604.

Dalpino, Catharin. 2012. "Thailand in 2011: High Tides and Political Tensions." *Asian Survey*, 52(1), 195–201.

Davis, Angela Y. 2001. "Race, Gender, and Prison History: From the Convict Lease System to the Supermax Prison." *Prison Masculinities*, 35–45.

———. 2011. *Are Prisons Obsolete?* New York: Seven Stories Press.

Dear, Michael. 1992. "Understanding and Overcoming the NIMBY Syndrome." *Journal of the American Planning Association*, 58(3), 288–300.

De Genova, Nicholas, and Natalie Peutz. 2010. *The Deportation Regime: Sovereignty, Space, and the Freedom of Movement*. Durham, NC: Duke University Press.

Della Porta, Donatella, and Sidney Tarrow. 2005. *Transnational Protest and Global Activism*. Lanham, MD: Rowman and Littlefield.

Della Porta, Donatella. 2006. *Social Movements, Political Violence, and the State: A Comparative Analysis of Italy and Germany*. Cambridge: Cambridge University Press.

Della Porta, Donatella, and Raffaele Marchetti. 2011. *Transnational Activisms and the Global Justice Movement."* Pp. 428–38 in Gerard Delanty and Stephen Turner, eds., *Handbook of Contemporary Social and Political Theory.* London: Routledge.

Deng, Guosheng. 2010. "The Hidden Rules Governing China's Unregistered NGOs: Management and Consequences." *China Review, 10*(1), 183–206, 908–26.

Desai, Manisha. 2007. "The Messy Relationship between Feminisms and Globalizations." *Gender and Society, 21*(6), 797–803.

Ditmore, Melissa Hope. 2011. *Prostitution and Sex Work.* Santa Barbara, CA: Greenwood.

Doezema, Jo. 1998. "Forced to Choose: Beyond the Voluntary v. Forced Prostitution Dichotomy." Pp. 34–51 in Kempadoo and Doezema 1998. New York: Routledge.

———. 2000. "Loose Women or Lost Women? The Re-emergence of the Myth of White Slavery in Contemporary Discourse of Trafficking in Women." *Gender Issues, 18*(1), 23–50.

———. 2001. "Ouch! Western Feminists' 'Wounded Attachment' to the 'Third World Prostitute.'" *Feminist Review,* 16–38.

———. 2005. "Now You See Her, Now You Don't: Sex Workers at the UN Trafficking Protocol Negotiation." *Social and Legal Studies, 14*(1), 61–89.

———. 2010. *Sex Slaves and Discourse Masters: The Construction of Trafficking.* London: Zed Books.

Dong, Marianna. 2019. "The Issue of Trafficking in Women and Young Girls in China and the Chinese Criminal Justice." *Deportate, Esuli, Profughe, 40,* 68–88.

Dong, Yiming, and Charlotte Goodburn. 2020. "Residence Permits and Points Systems: New Forms of Educational and Social Stratification in Urban China." *Journal of Contemporary China, 29*(125), 647–66.

Du Bois, W. E. B. 1899. *The Philadelphia Negro: A Social Study.* Philadelphia: University of Pennsylvania.

Dummermuth, Matt. 2019. "Human Trafficking: Hidden in Plain Sight.'" US Department of Justice, Office of Justice Programs. https://www.ojp.gov/files /archives/blogs/2019/human-trafficking-hidden-plain-sight.

Dwyer, Arienne M. 2005. "The Xinjiang Conflict: Uyghur Identity, Language Policy, and Political Discourse." Washington, DC: East-West Center.

Einstein, Mara. 2012. *Compassion, Inc.: How Corporate America Blurs the Line between What We Buy, Who We Are, and Those We Help.* Berkeley: University of California Press.

Elias, Robert. 1986. *The Politics of Victimization: Victims, Victimology, and Human Rights.* Oxford: Oxford University Press.

Elyachar, Julia. 2005. *Markets of Dispossession: NGOs, Economic Development, and the State in Cairo.* Durham, NC: Duke University Press.

Empower Foundation. 2011a. *Bad Girls of Lanna: Our Story of Sex Work in Chiang Mai, Thailand.* Chiang Mai: Empower University Press.

———. 2011b. *Bad Girls Tales.* Chiang Mai: Empower University Press.

———. 2012. *Hit and Run: The Impact of Anti-Human Trafficking Policy and Practice on Sex Workers' Human Rights in Thailand.* Chiang Mai: Empower University Press.

———. 2016. *Moving toward Decent Sex Work.* Chiang Mai: Empower University Press.

———. 2017. "Sex Workers and the Thai Entertainment Industry." Report Submitted to the Committee on the Elimination of Discrimination against Woman Sixty-seventh session, July 3-21, 2017. https://www.nswp.org/sites /default/files/sex_workers_and_the_thai_entertainment_industry_empower_ foundation_-_2017.pdf

Enloe, Cynthia. 1989. *Bananas, Beaches, Bases: Making Feminist Sense of International Politics.* Berkeley: University of California Press.

———. 2000. *Maneuvers: The International Politics of Militarizing Women's Lives.* Berkeley: University of California Press.

Enting, Carolyn. 2014. "Mission Possible." *Mindfood.* August 15. https:// www.mindfood.com/article/mission-possible-sex-slavery-daniel-walker/.

Erzen, Tanya. 2006. *Straight to Jesus: Sexual and Christian Conversions in the Ex-gay Movement.* Berkeley: University of California Press.

Evans, Peter. 2005. "Fighting Marginalization with Transnational Networks: Counter-hegemonic Globalization." *Contemporary Sociology,* 29(1), 230–41.

Eyerman, Ron, and Andrew Jamison. 1991. *Social Movements: A Cognitive Approach.* University Park: Penn State University Press.

Fassin, Didier. 2011. *Humanitarian Reason: A Moral History of the Present.* Berkeley: University of California Press.

Feingold, David A. 2005. "Human Trafficking." *Foreign Policy,* 26–32.

———. 2013. "The Burmese Traffic-Jam Explored: Changing Dynamics and Ambiguous Reforms." *Cultural Dynamics,* 25(2), 207–27.

Fittipaldo, Ray. 2018. "Mike Tomlin and the Steelers Are Doing Their Part to End Child Sex Trafficking." *Pittsburgh Post-Gazette,* August 3. https://www .post-gazette.com/sports/steelers/2018/08/03/steelers-mike-tomlin- operation-underground-railroad-chris-ballard-book/stories/201808030138.

Friedman, Eli. 2009. "External Pressure and Local Mobilization: Transnational Activism and the Emergence of the Chinese Labor Movement." *Mobilization: An International Quarterly,* 14(2), 199–218.

———. 2014. *Insurgency Trap: Labor Politics in Postsocialist China.* Ithaca, NY: Cornell University Press.

———. 2022. *The Urbanization of People: The Politics of Development, Labor Markets, and Schooling in the Chinese City.* New York: Columbia University Press.

Friedman, Eli, and Ching Kwan Lee. 2010. "Remaking the World of Chinese Labour: A 30-Year Retrospective." *British Journal of Industrial Relations,* 48(3), 507–33.

Fukushima, Annie Isabel. 2019. *Migrant Crossings: Witnessing Human Trafficking in the U.S.* Stanford, CA: Stanford University Press.

Gaetano, Arianne M., and Tamara Jacka, eds. 2013. *On the Move: Women and Rural-to-Urban Migration in Contemporary China.* New York: Columbia University Press.

Gallagher, Anne T. 2001. "Human Rights and the New UN Protocols on Trafficking and Migrant Smuggling: A Preliminary Analysis." *Human Rights Quarterly*, 23(4), 975–1004.

———. 2006. Human Rights and Human Trafficking in Thailand: A Shadow TIP Report." Pp. 139–64 in Karen Beeks and Delila Amir, eds., *Trafficking and the Global Sex Industry*. Lanham, MD: Lexington Books.

———. 2010. *The International Law of Human Trafficking*. Cambridge: Cambridge University Press.

———. 2014. "The Global Slavery Index Is Based on Flawed Data—Why Does No One Say So?" *The Guardian*, November 28. http://www.theguardian.com/global-development/poverty-matters/2014/nov/28/global-slavery-index-walk-free-human-trafficking-anne-gallagher.

Galusca, Roxana. 2012. "Slave Hunters, Brothel Busters, and Feminist Interventions: Investigative Journalists as Anti-sex-trafficking Humanitarians." *Feminist Formations*, 24(2), 1–24.

Ganz, Marshall. 2000. "Resources and Resourcefulness: Strategic Capacity in the Unionization of California Agriculture, 1959–1966." *American Journal of Sociology*, 1003–62.

Gasaway, Brantley W. 2014. *Progressive Evangelicals and the Pursuit of Social Justice*. Chapel Hill: University of North Carolina Press.

Gereffi, Gary, and Miguel Korzeniewicz, eds. 1994. *Commodity Chains and Global Capitalism*. London: Greenwood.

Ghimire, Saurav. 2012. "The Three Rs of Justice to Human Trafficking Victims (Rescue, Rehabilitation and Reintegration)." *Kathmandu School Law Review*, 1, 104.

Gilroy, Paul. 2010. *Darker than Blue: On the Moral Economies of Black Atlantic Culture*. Cambridge, MA: Harvard University Press.

GAATW (Global Alliance Against Traffic in Women). 2005. "The GAATW Story." March 15. https://www.gaatw.org/98-gaatw-journey/gaatw-history.

———. 2007. *Collateral Damage: The Impact of Anti-Trafficking Measures on Human Rights Around the World*. Bangkok. http://www.gaatw.org/CollateralDamage_Final/singlefile_CollateralDamagefinal.pdf.

Global Labor Justice and Asia Floor Wage Alliance. 2019. "End Gender Based Violence and Harassment." Global Labor Justice. https://globallaborjustice.org/wp-content/uploads/2019/06/End-GBVH_GLJ_AFWA-2019.pdf.

Global Network of Sex Worker Projects. 2013. "NSWP Supports Chinese Sex Worker Rights Activist Ye Haiyan, Currently Detained by Police." NSWP. June 5. https://www.nswp.org/es/news/nswp-supports-chinese-sex-worker-rights-activist-ye-haiyan-currently-detained-police.

———. 2010. "APNSW Launches Bad Rehab Video." NSWP. Accessed October 28, 2022. https://www.nswp.org/timeline/apnsw-launches-bad-rehab-video.

Global Times. 2014. "Education without Trial." June 4. http://www.globaltimes.cn/content/863879.shtml, accessed 21/10/2018.

Goffman, Erving. 1961. *Asylums: Essays on the Social Situation of Mental Patients and Other Inmates*. New York: Doubleday.

Golash-Boza, Tanya Maria. 2012. *Immigration Nation: Raids, Detentions, and Deportations in Post-9/11 America*. Boulder, CO: Paradigm.

Gold, Thomas, Doug Guthrie, and David Wank, eds. 2002. *Social Connections in China: Institutions, Culture, and the Changing Nature of Guanxi*. Cambridge: Cambridge University Press.

Goldman, Michael. 2005. *Imperial Nature: The World Bank and Struggles for Social Justice in the Age of Globalization*. New Haven, CT: Yale University Press.

Goodburn, Charlotte. 2009. "Learning from Migrant Education: A Case Study of the Schooling of Rural Migrant Children in Beijing." *International Journal of Educational Development*, 29(5), 495–504.

Goodman, Michael K. 2004. "Reading Fair Trade: Political Ecological Imaginary and the Moral Economy of Fair Trade Foods." *Political Geography*, 23(7), 891–915.

———. 2005. *Imperial Nature: The World Bank and Struggles for Social Justice in the Age of Globalization*. New Haven, CT: Yale University Press.

Goodman, Ryan, and Derek Jinks. 2004. "International Law and State Socialization: Conceptual, Empirical, and Normative Challenges." *Duke Law Journal*, 54, 983–97.

Goodwin, Jeff, James M. Jasper, and Francesca Polleta, eds. 2001. *Passionate Politics: Emotions and Social Movements*. Chicago: University of Chicago Press.

GuideStar. 2022a. Operation Underground Railroad Inc. Accessed October 31. https://www.guidestar.org/profile/46-3614979.

———. 2022b. Polaris Project. Accessed October 31. https://www.guidestar.org/profile/03-0391561.

Guidry, John A., Michael D. Kennedy, and Meyer N. Zald, eds. 2000. *Globalizations and Social Movements: Culture, Power, and the Transnational Public Sphere*. Ann Arbor: University of Michigan Press.

Hafner-Burton, Emilie and Kiyoteru Tsutsui. 2005. "Human Rights in a Globalizing World: The Paradox of Empty Promises." *American Journal of Sociology*, 110(5), 1373–1411.

Halegua, Aaron. 2021. "Workplace Gender-Based Violence and Harassment in China: Harmonizing Domestic Law and Practice with International Standards." Global Labor Justice. https://globallaborjustice.org/wp-content/uploads/2021/06/Halegua-Workplace-GBVH-in-China-FINAL-2021.06.21-10-am-EST.pdf.

Han, Ju Hui Judy. 2010. "Neither Friends nor Foes: Thoughts on Ethnographic Distance." *Geoforum*, 41(1), 11–14.

Haney, Lynne A. 2010. *Offending Women: Power, Punishment, and the Regulation of Desire*. Berkeley: University of California Press.

Hanser, Amy. 2005. "The Gendered Rice Bowl: The Sexual Politics of Service Work in Urban China." *Gender and Society*, 19(5), 581–600.

———. 2008. *Service Encounters: Class, Gender, and the Market for Social Distinction in Urban China*. Stanford, CA: Stanford University Press.

Harney, Alexandra. 2015. "China Labor Activists Say Facing Unprecedented Intimidation." Reuters, January 21. http://www.reuters.com/article/us-china-labour-idUSKBN0KU13V20150121.

Hartman, Saidiya. 2008. *Lose Your Mother: A Journey along the Atlantic Slave Route*. New York: Macmillan.

Harvey, David. 2003. *The New Imperialism*. Oxford: Oxford University Press.

———. 2005. *A Brief History of Neoliberalism*. Oxford: Oxford University Press.

Haynes, Dina Francesca. 2006. "(Not) Found Chained to a Bed in a Brothel: Conceptual, Legal, and Procedural Failures to Fulfill the Promise of the Trafficking Victims Protection Act." *Georgetown Immigration Law Journal*, 21, 337.

Heiliger, Evangeline. 2008. "Ado(red), Abhor(red), Disappea(red): Re-scripting Race, Poverty, and Morality under Product (Red)." Paper presented at annual meeting of National Women's Studies Association, Cincinnati, OH.

———. 2013. "Coffee 'Tied with a Pink Ribbon': Transgender Phenomena and Transnational Feminisms in Twenty-First Century Ethical Consumer Movements." *Reconstruction: Studies in Contemporary Culture*, 13(2), 3–4.

Hershatter, Gail. 1997. *Dangerous Pleasures: Prostitution and Modernity in Twentieth-Century Shanghai*. Berkeley: University of California Press.

Hess, Steve. 2010. "Nail-Houses, Land Rights, and Frames of Injustice on China's Protest Landscape." *Asian Survey, 50*(5), 908–26.

Hewison, Kevin. 2014. "Thailand: The Lessons of Protest." *Journal of Critical Perspectives on Asia, 50*(1), 1–15.

Heyrick Research. 2022. "Research." Accessed October 31, 2021. https://www.heyrickresearch.org/research.

Hildebrandt, Timothy. 2011. "The Political Economy of Social Organization Registration in China." *China Quarterly, 208*, 970–89.

———. 2013. *Social Organizations and the Authoritarian State in China*. Cambridge: Cambridge University Press.

Hirono, Miwa. 2008. *Civilizing Missions: International Religious Agencies in China*. New York: Springer.

Hoang, Kimberly. 2015. *Dealing in Desire: Asian Ascendency, Western Decline, and the Hidden Currencies of Sex Work*. Berkeley: University of California Press.

Hoang, Kimberly, and Rhacel Parreñas, eds. 2014. *Human Trafficking Reconsidered: Migration and Forced Labor*. New York: Idebate Press of the International Debate Education Association.

Hodal, Kate, and Chris Kelly 2014. "Trafficked into Slavery on Thai Trawlers to Catch Food for Prawns." *The Guardian*. June 10.

Hondagneu-Sotelo, Pierrette, ed. 2006. *Religion and Social Justice for Immigrants*. New Brunswick, NJ: Rutgers University Press.

Huang, Yasheng. 2008. *Capitalism with Chinese Characteristics: Entrepreneurship and the State*. Cambridge: Cambridge University Press.

Hughart, Suh. 2020. "Hidden in Plain Sight." *Journal of Emergency Medical Services*, January 16. https://www.jems.com/exclusives/hidden-in-plain-sight/.

Huguet, Jerrold W., and Sureeporn Punpuing. 2005 *International Migration in Thailand*. Bangkok: International Organization for Migration, Regional Office.

Human Rights Watch. 2013. *"Swept Away": Abuses against Sex Workers in China.* May 13. http://www.hrw.org/sites/default/files/reports/china0513_ForUpload_0.pdf.

———. 2014. "Thailand: Don't Supply Prisoners to Fishing Boats." December 10. http://www.hrw.org/news/2014/12/10/Thailand-don-t-supply-prisoners-fishing-boats.

———. 2018. "The Hidden Costs of Jewelry." February 8. https://www.hrw.org/report/2018/02/08/hidden-cost-jewelry/human-rights-supply-chains-and-responsibility-jewelry.

Hung, Veron Mei-Ying. 2002. "Improving Human Rights in China: Should Re-education through Labor Be Abolished?" *Columbia Journal of Transnational Law, 41,* 303–26.

Hunt, Nancy Rose. 1988. "'Le Bébé en Brouss': European Women, African Birth Spacing, and Colonial Intervention in Breast Feeding in the Belgian Congo." *International Journal of African Historical Studies,* 21(3), 401–32.

Hwang, Maria Cecilia. 2017. "Offloaded: Women's Sex Work Migration across the South China Sea and the Gendered Antitrafficking Emigration Policy of the Philippines." *Women's Studies Quarterly,* 131–47.

———. 2018. "Gendered Border Regimes and Displacements: The Case of Filipina Sex Workers in Asia." *Signs: Journal of Women in Culture and Society,* 43(3), 515–37.

Hyde, Sandra Teresa. 2007. *Eating Spring Rice: The Cultural Politics of AIDS in Southwest China.* Berkeley: University of California Press.

International Justice Mission. 2022. "2021: Year in Review." IJM. February. https://www.ijm.org/2021-year-in-review.

International Labor Rights Forum and Warehouse Workers United 2014. "The Walmart Effect: Child and Worker Rights Violations at Narong Seafood, Thailand's Model Shrimp Processing Factory." Accessed December 1. Warehouse Workers United. http://www.warehouseworkersunited.org/wp-content/uploads/Narong-Shrimp-Report_Final.pdf

International Princess Project. 2012. "Punjammies: International Princess Project." Accessed October 2012. http://shop.intlprincess.org/.

Jacka, Tamara, and Arianne M. Gaetano. 2004. *On the Move: Women and Rural-to-Urban Migration in Contemporary China.* New York: Columbia University Press.

Jacobs, Harrison. 2019. "KFC Is by Far the Most Popular Fast Food Chain in China and It's Nothing like the US Brand—Here's What It's like." *Business Insider,* March 8.

Jaffee, Daniel. 2007. *Brewing Justice: Fair Trade Coffee, Sustainability, and Survival.* Berkeley: University of California Press.

James, Joy. 1996. *Resisting State Violence: Radicalism, Gender, and Race in US Culture.* Minneapolis: University of Minnesota Press.

Jeffrey, Leslie Ann. 2002. *Sex and Borders: Gender, National Identity, and Prostitution Policy in Thailand.* Chiang Mai, Thailand: Silkworm Books.

———. 2004. *China, Sex, and Prostitution.* London: Routledge.

———. 2006. *Sex and Sexuality in China.* London: Routledge.

———. 2010. "Exposing Police Corruption and Malfeasance: China's Virgin Prostitute Cases." *China Journal*, 63, 127–49.

Jeffreys, Elaine, and Huang Yingying. 2009. "Governing Sexual Health in the People's Republic of China." Pp. 163–85 in Elaine Jeffreys, ed., *China's Governmentalities: Governing Change, Changing Government.* New York: Routledge.

Jenkins, J. Craig, and Charles Perrow. 1977. "Insurgency of the Powerless: Farm Worker Movements (1946–1972)." *American Sociological Review*, 249–68.

Jie, Chen. 2006. "The NGO Community in China: Expanding Linkages with Transnational Civil Society and Their Democratic Implications." *China Perspectives*, 68, 29–40.

Johnson, C. Neal. 2011. *Business as Mission: A Comprehensive Guide to Theory and Practice.* Westmont, IL: InterVarsity Press.

Johnson, Kendall, Eric Larson, Trisha Oliver, David-Allen Sumner Sr., and Tunji Yerima. 2022. "Worker-Owned Cooperatives for Formerly Incarcerated People: Avenues for Racial and Economic Justice." Providence, RI: Break the Cycle Cooperative Hub.

Johnston, Lee. 1996. "What Is Vigilantism?" *British Journal of Criminology*, 36(2), 220–36.

Jordan, Ann. 2002. "Human Rights or Wrongs? The Struggle for a Rights-Based Response to Trafficking in Human Beings." *Gender and Development*, 10(1), 28–37.

Kara, Siddharth. 2017. *Sex Trafficking: Inside the Business of Modern Slavery.* New York: Columbia University Press.

Karim, Lamia. 2011. *Microfinance and Its Discontents: Women in Debt in Bangladesh.* Minneapolis: University of Minnesota Press.

Kaufman, Joan. 2012. "The Global Women's Movement and Chinese Women's Rights." *Journal of Contemporary China*, 21(76), 585–602.

Kay, Tamara. 2005. "Labor Transnationalism and Global Governance: The Impact of NAFTA on Transnational Labor Relationships in North America." *American Journal of Sociology*, 111(3), 715–56.

———. 2011. *NAFTA and the Politics of Labor Transnationalism.* Cambridge: Cambridge University Press.

Keck, Kathryn, and Margret Sikkink. 1998. *Activists beyond Borders: Advocacy Networks in International Politics.* Ithaca, NY: Cornell University Press.

Kedmey, Dan. 2013. "How Thailand's Botched Rice Scheme Blew a Big Hole in Its Economy." *Time*, July 12. http://world.time.com/2013/07/12/how-thailands-botched-rice-scheme-blew-a-big-hole-in-its-economy/.

Kelley, Robin D.G. 2002. *Freedom Dreams: The Black Radical Imagination.* Boston: Beacon Press.

Kempadoo, Kamala. 2001. "Women of Color and the Global Sex Trade: Transnational Feminist Perspectives." *Meridians*, 28–51.

———. 2007. "The War on Human Trafficking in the Caribbean." *Race and Class*, 49(2), 79–85.

———. 2015. "The Modern-day White (Wo)man's Burden: Trends in Anti-trafficking and Anti-slavery Campaigns" *Journal of Human Trafficking,* 1(1), 8–20.

Kempadoo, Kamala, and Elena Shih, eds. 2022. *White Supremacy, Racism, and the Coloniality of Anti-trafficking.* New York: Routledge.

Kempadoo, Kamala, and Jo Doezema, eds. 1998. *Global Sex Workers: Rights, Resistance, and Redefinition.* New York: Routledge Paradigm.

Kempadoo, Kamala, Jyoti Sanghera, and Bandana Pattanaik, eds. 2005. *Trafficking and Prostitution Reconsidered: New Perspectives on Migration, Sex Work, and Human Rights.* New York: Routledge.

Kent, Ann. 2011. *China, the United Nations, and Human Rights: The Limits of Compliance.* Philadelphia: University of Pennsylvania Press.

Kim, Kathleen, and Kusia Hreshchyshyn. 2004. "Human Trafficking Private Right of Action: Civil Rights for Trafficked Persons in the United States." *Hastings Women's Law Journal,* 16, 1.

Kinetz, Erika. 2017. "Making Ivanka Trump Shoes: Long Hours, Low Pay, and Abuse." *Associated Press,* June 28. https://apnews.com/article/north-america-ap-top-news-ivanka-trump-international-news-politics-6cfff3ca3c7d-422594556044369bfb86.

King, Brayden G., and Nicholas Pierce. 2010. "The Contentiousness of Markets: Politics, Social Movements, and Institutional Change in Markets." *Annual Review of Sociology,* 36, 249–67.

Kinney, Edi. 2006. "Appropriations for the Abolitionists: Undermining Effects of the US Mandatory Anti-prostitution Pledge in the Fight against Human Trafficking and HIV/AIDS." *Berkeley Journal of Gender Law and Justice,* 21, 158.

Kitiarsa, Pattana. 2008. *Religious Commodifications in Asia: Marketing Gods.* London: Routledge.

Knowles, Kitty. 2018. "This Startup Is Tackling Human Trafficking by Training Women in 3D-Printed Jewelry Design." *Forbes Business.* April 17.

Kotiswaran, Prabha. 2011. *Dangerous Sex, Invisible Labor.* Princeton, NJ: Princeton University Press.

Kraska, Peter. 1998. "Enjoying Militarism: Political/Personal Dilemmas in Studying US Police Paramilitary Units." Pp. 88–110 in Jeff Ferrell and Mark S. Hamm, eds., *Ethnography at the Edge: Crime, Deviance, and Field Research.* Boston: Northeastern University Press.

Kron, Josh. 2012. "Mission from God: The Upstart Christian Sect Driving Invisible Children and Changing Africa." *The Atlantic.* April 10.

Kuruvilla, Sarosh, Ching Kwan Lee, and Mary Gallagher, eds. 2011. *From Iron Rice Bowl to Informalization: Markets, Workers, and the State in a Changing China.* Ithaca, NY: Cornell University Press.

Lai, Patrick. 2006. *Tentmaking: The Life and Work of Business as Missions.* Palmer Lake, CO: Biblica.

Lam, Elene. 2018a. *Behind the Rescue: How Anti-trafficking Investigations and Policies Harm Migrant Sex Workers.* Toronto: Butterfly.

———. 2018b. *Survey on Toronto Holistic Practitioners' Experiences with Bylaw Enforcement and Police.* Toronto: Butterfly, Coalition Against Abuse by Law Enforcement, Canadian HIV/AIDS Legal Network, and Holistic Practitioners Alliance.

Lau, Mimi. 2013. "Activist Ye Haiyan Evicted from Home by Guangdong Police." *South China Morning Post,* July 7. http://www.scmp.com/news/china/article/1277003/activist-ye-haiyan-evicted-home-guangdong-police.

Lawrence, Felicity, and Kate Hodal. 2014. "Thai Government Condemned in Annual US Human Trafficking Report." *The Guardian,* June 20.

Lawson, Tamara F. 2012. "Fresh Cut in an Old Wound: A Critical Analysis of the Trayvon Martin Killing—The Public Outcry, the Prosecutors' Discretion, and the Stand Your Ground Law." *University of Florida Journal of Law and Public Policy,* 23, 271–310.

LeBaron, Genevieve, Jessica R. Pliley, and David W. Blight, eds. 2022. *Fighting Modern Slavery and Human Trafficking: History and Contemporary Policy.* Cambridge: Cambridge University Press.

LeBaron, Genevieve, Remi Edwards, Tom Hunt, Charline Sempéré, and Penelope Kyritsis. 2022. "The Ineffectiveness of CSR: Understanding Garment Company Commitments to Living Wages in Global Supply Chains." *New Political Economy,* 27(1), 99–115.

Lee, Ching Kwan. 1998. *Gender and the South China Miracle: Two Worlds of Factory Women.* Berkeley: University of California Press.

———. 2007. *Against the Law: Labor Protests in China's Rustbelt and Sunbelt.* Berkeley: University of California Press.

Lee, Ching Kwan, and Shen Yuan. 2009. "China: The Paradox and Possibility of a Public Sociology of Labor." *Work and Occupations,* 36(2), 110–25.

———. 2011. "The Anti-solidarity Machine? Labor Non-governmental Organizations in China." Pp 173–87 in Kuruvilla, Lee, and Gallagher 2011.

Lee, Ching Kwan, and Yonghong Zhang. 2013. "The Power of Instability: Unraveling the Microfoundations of Bargained Authoritarianism in China." *American Journal of Sociology,* 118(6), 1475–1508.

Leigh, Carol. 2015. "Anti-trafficking Industrial Complex Awareness Month (2nd Edition)." Gilder Lehrman Center for the Study of Slavery, Resistance, and Abolition, Yale University. https://glc.yale.edu/sites/default/files/pdf/anti-trafficking_industrial_complex_awareness_month_2nd_edition_with_images_carolleigh_stori.pdf.

Lekakis, Eleftheria J. 2022. *Consumer Activism: Promotional Culture and Resistance.* Los Angeles: SAGE.

Le Espiritu, Yen. 2001. "'We Don't Sleep Around like White Girls Do': Family, Culture, and Gender in Filipina American Lives." *Signs,* 26, 415–40.

Levitt, Peggy, and Sally Merry. 2009. "Vernacularization on the Ground: Local Uses of Global Women's Rights in Peru, China, India and the United States." *Global Networks,* 9(4), 441-61.

Lewis, David, and David Mosse, eds. 2006. *Development Brokers and Translators: The Ethnography of Aid and Agencies.* West Hartford, CT: Kumarian Press.

Lim, Lin Lean, ed. 1998. *The Sex Sector: The Economic and Social Bases of Prostitution in Southeast Asia.* International Labour Office.

Limoncelli, Stephanie. 2010. *The Politics of Trafficking: The First International Movement to Combat the Sexual Exploitation of Women*. Stanford, CA: Stanford University Press.

Ling, Bonny. 2018. "Prostitution and Female Trafficking in China: Between Phenomena and Discourse." *China Perspectives*, 1–2, 65–74.

Ling, Minhua. 2019. *The Inconvenient Generation: Migrant Youth Coming of Age on Shanghai's Edge*. Stanford, CA: Stanford University Press.

Linke, Uli. 2012. "Mobile Imaginaries, Portable Signs: Global Consumption and Representations of Slum Life." *Tourism Geographies*, 14(2), 294–319.

Liu, Fei. 2018. "Pi Village, with Occasional Music: Notes on the New Workers Art Troupe." *Inter-Asia Cultural Studies*, 19(3), 419–30.

Loar, Theresa 1999. "Statement by the Director of the Office of the Senior Coordinator for International Women's Issues before Representative Christopher Smith, House Subcommittee on International Operations and Human Rights," September 14. US Department of State. Accessed October 29, 2022. https://1997-2001.state.gov/www/picw/trafficking/tloar.htm.

Lloyd, Rachel. 2011. *Girls like Us: Fighting for a World Where Girls Are Not for Sale, an Activist Finds Her Calling and Heals Herself—A Memoir*. New York: HarperCollins.

Lui, Mary. 2009. "Saving Young Girls from Chinatown: White Slavery and Woman Suffrage, 1910–1920." *Journal of the History of Sexuality*, 18(3), 393–417.

Ma, Qiusha. 2002. "The Governance of NGOs in China since 1978: How Much Autonomy?" *Nonprofit and Voluntary Sector Quarterly*, 31(3), 305–28.

Mahdavi, Pardis. 2013. *From Trafficking to Terror: Constructing a Global Social Problem*. London: Routledge.

———. 2022. "Trafficking, Terror and their Tropes." Pp. 33-46 in Kempadoo and Shih 2022.

Mai, Nicola. 2013. "Between Embodied Cosmopolitism and Sexual Humanitarianism: The Fractal Mobilities and Subjectivities of Migrants Working in the Sex Industry." In V. Baby-Collins and L. Anteby, eds., *Borders, Mobilities, and Migrations: Perspectives from the Mediterranean in the 21st Century*. Brussels: Peter Lang.

Maney, Gregory M. 2000. "Transnational Mobilization and Civil Rights in Northern Ireland." *Social Problems*, 47(2), 153–79.

Maney, Gregory M., and Margaret Abraham. 2008. "Whose Backyard? Boundary Making in NIMBY Opposition to Immigrant Services." *Social Justice*, 35(4), 66–82.

Manning, Richard. 2006. "Will 'Emerging Donors' Change the Face of International Co-operation?" *Development Policy Review*, 24(4), 371–85.

Marks, Simon. 2014. "Somaly Mam: The Holy Saint (and Sinner) of Sex Trafficking," *Newsweek*, May 21, https://www.newsweek.com/2014/05/30/somaly-mam-holy-saint-and-sinner-sex-trafficking-251642.html.

Marcus, George. 1995. "Ethnography in/of the World System: The Mergence of Multi-sited Ethnography." *Annual Review of Anthropology*, 24, 95–117.

Masenior, Nicole Franck, and Chris Beyrer. 2007. "The US Anti-prostitution Pledge: First Amendment Challenges and Public Health Priorities." *PLOS Medicine*, 4(7), e207.

Mawby, Rob, and Sandra Walklate. 1994. *Critical Victimology: International Perspectives*. London: SAGE.

McAdam, Doug, John McCarthy, and Meyer Zald. 1998. *Comparative Perspectives on Social Movements: Political Opportunities, Mobilizing Structures, and Cultural Framings*. Cambridge: Cambridge University Press.

McAdam, Doug, Sidney Tarrow, and Charles Tilly. 1996. "To Map Contentious Politics." *Mobilization: An International Quarterly*, 1(1), 17–34.

McAdam, Doug. 1988. *Freedom Summer*. New York: Oxford University Press.

McDaniel, Justin T. 2010. *Gathering Leaves and Lifting Words: Histories of Buddhist Monastic Education in Laos and Thailand*. Seattle: University of Washington Press.

McKim, Allison. 2017. *Addicted to Rehab: Race, Gender, and Drugs in the Era of Mass Incarceration*. Rutgers: Rutgers University Press.

Melucci, Alberto. 1989. *Nomads of the Present: Social Movements and Individual Needs in Contemporary Society*. New York: Vintage.

Mensah, Betty, and Samuel Okyere. 2019. "How CNN Reported on Child Slaves Who Were Not Really Enslaved." *Al Jazeera*, March 18.

Merlan, Anna, and Tim Marchman. 2020. "A Famed Anti–Sex Trafficking Group Has a Problem with the Truth." *Vice*. December 10.

———. 2021a. "Inside a Massive Anti-trafficking Charity's Blundering Overseas Mission." *Vice*. March 8.

———. 2021b. "Operation Underground Railroad's Carefully Crafted Public Image Is Falling Apart." *Vice*. June 10.

Meyer, John W., et al. 1992. *School Knowledge for the Masses: World Models and National Primary Curricular Categories in the Twentieth Century*. Washington, DC: Falmer Press.

———. 1997. "World Society and the Nation-State." *American Journal of Sociology*, 103(1), 144–81.

Mies, Maria. 1999. "Towards a Methodology for Feminist Research." *Qualitative Research*, 4, 66–85.

Miller, Donald, and Tetsunao Yamamori. 2007. *Global Pentecostalism: The New Face of Christian Social Engagement*. Berkeley: University of California Press.

Miller-Young, Mireille. 2008. "Hip-Hop Honeys and da Hustlaz: Black Sexualities in the New Hip-Hop Pornography." *Meridians: Feminism, Race, Transnationalism*, 8(1), 261–92.

———. 2010. "Putting Hypersexuality to Work: Black Women and Illicit Eroticism in Pornography." *Sexualities*, 13(2), 219–35.

Minzner, Carl. 2013. "The Turn against Legal Reform." *Journal of Democracy*, 24(1), 65–72.

Mohanty, Chandra Talpade. 1988. "Under Western Eyes: Feminist Scholarship and Colonial Discourses." *Feminist Review*, 61–88.

———. 2004. *Feminism without Borders: Decolonizing Theory, Practicing Solidarity*. Durham, NC: Duke University Press.

Mohanty, Chandra Talpade, Ann Russo, and Lourdes Torres, eds. 1991. *Third World Women and the Politics of Feminism*. Bloomington: Indiana University Press.

Molland, Sverre. 2012. *The Perfect Business? Anti-trafficking and the Sex Trade along the Mekong*. Honolulu: University of Hawai'i Press.

Mostafanezhad, Mary. 2013. "'Getting in Touch with Your Inner Angelina': Celebrity Humanitarianism and the Cultural Politics of Gendered Generosity in Volunteer Tourism." *Third World Quarterly*, 34(3), 485–99.

Mukherjee, Roopali, and Sarah Banet-Weiser, eds. 2012. *Commodity Activism: Cultural Resistance in Neoliberal Times*. New York: New York University Press.

Musto, Jennifer Lynne. 2008. "The Ngo-ification of the Anti-trafficking Movement in the United States: A Case Study of the Coalition to Abolish Slavery and Trafficking." Special Issue. *Wagadu: Anti-Trafficking, Human Rights, Social Justice*, 5, 6–20.

———. 2010. "Carceral Protectionism and Multi-professional Anti-trafficking Human Rights Work in the Netherlands." *International Feminist Journal of Politics*, 12(3–4), 381–400.

———. 2011. "Institutionalizing Protection, Professionalizing Victim Management: Explorations of Multi-professional Anti-trafficking Efforts in the Netherlands and the United States." PhD dissertation, University of California, Los Angeles.

———. 2016. *Control and Protect: Collaboration, Carceral Protection, and Domestic Sex Trafficking in the United States*. Berkeley: University of California Press.

Myers, Ched, and Matthew Colwell. 2012. *Our God Is Undocumented: Biblical Faith and Immigrant Justice*. Maryknoll, NY: Orbis Books.

Nader, Laura. 1972. "Up the Anthropologist: Perspectives Gained from 'Studying Up.'" Pp. 284–311 in Dell Hymes, ed., *Reinventing Anthropology*. New York: Random House.

Napathorn, Chaturong, and Suchada Chanprateep. 2011. "Recent Labor Relations and Collective Bargaining Issues in Thailand." *Interdisciplinary Journal of Research in Business*, 1(6), 66–81.

National Institute of Justice. 2013. "The Prevalence of Labor Trafficking in the United States." NIJ. February 26. https://nij.ojp.gov/topics/articles/prevalence-labor-trafficking-united-states.

Nawaz, Faraha. 2019. *Microfinance and Women's Empowerment in Bangladesh: Unpacking the Untold Tales*. London: Palgrave Pivot.

Nealon, Sarah. 2014. "Daniel Walker Is a Sex-Trade Saviour." *Stuff*. November 7. https://www.stuff.co.nz/entertainment/63013361/.

Neill, Kevin Lewis. 2015. *Secure the Soul: Christian Piety and Gang Prevention in Guatemala*. Berkeley: University of California Press.

New Zealand Government 2022. "2021 Annual Returns" for LIFT International. Charity Services. June 24. https://register.charities.govt.nz/Charity/CC46932.

Ngai, Pun. 2005. *Made in China: Women Factory Workers in a Global Workplace*. Durham, NC: Duke University Press.

Ngai, Pun, and Sam Austin. 2018. "The Third Round of Migrant Labor Struggles in Post-Socialist Guangdong." Pp. 11–21 in Fan Shigang, ed., *Striking to Survive: Workers' Resistance to Factory Relocations in China.* Chicago: Haymarket.

Nguyen, Mimi Thi. 2011. "The Biopower of Beauty: Humanitarian Imperialisms and Global Feminisms in an Age of Terror." *Signs: Journal of Women in Culture and Society,* 36(2), 359–83.

———. 2012. *The Gift of Freedom: War, Debt, and Other Refugee Passages.* Durham, NC: Duke University Press.

———. 2022. "The Right to Be Beautiful." Talk at Brown University. March 22.

Nomi Network. 2021. "2021 Annual Report." https://nominetwork.org/2021-annual-report/.

Not For Sale. 2013. "Become an Abolitionist." Accessed March 2013. http://209.68.62.130/content/08/10/03/not-sale-i-am-not-sale-you-are-not-sale-no-one-should-be-sale-become-abolitionist.

O'Connell Davidson, Julia. 1998. *Prostitution, Power, and Freedom.* Ann Arbor: University of Michigan Press.

———. 2014. *Modern Slavery: The Margins of Freedom.* New York: Springer.

Office of the NESDC (National Economic and Social Development Council). 2018. *Gross Regional and Provincial Product.* https://www.nesdc.go.th/ewt_dl_link.php?nid=5628&filename=gross_regional.

Ogunlesi, Tolu. 2013. "Hijacking Nigeria's #BringBackOurGirls Campaign." *Al Jazeera.* October 22.

Okazaki, Sumie. 2002. "Influences of Culture on Asian Americans' Sexuality." *Journal of Sex Research,* 39(1), 34–41.

Okyere, Samuel. 2013. "Are Working Children's Rights and Child Labour Abolition Complementary or Opposing Realms?" *International Social Work,* 56(1), 80–91.

———. 2017. "'Shock and Awe': A Critique of the Ghana-centric Child Trafficking Discourse." *Anti-Trafficking Review,* 9, 92–105.

———. 2022. "Moral Economies and Child Labour in Artisanal Gold Mining in Ghana." Pp. 29–55 in Neil Howard and Samuel Okyere, eds., *International Child Protection.* London: Palgrave Macmillan.

Ong, Aihwa. 1999. *Flexible Citizenship: The Cultural Logics of Transnationality.* Durham, NC: Duke University Press.

Ono, Yukako. 2017. "Thai PM Confirms Yingluck Fled to Dubai: Emirate Does Not Have an Extradition Treaty with Bangkok." *Nikkei Asia.* September 28. https://asia.nikkei.com/Politics/Thai-PM-confirms-Yingluck-fled-to-Dubai.

Operation Underground Railroad. 2021. "Annual Report." Accessed October 17, 2022. https://www.ourrescue.org/reports/2021-annual.pdf

Opie, Anne. 1992. "Qualitative Research: Appropriation of the Other and Empowerment." *Feminist Review,* 40, 52–69.

Otis, Eileen M. 2011. *Markets and Bodies: Women, Service Work, and the Making of Inequality in China.* Stanford, CA: Stanford University Press.

Owens, Emily A. 2017. "Promises: Sexual Labor in the Space between Slavery and Freedom." *Louisiana History: The Journal of the Louisiana Historical Association,* 58(2), 179–216.

Paitoonpong, Srawooth, and Nipanan Akkarakul. 2009. "The Impact of the Global Financial Crisis on Women Workers in Thailand." *TDRI Quarterly Review,* 24(4), 3–13.

Palaung Women's Organization. 2011. *Stolen Lives: Human Trafficking from Palaung Areas of Burma to China.* Palaung, China: Palaung Women's Organization.

Pan, Suiming. 1999. *Cunzai yu Huangmiu: Zhongguo Dixia "Xing Chanye" Kaocha (Reality and Absurdity: An Investigation of China's Underground Sex Industry).* Beijing: Qunyan Press.

Pangsapa, Piya. 2015. "When Battlefields Become Marketplaces: Migrant Workers and the Role of Civil Society and NGO Activism in Thailand." *International Migration,* 53(3), 124–149.

Parreñas, Rhacel Salazar. 2011. *Illicit Flirtations: Labor, Migration, and Sex Trafficking in Tokyo.* Stanford, CA: Stanford University Press.

Parreñas, Rhacel Salazar, Hung Cam Thai, and Rachel Silvey. 2016. "Introduction: Intimate Industries—Restructuring (Im)material Labor in Asia." *Positions: East Asia Cultures Critique,* 24(1), 1–15.

Parreñas, Rhacel Salazar, Maria Cecilia Hwang, and Heather Ruth Lee. 2012. "What Is Human Trafficking? A Review Essay." *Signs,* 37(4), 1015–29.

Pascoe, Peggy. 1990. *Relations of Rescue: The Search for Female Moral Authority in the American West, 1874–1939.* New York: Oxford University Press.

Pathmanand, Ukrist. 1998. "The Thaksin Shinawatra Group: A Study of the Relationship between Money and Politics in Thailand." *Copenhagen Journal of Asian Studies,* 13(1), 60.

Patterson, Orlando. 2012. "Trafficking, Gender, and Slavery—Past and Present." Pp. 322–59 in Jean Allain, ed., *The Legal Understanding of Slavery: From the Historical to the Contemporary.* Oxford: Oxford University Press.

Permani, Risti, and David Vanzetti. 2014. "Rice Mountain Assessment of the Thai Rice Pledging Program." Paper presented at the Australian Agricultural and Resource Economics Society Conference, February 4–7, 2014, Port Maquarie, Australia.

Peters, Heather A. 2013. "Dancing in the Market: Reconfiguring Commerce and Heritage in Lijiang." Pp. 115-40 in Tami Blumenfield and Helaine Silverman, eds., *Cultural Heritage Politics in China.* New York: Springer.

Petrova, Daniela. 2017. "A Vacation with a Purpose: Fighting Trafficking in Thailand." *New York Times,* May 11. https://www.nytimes.com/2017/05/11/travel/Thailand-vacation-fighting-trafficking-exploitation-altruvistas.html.

Phananiramai, Mathana 2002. "Changes in Women's Economic Role in Thailand." Pp. 274–306 in Susan Horton, ed., *Women and Industrialization in Asia.* New York: Routledge.

Phongpaichit, Pasuk. 2004. *Thailand under Thaksin: Another Malaysia?* Bangkok: Asia Research Centre.

Phongpaichit, Pasuk, and Christopher John Baker. 1998. *Thailand's Boom and Bust.* Chiang Mai: Silkworm Books.

———. 2004. *Thaksin: The Business of Politics in Thailand.* Copenhagen: NIAS Press.

———. 2008. "Thaksin's Populism." *Journal of Contemporary Asia,* 38(1), 62–83.

Plambech, Sine. 2014. "Between 'Victims' and 'Criminals': Rescue, Deportation, and Everyday Violence among Nigerian Migrants." *Social Politics: International Studies in Gender, State, and Society,* 21(3), 382–402.

Pliley, Jessica R. 2014. *Policing Sexuality: The Mann Act and the Making of the FBI.* Cambridge, MA: Harvard University Press.

Polanyi, Karl. 2001 (1944). *The Great Transformation: The Political and Economic Origins Of Our Time.* Boston: Beacon Press.

Polaris Project. 2019. "Human Trafficking in Illicit Massage Businesses: Executive Summary." Polaris Project. September. https://polarisproject.org/wp-content/uploads/2019/09/Human-Trafficking-in-Illicit-Massage-Businesses-Executive-Summary.pdf.

Polletta, Francesca, and James M. Jasper. 2001. "Collective Identity and Social Movements." *Annual Review of Sociology,* 283–305.

Pollock, Jackie, and Soe Lin Aung. 2010. "Critical Times: Gendered Implications of the Economic Crisis for Migrant Workers from Burma/Myanmar in Thailand." *Gender and Development,* 18(2), 213–27.

Ponnudurai, Parameswaran. 2013. "Controversy behind Human Trafficking Rankings." *Radio Free Asia.* April 24. https://www.rfa.org/english/commentaries/east-asia-beat/trafficking-04252013232758.html.

Qiu, Geping, Sheldon X. Zhang, and Weidi Liu. 2019. "Trafficking of Myanmar Women for Forced Marriage in China." *Crime, Law, and Social Change,* 72(1), 35–52.

Qiu, Jack Linchuan, and Hongzhe Wang. 2012. "Working-Class Cultural Spaces: Comparing the Old and the New." Pp. 124–46 in Beatriz Carrillo and David Goodman, eds., *China's Peasants and Workers: Changing Class Identities.* Cheltenham, UK: Edward Elgar.

Radhakrishnan, Smitha. 2021. *Making Women Pay: Microfinance in Urban India.* Durham, NC: Duke University Press.

Radosh, Daniel. 2008. *Rapture Ready! Adventures in the Parallel Universe of Christian Pop Culture.* New York: Simon and Schuster.

Rahman, Shams, and Aswini Yadlapalli. 2021. "Years after the Rana Plaza Tragedy, Bangladesh's Garment Workers Are Still Bottom of the Pile." *The Conversation.* April 22.

Ramachandran, Vibhuti, and Kimberly Walters. 2018. "A Recipe for Injustice: India's New Trafficking Bill Expands a Troubled Rescue, Rehabilitation, and Repatriation Framework." *Open Democracy.* July 30.

Rapley, John. 2004. "Development Studies and the Post-development Critique." *Progress in Development Studies,* 4(4), 350–54.

Raymond, Janice G., Donna M. Hughes, and Carol J. Gomez. 2001. "Sex Trafficking of Women in the United States." Pp. 3–14 in Leonard Territo and George Kirkham, eds., *International Sex Trafficking of Women and Children: Understanding the Global Epidemic.* Flushing, NY: Looseleaf Law.

Reeb, Lloyd, and Bill Wellons. 2006. *Unlimited Partnership: Igniting a Marketplace Leader's Journey to Significance.* Nashville: B&H.

Risse-Kappen, Thomas, Stephen Ropp, and Kathryn Sikkink, eds. 1999. *The Power of Human Rights: International Norms and Domestic Change*. Cambridge: Cambridge University Press.

Royal Thai Government. 2021. "Royal Thai Government's Country Report on Anti-Trafficking Efforts." https://aseanactpartnershiphub.com/wp-content/uploads/2022/02/Thailands-Country-Report-on-Anti-Human-Trafficking-Efforts-2021.pdf.

Rudrappa, Sharmila. 2015. *Discounted Life: The Price of Global Surrogacy in India*. New York: New York University Press.

Rundle, Steven L. 2012. "'Business as Mission' Hybrids: A Review and Research Agenda." *Journal of Biblical Integration in Business*, 15(1), 66–79.

Rundle, Steven, and Tom A. Steffen. 2011. *Great Commission Companies: The Emerging Role of Business in Missions*. Westmont, IL: InterVarsity Press.

Saich, Tony. 2000. "Negotiating the State: The Development of Social Organizations in China." *China Quarterly, 161*, 124–41.

Salt, John, and Jeremy Stein. 1997. "Migration as a Business: The Case of Trafficking." *International Migration, 35*(4), 467–94.

Sassen, Saskia. 2006. *Territory, Authority, Rights: From Medieval to Global Assemblages*. Princeton, NJ: Princeton University Press.

Sawasdipakdi, Pongkwan. 2014. "The Politics of Numbers: Controversy Surrounding the Thai Rice-Pledging Scheme." *SAIS Review of International Affairs, 34*(1), 45–58.

Scheer, Catherine, Philip Fountain, and R. Michael Feener. 2018. *The Mission of Development: Religion and Techno-politics in Asia*. Leiden, Netherlands: Brill Press.

Scott, James C. 1977. *The Moral Economy of the Peasant: Rebellion and Subsistence in Southeast Asia*. New Haven, CT: Yale University Press.

Seidman, Gay. 2007. *Beyond the Boycott: Labor Rights, Human Rights, and Transnational Activism*. New York: Russell Sage Foundation.

Shah, Svati P. 2014. *Street Corner Secrets: Sex, Work, and Migration in the City of Mumbai*. Durham, NC: Duke University Press.

Sharma, Nandita. 2005. "Anti-trafficking Rhetoric and the Making of a Global Apartheid." *NWSA Journal, 17*(3), 88–111.

———. 2006. *Home Economics: Nationalism and the Making of "Migrant Worker" in Canada*. Toronto: University of Toronto Press.

———. 2017. "'The New Order of Things': Immobility as Protection in the Regime of Immigration Controls." *Anti-Trafficking Review, 9*, 31–47.

———. 2020. *Home Rule: National Sovereignty and the Separation of Natives and Migrants*. Durham, NC: Duke University Press.

Shieh, Shawn, and Guosheng Deng. 2011. "An Emerging Civil Society: The Impact of the 2008 Sichuan Earthquake on Grass-Roots Associations in China." *China Journal, 65*, 181–94.

Shih, Elena. 2013a. "Globalising Rehabilitation Regimes: The Moral Economy of Vocational Training in After-Trafficking Work." Pp. 64–78 in Sallie Yea, ed., *Forcing Issues: Rethinking and Rescaling Human Trafficking in the Asia-Pacific Region*. London: Routledge.

———. 2013b. "Health and Rights at the Margins: Human Trafficking and HIV/AIDS amongst Jingpo Ethnic Communities in Ruili City, China." *Anti-Trafficking Review*, 2, 119–36.

———. 2014. "The Anti-Trafficking Rehabilitation Complex." *Contexts*, 13(1), 21–22.

———. 2016. "'Not in My Backyard' Abolition: Vigilante Rescue against American Sex Trafficking." *Sociological Perspectives*, 59(1), 66–90.

———. 2017. "Freedom Markets: Consumption and Commerce across Human Trafficking Rescue in Thailand." *Positions: Asia Critique*, 25(4), 769–94.

———. 2018a. "Duplicitous Freedom: Moral and Material Care Work of Sex and Migration." *Critical Sociology*, 44(7–8), 1077–86.

———. 2018b. "Evangelizing Entrepreneurship: Technopolitics of Vocational Training in the Global Anti-Trafficking Movement." Pp. 243–63 in Catherine Scheer, Philip Fountain, and Michael Feener, eds., *The Mission of Development: Religion and Techno-politics in Asia*. Leiden, Netherlands: Brill.

Shih, Elena, Jennifer JJ Rosenbaum, and Penelope Kyritsis. 2021. "Undermining Labor Power." Pp. 141–55 in LeBaron, Pliley, and Blight 2021.

Shimizu, Celine Parreñas. 2007. *The Hypersexuality of Race: Performing Asian/American Women on Screen and Scene*. Durham, NC: Duke University Press.

Shohat, Ella. 1998. *Talking Visions: Multicultural Feminism in a Transnational Age*. New York: New Museum of Contemporary Art.

Siddiqi, Dina M. 2009. "Do Bangladeshi Factory Workers Need Saving? Sisterhood in the Post-sweatshop Era." *Feminist Review*, 91(1), 154–74.

Silver, Beverly J. 2003. *Forces of Labor: Workers' Movements and Globalization since 1870*. Cambridge: Cambridge University Press.

Silvoso, Ed. 2010. *Transformation: Change the Marketplace and You Change the World*. Delight, AK: Gospel Light.

Skocpol, Theda, and Margeret Somers. 1980. "The Uses of Comparative History in Macrosocial Inquiry." *Comparative Studies in Society and History*, 22, 174–281.

Skrobanek, Siriporn, Nattaya Boonpakdi, and Chutimā Čhanthathīrō. 1997. *The Traffic in Women: Human Realities of the International Sex Trade*. London: Zed Books.

Smith, Linda Tuhiwai. 2012. *Decolonizing Methodologies: Research and Indigenous Peoples*. 2nd ed. London: Zed Books.

Snow, David A., and Robert D. Benford. 1988. "Ideology, Frame Resonance, and Participant Mobilization." *International Social Movement Research*, 1(1), 197–217.

Soderlund, Gretchen. 2005. "Running from the Rescuers: New US Crusades against Sex Trafficking and the Rhetoric of Abolition." *NWSA Journal*, 17(3), 64–87.

Soerens, Matthew, and Jenny Yang. 2018. *Welcoming the Stranger: Justice, Compassion, and Truth in the Immigration Debate*. Westmont, IL: InterVarsity Press.

Somers, Margaret, and Gloria Gibson. 1994. "Reclaiming the 'Epistemological Other': Narrative and the Social Constitution of Identity." Pp. 37–99 in

Craig Calhoun, ed., *Social Theory and the Politics of Identity*. Oxford: Basil Blackwell.

Soysal, Yasemin N. 2012. "Citizenship, Immigration, and the European Social Project: Rights and Obligations of Individuality." *British Journal of Sociology* 63(1), 1–21.

Spengler. 2007. "Christianity Finds a Fulcrum in Asia." *Asia Times*. August 7.

Spivak, Gayatri Chakravorty. 1988. "Can the Subaltern Speak?" Pp. 271–313 in Cary Nelson and Lawrence Grossberg, eds., *Marxism and Interpretation of Culture*. Urbana: University of Illinois Press.

———. 1999. *A Critique of Postcolonial Reason: Toward a History of the Vanishing Present*. Cambridge, MA: Harvard University Press.

Srikantiah, Jayashri. 2007. "Perfect Victims and Real Survivors: The Iconic Victim in Domestic Human Trafficking Law." *Immigration and Nationality Law Review*, 28, 157–211.

Stacey, Judith. 1988. "Can There Be a Feminist Ethnography?" *Feminist Anthropology Review*, 4, 23–30.

Steinbrink, Malte. 2012. "'We did the Slum!': Urban Poverty Tourism in Historical Perspective." *Tourism Geographies*, 14(2), 213–34.

Su, Yihui. 2010. "Student Workers in the Foxconn Empire: The Commodification of Education and Labor in China." *Journal of Workplace Rights* 15(3), 341–62.

Surtees, Rebecca. 2008. "Why Shelters? Considering Residential Approaches to Assistance." Vienna: NEXUS Institute to Combat Human Trafficking. https://nexusinstitute.net/wp-content/uploads/2015/03/why-shelters-residential-approaches-to-trafficking-assistance-nexus-2008.pdf.

———. 2013. *After Trafficking: Experiences and Challenges in the (Re)integration of Trafficked Persons in the Greater Mekong Sub-region*. Bangkok: UNIAP (United Nations Inter-agency Project on Human Trafficking in the Greater Mekong Sub-region); Washington, DC: NEXUS Institute to Combat Human Trafficking.

Swider, Sarah. 2016. *Building China: Informal Work and the New Precariat*. Ithaca, NY: Cornell University Press.

Swidler, Ann, and Susan Cotts Watkins. 2009. "'Teach a Man to Fish': The Sustainability Doctrine and Its Social Consequences." *World Development*, 37(7), 1182–96.

Tan, Vivian. 2014. "As Thousands Continue to Flee Myanmar, UNHCR Concerned about Growing Reports of Abuse." United Nations High Commission on Refugees. June 10. https://www.unhcr.org/5396ee3b9.html.

Tansubhapol, Thanida. 2014. "Poor Trafficking Record 'Inaccurate.'" *Bangkok Post*, May 5. http://www.bangkokpost.com/news/local/408138/govt-disputes-poor-human-trafficking-record-claims.

Tarrow, Sidney. 2005. *The New Transnational Activism*. Cambridge: Cambridge University Press.

Taylor, Lisa Rende, and Elena Shih. 2019. "Worker Feedback Technologies and Combatting Modern Slavery in Global Supply Chains." *Journal of the British Academy*, 7(s1), 131–65. https://doi.org/10.5871/jba/007s1.131.

Thailand Anti–Trafficking in Persons Act B.E. 2551 (2008).

Thompson, E. P. 1971. "The Moral Economy of the English Crowd in the Eighteenth Century." *Past and Present,* 50(1), 76–136.

Ticktin, Miriam. 2014. "Transnational Humanitarianism." *Annual Review of Anthropology,* 43(1), 273–89.

Tilly, Charles. 1978. *From Mobilization to Revolution.* Reading, MA: Addison-Wesley.

Tilly, Charles, and Sidney Tarrow. 2007. *Contentious Politics.* Boulder, CO: Paradigm.

Toone, Trent. 2017. "Glenn Beck and Tim Ballard Team Up in Operation Underground Railroad Video in Thailand." *Deseret News* (Salt Lake City), May 9. https://www.deseret.com/2017/5/9/20611918/glenn-beck-and-tim-ballard-team-up-in-operation-underground-railroad-video-in-thailand.

Trinh, Minh-Ha T. 1989. *Woman, Native, Other.* Bloomington: Indiana University Press.

———. 1997. "Not You/Like You: Postcolonial Women and the Interlocking Questions of Identity and Difference." *Cultural Politics,* 11, 415–19.

Trump, Ivanka. 2018. "Opinion: The Trump Administration Is Taking Bold Action to Combat the Evil of Human Trafficking." *Washington Post,* November 29. https://www.washingtonpost.com/opinions/the-trump-administration-is-taking-bold-action-to-combat-the-the-evil-of-human-trafficking/2018/11/29/3e21685c-f411-11e8-80d0-f7e1948d55f4_story.html.

Tsing, Anna. 2005. *Friction: An Ethnography of Global Connections.* Princeton, NJ: Princeton University Press.

Tuck, Eve. 2013. "Commentary: Decolonizing Methodologies 15 Years Later." *AlterNative: An International Journal of Indigenous Peoples,* 9(4), 365–72.

Tucker, Joseph, Xin Ren, and Flora Sapio. 2010. "Incarcerated Sex Workers and HIV Prevention in China: Social Suffering and Social Justice Countermeasures." *Social Science and Medicine,* 70(1), 121–29.

UNIAP (United Nations Inter-Agency Project to Combat Human Trafficking). 2009. "Siren Report: Exploitation of Cambodian Men at Sea: Facts about the Trafficking of Cambodian Men onto Thai Fishing Boats." Phnom Penh, April 9.

United Nations Convention Against Transnational Organized Crime, U.N. Doc. A/RES/55/25.

United Nations Protocol to Prevent, Suppress, and Punish Trafficking in Persons, Especially Women and Children, Supplementing the U.N. Convention against Transnational Organized Crime. U.N. Doc. A/55/383.

Uretsky, Elanah. 2016. *Occupational Hazards: Sex, Business, and HIV in Post-Mao China.* Stanford, CA: Stanford University Press.

Urry, John. 2002 (1991). *The Tourist Gaze.* New York: Sage.

US Congress Committee on Foreign Affairs. 2015. "Hearing Before the Subcommittee on Africa, Global Health, Global Human Rights, and International Organizations." Serial No. 114-67, May 14. https://docs.house.gov/meetings/FA/FA16/20150514/103457/HHRG-114-FA16-Wstate-BallardT-20150514.pdf.

US Department of Health and Human Services. 2004. "The Campaign to Rescue and Restore Victims of Human Trafficking." http://www.acf.hhs.gov/trafficking/rescue_restore/index.html.

US Department of State, Office to Monitor and Combat Trafficking in Persons. 2008–10, 2013–14, 2021. *Trafficking in Persons Report.* https://www.state.gov/reports/2022-trafficking-in-persons-report/.

US GAO (Government Accountability Office). 2007. "Human Trafficking: Monitoring and Evaluation of International Projects Are Limited, but Experts Suggest Improvement." July. https://www.gao.gov/assets/gao-07-1034.pdf.

———. 2006. Report to the Chairman, Committee on the Judiciary, and the Chairman, Committee on International Relations, House of Representatives. *Human Trafficking: Better Data, Strategy, and Reporting Needed to Enhance US Antitrafficking Efforts Abroad* (GAO-06-825). Washington, DC, July. http://www.gao.gov/new.items/do6825.pdf.

US TVPA (Trafficking Victims Protection Act). 2000. Pub. L. no. 106-386, 114 Stat 1467.

Varley, Teresa. 2018. "Tomlin Helping to Tell a Tough Story." Pittsburgh Steelers. August 3. https://www.steelers.com/news/tomlin-helping-to-tell-a-tough-story.

———. 2012. "Innocence and Experience: Melodramatic Narratives of Sex Trafficking and Their Consequences for Law and Policy." *History of the Present,* 2(2), 200–218.

Vincent, Susan. 2003. "Preserving Domesticity: Reading Tupperware in Women's Social, Domestic, and Economic Roles." *Canadian Review of Sociology and Anthropology,* 40(2), 171–96.

Vrasti, Wanda. 2012. *Volunteer Tourism in the Global South: Giving Back in Neoliberal Times.* London: Routledge.

Walder, Andrew G. 1984. "The Remaking of the Chinese Working Class, 1949–1981." *Modern China,* 3–48.

———. 2002. "Markets and Income Inequality in Rural China: Political Advantage in an Expanding Economy." *American Sociological Review,* 231–53.

Walker, Edward, Andrew Martin, and John McCarthy. 2008. "Confronting the State, the Corporation, and the Academy: The Influence of Institutional Targets on Social Movement Repertoires." *American Journal of Sociology,* 114(1), 35–76.

Walker, Kathy Le Mons. 2008. "From Covert to Overt: Everyday Peasant Politics in China and the Implications for Transnational Agrarian Movements." *Journal of Agrarian Change,* 8(2–3), 462–88.

Walters, Kimberly. 2016. "The Stickiness of Sex Work: Pleasure, Habit, and Intersubstantiality in South India." *Signs: Journal of Women in Culture and Society,* 42(1), 99–121.

Wang, Alex. 2006. "The Role of Law in Environmental Protection in China: Recent Developments." *Vermont Journal of Environmental Law,* 8, 195–217.

Waterman, Peter. 2001. *Globalization, Social Movements, and the New Internationalism*. New York: Bloomsbury.

Weeks, Kathi. 2011. *The Problem with Work: Feminism, Marxism, Antiwork Politics, and Postwork Imaginaries*. Durham, NC: Duke University Press.

Weiss, Robert P. 2001. "'Repatriating' Low-Wage Work: The Political Economy of Prison Labor Reprivatized in the Postindustrial United States." *Criminology*, 39(2), 253–92.

Weitzer, Ronald, ed. 2010. *Sex for Sale: Prostitution, Pornography, and the Sex Industry*. London: Routledge.

Wesley, Luke. 2004. "Is the Chinese Church Predominantly Pentecostal?" *American Journal of Pentecostal Studies*, 7(2), 225–54.

Wherry, Frederick. 2008. *Global Markets and Local Crafts: Thailand and Costa Rica Compared*. Baltimore: Johns Hopkins Press.

White House, Office of the Press Secretary. 2010. "Presidential Proclamation—National Slavery and Human Trafficking Prevention Month." The White House: President Barack Obama, December 22. https://obamawhitehouse.archives.gov/the-press-office/2010/12/22/presidential-proclamation-national-slavery-and-human-trafficking-prevent.

Whyte, Martin King. 1985. *Urban Life in Contemporary China*. Chicago: University of Chicago Press.

Wilson, Ara. 2004. *The Intimate Economies of Bangkok: Tomboys, Tycoons, and Avon Ladies in the Global City*. Berkeley: University of California Press.

Wilson, Kalpana. 2011. "'Race,' Gender, and Neoliberalism: Changing Visual Representations in Development." *Third World Quarterly*, 32(2), 315–31.

Winship, Christopher, and Robert D. Mare. 1992. "Models for Sample Selection Bias." *Annual Review of Sociology*, 18, 327–50.

Wolf, Diane. 1996. *Feminist Dilemmas in Fieldwork*. Boulder, CO: Westview Press.

Wongsamuth, Nanchanok. 2020. "Thailand's Migrant Sex Workers Fear for the Future." Reuters. July 1.

Wooditch, Alese. 2010. "The Efficacy of the Trafficking in Persons Report: A Review of the Evidence." *Criminal Justice Policy Review*, 22(4), 471–93.

Woods, Tryon P. 2013. "Surrogate Selves: Notes on Anti-trafficking and Anti-blackness." *Social Identities*, 19(1), 120–34.

World Vision. 2022. "Our Mission Statement." https://www.wvi.org/our-mission-statement.

Xin, Katherine K., and Jone L. Pearce. 1996. "Guanxi: Connections as Substitutes for Formal Institutional Support." *Academy of Management Journal*, 39(6), 1641–58.

Xin Ren. 1999. "Prostitution and Economic Modernization in China." *Violence Against Women*, 5(12), 1411–36.

Yanagisako, Sylvia and Delaney, Carol. 1995. "Naturalizing Power." Pp. 1–24 in Sylvia Yanagisako and Carol Delaney, eds., *Naturalizing Power: Essays in Feminist Cultural Analysis*. New York: Routledge.

Yancy, George, and Janine Jones, eds. 2013. *Pursuing Trayvon Martin: Historical Contexts and Contemporary Manifestations of Racial Dynamics*. Lanham, MD: Rowman and Littlefield.

Yang, Quanhe, and Fei Guo. 1996. "Occupational Attainments of Rural to Urban Temporary Economic Migrants in China, 1985–1990." *International Migration Review,* 30(3), 771–87.

Yang, Guobin. 2005. "Environmental NGOs and Institutional Dynamics in China." *China Quarterly,* 181(1), 44–66.

Yang, Jie. 2010. "The Crisis of Masculinity: Class, Gender, and Kindly Power in Post-Mao China." *American Ethnologist,* 37(3), 550–62.

Yu, Jess M. 2014. "Ye Haiyan, Rights Campaigner, Is Detained over Photo Posted Online." *New York Times Blog,* November 11. http://sinosphere.blogs.nytimes.com/2014/11/04/ye-haiyan-rights-campaigner-is-detained-over-photo-posted-online/.

Zaloznaya, Marina, and John Hagan. 2012. "Fighting Human Trafficking or Instituting Authoritarian Control." Pp. 344–364 in Kevin Davis et al., eds., *Governance by Indicators: Global Power through Classification and Rankings.* Oxford: Oxford University Press.

Zavella, Patricia. 1993. "Feminist Insider Dilemmas: Constructing Ethnic Identity with 'Chicana' Informants." *Frontiers: A Journal of Women Studies,* 53–76.

Zelizer, Viviana. 1979. *Morals and Markets: The Development of Life Insurance in the United States.* New York: Columbia University Press.

———. 1985. *Pricing the Priceless Child: The Changing Social Value of Children.* Princeton, NJ: Princeton University Press.

———.1994. *The Social Meaning of Money.* Princeton, NJ: Princeton University Press.

———. 2005. *The Purchase of Intimacy.* Princeton, NJ: Princeton University Press.

Zhang, Chenchen. 2018. "Governing Neoliberal Authoritarian Citizenship: Theorizing Hukou and the Changing Mobility Regime in China." *Citizenship Studies,* 22(8), 855-881.

Zhang, Naihua. 2020. "Searching for 'Authentic' NGOs: The NGO Discourse and Women's Organizations in China." Pp. 159–90 in Ping-Chun Hsiung, Maria Jaschak, and Cecilia Milwertz, eds., *Chinese Women Organizing.* New York: Routledge.

Zheng, Tiantian. 2009a. *Red Lights: The Lives of Sex Workers in Postsocialist China.* Cambridge: Cambridge University Press.

———. 2009b. *Ethnographies of Prostitution in Contemporary China: Gender Relations, HIV/AIDS, and Nationalism.* Chicago: Palgrave Macmillan.

Zimmerman, Yvonne C. 2013. *Other Dreams of Freedom: Religion, Sex, and Human Trafficking.* London: Oxford University Press.

Zin, Salai Thant. 2019. "Myanmar Garment Workers Continue Strike, Demand Regional Minister Resign." *Irawaddy.* December 24.

Index

AAPTIP (Australian-Asia Program to
Combat Trafficking in Persons), 153
abolition of prostitution, 9, 15, 141, 149,
158, 189; abolitionist nostalgia, and,
11, 158, 232n37; faith-based organizing, and, 15, 17, 141
Acting for Women in Distressing Situations
(AFESIP), 86, 110, 143, 144
Agustín, Laura, 9, 21, 217. *See also* "rescue
industry"
Akha ethnicity, Thailand, 143, 146
All-China Women's Federation (ACWF),
115, 124, 125, 129
Almeling, Rene, 18
American empire, 4, 8–12, 19–22, 82, 109,
164, 186
American slavery, *xi*, 11, 81, 158, 164,
229n45
American vigilantism. *See* paramilitary
operations
"anti-solidarity machine." *See* Lee, Ching
Kwan; Shen Yuan
anti-trafficking fairs, 29, 83, 209
anti-trafficking movement: American
organizations (*see names of individual
groups*); defunding, 197–98; fraudulent
anti-trafficking schemes, 110, 143, 144;
harm to sex-worker rights, 147, 149–52,
154–57; inequalities in global movement, 130, 131; profitability, 5, 9, 29,
143–44, 178, 182; religiosity, 29,

32–38, 62, 65, 66, 73, 74, 81, 97, 182,
211–13, 223n33 (*see also under*
Christianity, evangelical; World Vision);
sex trafficking and labor trafficking
debates and conflations, 9, 23, 36, 117,
191, 222n8; vocational training and
rehabilitation organizations (*see*
rehabilitation; vocational training)
anti-trafficking rehabilitation programs. *See*
rehabilitation
anti-trafficking rescue industry. *See* Agustín,
Laura; "rescue industry"
APNSW. *See* Asia Pacific Network of Sex
Workers
Asia Floor Wage Alliance, 196
Asian Pacific American Legal Center
(APALC), *ix*
Asia Pacific Network of Sex Workers
(APNSW), 22, 85–87, 119, 187, 191,
195, 201
Austin, Sam, 116
Australian-Asia Program to Combat
Trafficking in Persons (AAPTIP), 153

"Bad Rehab" (song), 84–87. *See also* Asia
Pacific Network of Sex Workers
Ballard, Tim. *See* Operation Underground
Railroad (OUR)
Bandy, Joe, 130
Bangladesh Accord, 194
Beck, Glenn, 135–37, 157

Beijing University Center for Women's Law
Studies and Legal Aid. *x, xi,* 107, 170
Bernstein, Elizabeth, 8, 28, 36, 136, 144,
202, 215, 230n5. *See also* abolition of
prostitution: faith-based organizing, and
Beutin, Lyndsey, xi, 11, 20
Blee, Katherine, 213
Body Shop, The, 86–87
Bose, Diya, 94, 202
Brennan, Denise, 165
Brooks, Ethel, 20
Burawoy, Michael, 69, 186

California Supply Chain Transparency Act
(SB 657), 193
Cambodia, 11, 15, 22, 96, 140, 152, 197,
223n33. *See also* "Bad Rehab"; Chab
Dai Charter; Mam, Somaly
Can-Do Bar, Chiang Mai, Thailand, 148,
152, 155, 195, 215. *See also* Empower
Foundation
CEDAW, 155. *See also* United Nations
Committee on the Elimination of
Discrimination Against Women
Chab Dai Charter, 96, 97, 226n14
Chan, Debby, 127
Chasin, Alexandra, 18
Chen Huihai, 116. *See also* China: labor
movement, repression against; labor
organizing
childcare and other care work, 72, 80,
167–68, 170, 172–79, 194. *See also*
daycare in anti-trafficking organizations
child labor, 20, 126, 129–31, 155
Chin, Angelina, 80
China: anti-trafficking definition and, 13,
117–18, 120–22, 125–30, 132, 192;
brides from Myanmar, selling of, 119;
censorship, 63, 65, 74, 124, 132–33,
185; child kidnapping, 13, 117, 130–31,
228n38; *danwei,* 185; Foxconn workers,
112–13, 126–27; *hukou,* 12, 108, 111,
168, 219n22 (*see also* migrant workers);
labor movement, repression against, *xi,*
14, 112–116, 120, 127, 133, 192;
migrant populations and, *x–xi,* 3, 4, 12,
62, 64, 70, 72, 91, 108, 111–16, 124,
128–33; movement and, 13–14, 113–19,
121–24, 133–34; movement and
co-optation, 14, 114, 116, 127–28, 133;
organizations and agencies (*see names
of individual agencies*); sex work, 13,
14, 62, 65, 108, 117, 119; sex work,
policing of, 13, 14, 62, 63, 108, 119,
233n16; United Nations Inter-Agency
Project on Human Trafficking, China
office of the (UNIAP China), 95, 97, 98,
118, 120–27, 129, 130, 143, 214,
227n34; wealth disparities, rural and
urban, 6, 7, 12, 13, 219n22; World
Vision coalition, 33, 115, 122–24, 129.
See also Christian missionary work:
outlawed in China; National Plan of
Action (NPA), China
China Labor Watch, 132, 229n47
Chootesa, Mickey, 143
Christianity, evangelical: anti-trafficking
movement and, 8, 16, 17, 21, 26, 29,
30, 32–38, 82, 197–99, 214, 223n33;
anti-sex trafficking vocational and
rehabilitation centers (*see* Cowboy
Rescue; Freedom Unchained; rehabilitation; vocational training); faith-based
objectives, obfuscation of, 29, 34–35,
123 (*see also* anti-trafficking movement:
religiosity; World Vision); progressive
Pentecostal, 38
Christian missionary work: authoritarianism
of Chinese government, replicated in,
74, 185; China, outlawed in, 44, 62, 65,
73–74; government oversight, avoidance
of, 33, 97; and state posture against
sexual commerce, 37, 97, 182; Thailand,
reception in, 54–56, 59, 73–74, 185
Chuang, Janie, 9–10, 21, 141, 157, 230n17.
City Light, 145. *See also* human trafficking
reality tours
Coalition to Abolish Slavery and Trafficking
(CAST), *ix,* 223n33
contract, employment: emotional labor,
75–76, 167; penalties, 59, 92, 98;
religiosity rewards, 72–74, 97;
"repentant labor," 58, 59, 72–74, 81,
211; restrictions: sexual commerce
forbidden, 60–61, 65, 98, 100, 102;
restrictions: socializing in former
workplaces forbidden, 3, 58, 60–61, 72,
98, 100; salary and benefits, 58, 60–61,
63, 71–72, 91, 177; surveillance of
workers, 61, 64–65, 107, 211. *See also*
Cowboy Rescue; Freedom Unchained;
maternalist control
COSA. *See* anti-trafficking movement:
fraudulent
Cowboy Rescue, 53–61; contract restrictions, 58, 60, 100, 102 (*see also under*
contract); co-optation of workers'
stories, 103, 106–107; dependence on

by "victims", 24, 102–103; discipline, 61, 82, 100, 102, 189; funding, 37, 47; moral rehabilitation, 61; religiosity, 34, 59, 81; religiosity rewards, 72–74, 97; salary and benefits, 58, 60–61, 71–72, 91; staff and volunteers, 53–55, 57, 59

cultural scapegoating, 33, 42, 43, 82, 92, 109: Buddhist values, 42–43, 56, 77; Chinese culture, 92; Thai culture and religion, 42–43, 56

daycare in anti-trafficking organizations, 58, 72, 104–105. See also childcare and other care work

Department of Special Investigations (DSI), Thailand, 135

discipline, 32, 46, 61, 82, 88, 98, 168, 189

Doezema, Jo, 42

Echo Foundation, 143, 146

Empower Foundation, 147–52, 159–60, 195, 215, 225n2, 231n27: entrapment, commentary on, 155 (see also United Nations Committee on the Elimination of Discrimination Against Women, CEDAW); Hit and Run report, 93–94, 151, 155, 199; Last Rescue of Siam, The, 149–50, 187; Mida tapestry, 93–94; "rights, not rescue," 88, 152, 191; "solidarity, not sewing machines," 148, 151–52, 190–91

End Child Prostitution and Trafficking (ECPAT), 143

End Slavery Now, 143

End Trafficking Now, 1, 2, 8

Erzen, Tanya, 212

ethical consumption, 3, 5, 17–19, 21, 26–31, 52, 58, 186, 221n57

evangelical Christianity. See Christianity, evangelical

expertise: local and indigenous knowledge, 11, 128, 198; workers' voices, 186

fair trade movement. See ethical consumption

Fassin, Didier, 19

Feingold, David, 121, 201

Free-D, 181–183

freedom, concept of, 3, 8, 164

Freedom and Fashion, 169, 190.

Freedom Unchained, 61–70: Beijing Christian International Fellowship (BCIF), 61–62; contract prohibitions, 3, 58, 60–61, 65, 72, 98, 100, 102 (see also under contract,

employment: penalties); co-optation of workers' stories, 105–107; discipline, 63, 98, 82, 90, 168, 189; dormitory living, 64, 65, 78, 89–91, 98; founding, 61; funding, 37, 62; government surveillance over, 67, 107–8; moral rehabilitation, 51, 93, 98, 104; religiosity, 66, 73, 75–77, 168; religiosity rewards, 73, 97, 111–12, 168; salary and benefits, 58, 63, 71–72, 74, 91, 168, 177; self-censorship, 63, 74, 185; staff relationships with workers, 67, 68, 77–78, 106–7; housemoms, 62, 65, 77, 78, 90 (see also "imperialist motherhood"; maternalist control); volunteers, 61–62, 209; working conditions, 58, 63–65, 67–68, 70; vocational programs, 66

Fude, Kunming City, Yunnan Province, China, 114, 129, 131

funding, 37, 47, 62

Ghana: child labor, 20, 131; colonial context, 131; raid and rescue, 20, 136, 155, 197

Global Alliance Against Traffic in Women (GAATW), 143, 214, 218n14

Global Labor Justice, 71, 195–96

Global Slavery Index, 141. See also International Labor Organization

Goldman, Michael, 128

Goffman, Erving, 93

Grey Man, The, 143

Hagan, John, 121

Han, Judy Ju Hui, 213

Haney, Lynne, 45

Harriet Tubman Award, 11, 158, 232n37

Hildebrandt, Timothy, 123

housemoms, 62, 65, 77, 78, 90. See also maternalist control

Hoang, Kimberly Kay, 58, 231n24

human trafficking: identifying victims, 16, 37, 53, 96, 188, 209, 211n57; "modern-day slavery" and, xi, xii, 8, 11, 132, 139, 144, 158, 165, 232n37; nonsexual-labor trafficking, 8–9, 13, 17, 23, 36, 79, 127, 199, 220n41. See also human trafficking definition

human trafficking definition: China, 13, 117, 120–127, 133; fluidity, 9, 225n14; Thailand, 16

human trafficking reality tours, 145, 215, 136: accountability to host governments, 145; profitability, 146–148, 153

human trafficking visas (T-visas), 46
Hunt, Nancy Rose, 80

"imperialist motherhood," 80, 89
India, 18, 27, 29, 93, 160, 181, 197
IndustriALL, 194
International Labor Organization (ILO),
    125–27, 129, 141, 222n9
International Organization for Migration
    (IOM), 141
Inter-Ministerial Office Against Trafficking
    (IMOAT), China, 13, 118, 227n34,
    228n38
Isaan province, Thailand, 60

Jaffee, Daniel, 19
jewelry parties, 21, 26–28, 39, 210
jewelry work: capitalist production, and,
    82; physical risk, 71; prestige, 80; wage
    labor, 72, 75, 78, 80. See also salary;
    vocational training: economic benefits,
    goals vs. realities, manual labor and
    moral transformation

Karim, Lamia, 28
Keck, Kathryn, 33
Kempadoo, Kamala, 11, 20, 203
Kitiarsa, Pattana, 38

labor organizing, 114, 121, 134, 183, 202,
    203, 206
Lady Gaga, song "Bad Romance," 22, 85
language barriers, 95; skills of volunteers,
    lack of, 57, 121; translations, disso-
    nance in, 104, 164
Laos, 15, 140, 152, 228n39
Last Rescue in Siam, The, 149–150, 187
Lee, Ching Kwan, 14, 114, 117, 202
Leigh, Carol, xii, 88, 203
LIFT International (formerly Nvader), 153,
    197
Ling, Bonny, 117
Lui, Mary, 81

Mahdavi, Parvis, 108
Mai, Nicola, 9, 171, 230
Mam, Somaly, 86, 110, 144
market-based social movements, 5, 17
marriage, 24, 81, 119, 166–74, 189; and
    rehabilitation and redemption,
    166–174
maternalist control: in shelters, 145; and
    boys, 225n5
McKim, Alison, 45

migration, rural and urban inequality, 12,
    139, 219n19
"Migrant Worker Band Project," 23, 122,
    124. See also New Workers' Artist
    Troupe
migrant workers, 24, 62, 89, 114, 158, 170;
    agency and storytelling, 160, 166, 188;
    childcare options, 58, 72; hukou, 12,
    108, 111, 168, 219n; solidarity with,
    79, 190; undocumented sex workers,
    113, 154
military interventions, civilian-led. See
    paramilitary operations
Ministry of Public Security (MPS), China,
    13, 228n34, 233n16
missionaries. See Christian missionary work
"modern-day slavery," 27, 132, 144, 158,
    165; antiblackness and, xi, 11; human
    trafficking, synonymous with, xi, 199;
    metaphor, 165, 169. See also human
    trafficking: "modern day slavery"
moral economy, 22, 28, 224n4; low wage
    women's work, 22, 58, 82; bootstrap
    entrepreneurship, 47–50
moral market. See ethical consumption
moral panic, xi, 9, 60, 182
MTV EXIT ("End Exploitation and
    Trafficking"), 120, 121
Musto, Jennifer, 74, 202
Myanmar, 15, 196; China-Myanmar border,
    119, 201, 209, 229n49; Federation of
    Garment Workers Myanmar (FGWM),
    195

Nataree, Thai massage raid, 154
National Plan of Action (NPA), China, 13,
    117, 127
Neelapaljit, Ankaka, 155
New Workers' Artist Troupe: Migrant
    Worker's Home, 122, 192, 214; Migrant
    Worker Culture and Art Museum, 122
Nguyen, Mimi Thi, 43, 164, 203
Nvader, 11, 153, 154, 159, 197. See also
    paramilitary operations

Okyere, Samuel, 20, 131, 203. See also
    Ghana
Operation Underground Railroad (OUR),
    11; Ballard, Tim, founder, 135, 154;
    Operation Toussaint, 156; and rejection
    of state-led forms of activism, 158. See
    also paramilitary operations
outreach, 3, 37, 53–57, 107, 107, 209–215
Owens, Emily, 164, 205

Paladin Rescue, 153. *See also* paramilitary operations

Panyu Migrant Workers Center, Guangzhou, 115. *See also* China: labor movement, repression against

paramilitary operations, 23, 138; entrapment, 153–158; limited transparency, 138; relationship with local law enforcement, 138. *See also* AAPTIP; LIFT International; Nvader; OUR; Walker, Daniel

Pascoe, Peggy, 32, 81

Perfectly Imperfect, 181. *See* Free-D; jewelry work

Peters, Heather, 121, 201

Phongpaichit, Pasuk, 139

Pliley, Jessica, 81, 225n15

Polanyi, Karl, 18

Po Leung Kuk (PLK), 80

policing, 5, 11; law enforcement, 118, 133; NGOs, and, 81, 99, 234n29; vigilante, 138

Pun Ngai, 116

Quanhe Yang, 62

racialization of Asian women, and sexuality, 61

racialized redemptive labor, 4–6, 58, 82, 182. *See also* redemptive labor

racial wages of rescue, 81–83, 183

racism, 11, 21, 42, 81, 183, 189, 199, 213

Radhakrishnan, Smitha, 28

raid and rescue operations, 15, 153–158, 195. *See also* paramilitary operations

Ramachandran, Vibhuti, 93

Rana Plaza building collapse, 193

reality tourism. *See* human trafficking reality tours

recruitment. *See* outreach

Red Canary Song, 234n29

redemptive labor, 4, 82, 88, 91, 182. *See also* racialized redemptive labor

rehabilitation: life after, 175–180; mandatory shelter housing, 57, 63–64, 75, 91; market-based strategy for redemption and reform, 82; monitoring of social behavior, 61, 74, 79, 93, 109 (*see also under* contract, employment); quitting, 166, 174, 177–180; virtuous wages, 4, 58, 69, 81, 189. *See also* rights-based sex worker organizing; vocational training

religiosity in anti-trafficking organizations, 72–74, 77, 212. *See also* Christianity, evangelical

repentant labor, 58, 72, 81

"rescue industry," 9, 21, 81, 86, 182, 219n19; China, 73, 184, 192; Thailand, 16, 23, 134, 139, 159. *See also* Agustín, Laura

resistance, workplace, 110, 183, 190, 196: co-optation of by activist organizations, 68–69, 105

rights-based sex worker organizing: anti-sex trafficking movement, invisibility in, 146–148; policing in anti-trafficking movement, critique of, 147, 151, 152, 155; vs. religious imperatives, 97; vs. rescue and rehabilitation, 21, 88; solidarity with, 138, 151, 152, 186, 188, 190. *See also* Empower Foundation; Sex Workers of ASEAN (SWASEAN)

Rudrappa, Sharmila, 18

SACOM. *See* Students and Scholars Against Corporate Misbehavior

salary: as compared to sex work, 60, 91–92; benefits, 60, 91, 177; jewelry workers in anti-trafficking organizations, 48, 55, 58, 60, 73, 163, 168, 224n3; life after rehab, 175; racial wages of rescue, 81–83, 183; remittances, 172

salvific evangelism, 22, 31, 51, 182

sex commerce. *See* sex work

sex-tourism, 15, 62, 141–143, 230n14

"sexual humanitarianism," 9, 171, 230

sex work: addiction lens of anti-trafficking activists, 60; conflation with sex trafficking, 6–8, 55, 82, 105, 106, 148; economic alternatives to, 48, 57, 81, 102, 177; manual labor and, 7, 8, 70, 79; quitting, 67, 176; voluntary, 7, 79

sex-worker rights organizations. *See* rights-based sex worker organizing

Sex Workers of ASEAN (SWASEAN), 148, 190

Shen Yuan, 114. *See also* Lee Ching Kwan

shop floor discontent. *See* resistance, workplace

shelters: China, 63–68, 95–96, 177; criticisms of and improvements, 149–55; Thailand, 94–95, 99–100, 142; UNIAP project, 96–99. *See also* Empower Foundation: *Hit and Run* report; vocational training

Sikkink, Margaret, 33
"slave-free goods": global commodity chain, 3, 47; jewelry, 3, 17, 114, 138, 165, 169, 178, 182, 208
Smith, Jackie, 130
Soi Cowboy red-light district, 3, 53, 57, 58, 100, 102
Students and Scholars Against Corporate Misbehavior (SACOM), 127
Surtees, Rebecca, 93, 203, 214
surveillance, 61, 98, 119, 135, 151, 159, 207, 211
Swider, Sarah, 64
SWING, 175. See also rights-based sex worker organizing

Tarrow, Sid, 42
Thailand: Anti-Trafficking in Persons Act (B.E. 2551; 2008), 16, 220n41; Buddhism, 42, 219n32; Covid-19 response plan, 175; economy, 15, 137–141; fishing industries, deep-sea, 145, 220n41; Global Slavery Index, ranking, 141; as humanitarian aid hub, 143; human rights abuses, 156; labor-trafficking, 16; migrant populations and, 60; military repression, 219n19; organizations and agencies (see names of individual agencies); public relations campaign, 142; "rice-pledging schemes," 160; Rohingya refugees, 142, 230n19; sex work activism, 191 (see also Empower Foundation: Hit and Run Report); sex work, prevalence and visibility of, 54, 160; TIP report, ranking, 142; US militarism legacy and, 144; wealth disparities, rural and urban, 60, 160
trafficking. See human trafficking; human trafficking definition
Trafficking in Persons Report (TIP): as "global sheriff," 157 (see also under Chuang, Janie; United States); China ranking, 131–133; Operation Underground Railroad (OUR) and, 156; Thailand ranking, 141, 142; tiers, 10; US State Department, 10
transgender sex workers, 81, 162
Truckers Against Trafficking, 11, 158
Trump, Ivanka: China labor abuses, 132; op-ed in Washington Post, 132; White House anti-trafficking efforts, 135
T-visas, 46
TVPA. See United States Trafficking Victims Protection Act

undocumented migration, 15, 37, 108, 120, 160
UNI Global Union, 194
UN Action for Cooperation Against Trafficking in Persons (UN-ACT, formerly UNIAP), 214
UN Committee on the Elimination of Discrimination Against Women (CEDAW), 155
UN Inter-Agency Project on Human Trafficking, China office of the (UNIAP China), 95, 97, 118, 120, 143, 214
UN Palermo Protocol, 9, 17, 183
United States: commodity chains, 3, 51, 133, 178; definition of trafficking, 10, 35, 46 (see also under human trafficking definition, United States TVPA); "global sheriff" in anti-trafficking movement, 10, 21, 141, 157; human trafficking visas (T-visas), 46; imperialism, 20, 82, 109, 139, 164, 199, 286 (see also US Empire); surveillance of communities of color, 158; Trump family, 131–133
US Empire, 4, 8–12, 19–22, 82, 109, 164, 186
United States State Department's Trafficking in Persons (TIP). See Trafficking in Persons Report (TIP)
United States Trafficking Victims Protection Act (TVPA), ix, 10, 35, 46
Urry, John, 103

Vance, Carol, x, 27
"victim of trafficking": realities vs. marketed portrayals, 7–8, 149, 171, 177; protection and rights based on victim status, 96, 108, 190
vigilante humanitarianism, 152. See also paramilitary operations
vigilantism, 25, 137, 138; global racial, 138. See also paramilitary operations
Violence Against Women Act (VAWA), xi
virtuous labor, 22, 51, 58, 182
vocational training: in China, 49, 65, 66, 98, 126, 127, 131 (see also Freedom Unchained); economic benefits, 26–30, 44–51, 65, 67, 166, 179, 181–83; goals vs. realities, 49–51, 66, 89, 131, 165, 178, 183, 197; manual labor and moral transformation, 49–51, 66, 131, 165, 166, 178, 183, 197; in NGO shelters, 94, 95, 146; in state-run shelters, 93–96;

in Thailand, 48, 94, 95, 183 (*see also* Cowboy Rescue); in United States, 169. *See also* rehabilitation

Walker, Daniel, 153–154. *See also* LIFT International; Nvader
Walk Free Foundation, 141
Walters, Kimberly, 93
"war on trafficking," 11
Weber, Max, 35
Wherry, Frederick, 18
white saviors, 11, 20, 82, 109
white supremacy, 21, 213
Wilberforce, William, 11
Wilson, Ara, 140
women's work, low-wage: jewelry work, 47, 71–72, 78, 175–178; manual labor, 82, 131, 167, 182; and racialized hierarchies (*see* racialized redemptive labor); sexual abuse in workplace, 71, 195; and white Western feminists, 58

World Vision, 33, 115, 123, 129
World Vision and obfuscation of Christianity in China, 122, 123
worker organizing, 116, 147, 195–197. *See also* labor organizing

Xin Ren, 13

Yasheng Huang, 117
Ye Haiyan, 192
Yihui Su, 126
Yin Q, 198, 203
Yonghong Zhang, 17
Yunus, Muhammed, 27

Zaloznaya, Marina, 121
Zelizer, Viviana, 18
Zeng Feiyang, 115
Zhongze Women's Legal Counseling and Service Center, x, xi, 107, 170
Zimmerman, Yvonne, 35–36

Founded in 1893,
UNIVERSITY OF CALIFORNIA PRESS
publishes bold, progressive books and journals
on topics in the arts, humanities, social sciences,
and natural sciences—with a focus on social
justice issues—that inspire thought and action
among readers worldwide.

The UC PRESS FOUNDATION
raises funds to uphold the press's vital role
as an independent, nonprofit publisher, and
receives philanthropic support from a wide
range of individuals and institutions—and from
committed readers like you. To learn more, visit
ucpress.edu/supportus.